The Cross and the Serpent

CONZEDERACIOU
CIVDAD·DE·LIINFIERNO

princepe selas tinieblas

castigo delos soberbios piadores y rricos queno teniais quese aqui

THE CROSS
AND THE SERPENT

Religious Repression
and Resurgence
in Colonial Peru

By Nicholas Griffiths

University of Oklahoma Press : Norman and London

Library of Congress Cataloging-in-Publication Data

Griffiths, Nicholas, 1962–
    The cross and the serpent : religious repression and resurgence
in colonial Peru / by Nicholas Griffiths.
        p   cm.
    Includes bibliographical references and index.
    ISBN 0-8061-2800-3 (alk. paper)
    1. Indians of South America—Peru (Viceroyalty)—Religion.
2. Indians, Treatment of—Peru (Viceroyalty)—History. 3. Indians
of South America—Peru (Viceroyalty)—Social conditions.
4. Catholic Church—Missions—Peru (Viceroyalty)—History.
5. Persecution—Peru (Viceroyalty)—History. 6. Freedom of
religion—Peru (Viceroyalty)—History. 7. Peru (Viceroyalty)—
History. I. Title.
F3429.3.R3G74   1995
299′.895—dc20   95-24751
                                                                       CIP

Text design by Bill Cason

1 2 3 4 5 6 7 8 9 10

To my father

CONTENTS

ILLUSTRATIONS

Illustrations on frontispiece and at heads of chapters from Felipe Guaman Poma de Ayala, *El primer nueva corónica y buen gobierno.*

ACKNOWLEDGMENTS

I would like to express my thanks to the following for their advice, assistance, and professional guidance: Dr. Antonio Acosta Rodríguez, D. W. Baubeta, Dr. Fernando Cervantes, Dr. Marco Curatola, Professor Trevor Dadson, Dr. John Edwards, Dr. Luis Miguel Glave, Dr. Margarita Guerra, Dr. José Hernández Palomo, Dr. Mervyn Lang, the late Professor Derek Lomax, Professor John Lynch, Professor David Mackenzie, Professor Félix de Negri Luna, Armando Nieto S.J., Dr. Patricia Odber de Baubeta, Dr. Anthony Pagden, Gilbert Pleuger, Professor Franklin Pease, and Dr. R. W. Scribner. Above all, I owe a particular debt of gratitude to Dr. David Brading and to his wife, Dr. Celia Wu Brading. I would also like to express my special debt to, and affection for, the late Charles W. Parkin.

The staff of the various archives I have consulted, in particular, Mario E. Ormeño, José María Sánchez-Blanco S.J., and José Torres García S.J., have provided kind, devoted attention. Research was made possible by awards from the British Academy and Jesus College, Cambridge, which I thank most heartily.

I gratefully remember the warm and generous hospitality and friendship offered to me by Victor and Salwa Fuentes, Marcelo Martín, Elia Olmo, Bertha and Carla Rubio, Pablo Sanz Martín and his family and friends, Alberto and Catalina de Souza-Ferreira and their family, Ingrid Terrile, and Antonio Ugarte.

Finally, I wish to express my appreciation to my mother and my grandmother for their kind generosity and, above all, to my wife for her ceaseless patience and support.

THE CROSS AND THE SERPENT

Introduction

675 CAPITVLOPRIMERODEVECT
CHRISTOBA DE ALBOR
nos una madry gene val dela madre ya teusa buena jusa hija

The Visitor-General Cristóbal de Albornoz.

*One day, there was a great fire in a large house where the Indians
used to consult with the Devil . . . and, in full view of all, among
the flames and embers there passed a huge serpent which, not once
but many times, slid through the centre of the blaze without being
burned. . . . [T]he magicians and sorcerers gathered together to
speak with the Devil (for that was who the snake was) and ask the
meaning of his passage through the flames. The Devil replied that
soon a great fire would come upon them and there would be great
spilling of blood as a punishment for the murder of the priest [the
Augustinian missionary Diego de Ortiz]. And it came to pass.*
—Antonio de la Calancha, *Corónica moralizada* (1639)

ASTRIDE THE RUINS OF THE FORMER DOMAIN OF TAWAN-
tinsuyu, victorious Spaniards determined to inscribe into
the very pattern of the heavens their conquest of the Andean world. The ancient native sacred universe, eclipsed

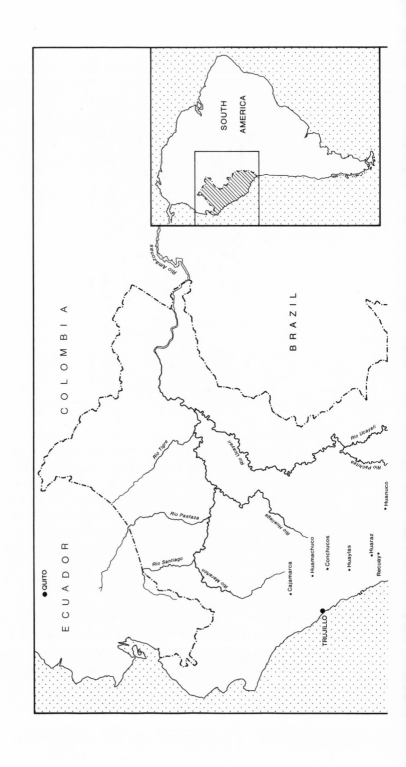

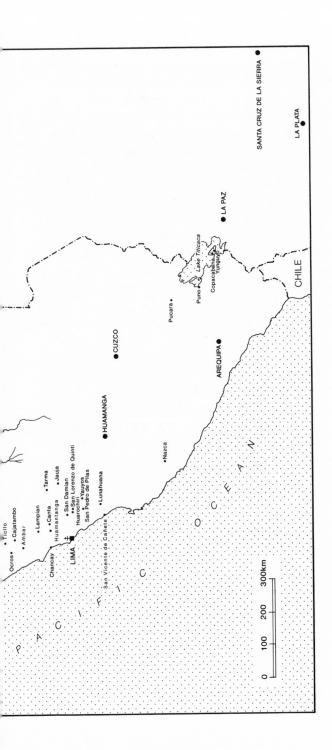

by the advent of the One True God, would now capitulate to Spanish hegemony, as surely as the material world on which it had been predicated. The mighty Andean deities, formerly revered as the founders and guardians of civilization, stood dispossessed, their authority dishonored, their treasures dispersed, and their temples razed to the ground. The conquest itself had already proved their inability to repel the invaders; now they also stood powerless to preserve from destruction their own representations in the material world (which Spaniards called "idols").

The advent of uncompromising militant Christianity confirmed that the subjugation of Andean peoples to their new colonial overlords would be reinforced by what one scholar has evocatively called "the colonization of the *imaginaire*"; native experiences of the numinous were to be appropriated by the only legitimate interpreters of the supernatural, Christian priests and missionaries.[1] Thus the passage of the serpent through the flames was encoded according to Christian symbolism (the identification of the serpent with the Devil), as part of a broader process whereby indigenous manifestations of the supernatural were channeled into a new Christian discourse of diabolism. But although both Spaniards and Andeans recognized the numinous resonance of this story, they did not attribute the same significance to it: a religious symbol may be shared by two groups of people and yet mean something different to each of them.[2] The serpent has always been as powerful a symbol in Andean culture as in European culture. If for Christians the serpent embodied the forces of evil, for Andeans it represented *amaru*, a destructive force erupting from beneath the earth in an attempt to re-create balance when relations of equilibrium were not maintained in the social and natural universe.[3] Thus, according to an Andean reading of the event, the manifestation of amaru testifies not to the defeat of satanic forces but, on the contrary, to the revi-

talization of the native supernatural world. It was this revitalization that was to subvert the self-confident triumphalism of the Spaniards.

For just as the subjugation of native Andeans to Spanish rule had not destroyed the framework of indigenous
society, so the humbling of traditional religion by the
emissaries of the Christian god did not signify the annihilation of the Andean supernatural. To be sure, the experience of defeat brought in its wake unprecedented
disorder in the native spiritual realm; the serpent was not
left unscathed by its passage through the flames of Christian persecution. But nor was it reduced to a smoldering
pile of ashes. In effect, native religion stood in relation to
Christianity much as native Andeans stood in relation
to Spaniards: subordinate but not obliterated. However,
whereas native submission to Spanish rule could not easily be reversed, the realm of the supernatural might furnish a battleground where Andeans could challenge their
oppressors. Indeed, the response of the native supernatural to the challenge of Christianity was to take the form
of a complex dichotomy of submission and resurgence.[4]

The Spanish reaction to the ostensible victory of Christianity over native religion was also characterized by a
curious dichotomy. On the one hand, the successful establishment of a visible Church seemed ample evidence
that Satan had been expunged from his lair. Within a generation of the conquest, Christian places of worship had
sprung up across the viceroyalty, a network of *doctrinas*,
or missionary parishes, had been created, and a vast re-
location program, whereby rural inhabitants were moved
from scattered settlements to larger villages, had been
initiated to facilitate the propagation of the gospel.[5] Even
if early missionary activity in Peru was not accompanied
by the euphoria that characterized the evangelization of
New Spain, the apparent rapid advance of the faith, as
the Indians succumbed to mass baptism, gave cause for

an unquestioning confidence that within the foreseeable future the inhabitants of the entire continent would be brought within the fold.

On the other hand, triumphalism with regard to the accomplishments of the visible Church contrasted starkly with deep-seated pessimism, verging on despair, concerning the apparent impermanence of native conversion. As the sixteenth century progressed, the conviction hardened that the much-heralded evangelization had been nothing but an illusion. In part, this was a reaction against earlier exaggerations, but it also derived from an increasing awareness that the native religious world had not been supplanted by Christianity.

The "spiritual conquest" of Peru had always been, in effect, little more than a religious decapitation. If the official religion of the Cuzqueño Inca elite disappeared relatively rapidly after the conquest, the regional worship of *huacas* (local deities or supernatural entities), liberated from central control, not only continued but grew and developed.[6] Whereas the imperial Inca priesthood had succumbed to the Spanish onslaught, the popular Andean priesthood, which sustained the worship of localized sacred entities, survived relatively intact. As Frank Salomon and George L. Urioste have stressed, the overarching, abstract, and universalizing philosophy of Inca elite religion bore little relevance to the lives of most of the subject peoples of Tawantinsuyu. Instead, local religious life was expressed in terms of place and descent and was focused on sacred beings (rocks, stones, mountains, and canals and other bodies of water) peculiar to particular communities, kin groups, families, or individuals. The Spaniards were no more successful at eliminating this strong current of religious particularism than the Incas had been.[7]

The militant revitalization of these regional and local cults was manifested most clearly in the Taki Onqoy, a religious revivalist movement that broke out in central Peru around Huamanga after 1560. The *taquiongos*, or disseminators of the movement's message, preached that a pan-Andean alliance of deities would soon defeat the Christian god and restore to the Andean world its own principles of harmony and order, which had been so brutally shattered by the advent of the Spaniards. The movement's millenarian message was given credence by the unprecedented outbreaks of disease that had afflicted native Andeans since the conquest. Only the wrath of the huacas, provoked by the neglect of their worship since the triumph of the Christian god, could explain the calamities that had befallen the native world. Now the huacas would wreak their revenge on the Europeans by attacking them with the same diseases to which the Indians had succumbed. In order to escape the vengeance of the revitalized deities, native peoples were exhorted to return to traditional cults, to revile Christian worship, and to reject all forms of cooperation with Spaniards. Only in this way would they be able to participate in the imminent regeneration of the Andean world and enjoy the dawn of a new era purified of Hispanic traces, free of colonial exploitation and uncontaminated by disease.[8] Taki Onqoy essentially served notice that native religion's subordination to Christianity might be overturned; and, indeed, this threat outlived the movement since the brutality with which the taquiongos were successfully repressed between 1568 and 1571, by Visitor-General Cristóbal de Albornoz, failed to halt the revitalization of local huaca religion in a broader sense.[9]

However, it was not until the beginning of the seventeenth century, in 1609, that the ecclesiastical authorities again became alarmed at apparent widespread native religious recidivism. In that year, Francisco de Avila, the parish priest of San Damián de Checa de Huarochirí, raised the alarm that the Indians in his doctrina continued in their native practices, just as before the conquest, having simply adapted them to clandestinity. The response of the colonial authorities was the initiation of a series of persecutory "campaigns of extirpation," organized and coordinated centrally by the archbishop of Lima and characterized by judicial trials for the offense of idolatry. Such a reaction confirmed that the survival of native religion was to be countered principally by coercion rather than by persuasion.[10]

Although successive visitations were conducted in the provinces of the archbishopric, the enterprise always remained intermittent. In the seventeenth century, there were two periods of activity, the first between 1609 and 1622 (with an epilogue in 1625–26) and the second between 1649 and 1670. The latter campaigns represented the zenith of the Extirpation. Thereafter, despite some prosecutions in the 1690s, there was no such attempt to organize a coordinated, centralized campaign until 1725. This final initiative faded almost as soon as it had begun, failing to follow the model established by its seventeenth-century predecessors. But despite their intermittent occurrence, these campaigns were characterized by a consistency of ideology, aims, and methods that permits them to be considered as a distinct movement. It is these campaigns that are the principal focus of this book.

Previous studies of the Extirpation have tended to concentrate upon the earlier periods of the sixteenth century and the first half of the seventeenth century. Pierre Duviols restricted his survey, *La lutte*, to the years between 1532 and 1660, and his more recent work, *Cultura andina y represión*, was confined to the Cajatambo trials that took place between 1656 and 1664.[11] This emphasis reflects agreement with the thesis of George Kubler that by 1660 persecution had succeeded in overturning the cultural basis of the Quechua colonial world and in effectively Catholicizing the native inhabitants.[12] As a result, the history of the eradication of native religion in the second half of the seventeenth century and first quarter of the eighteenth century has generally been neglected.[13] Even the recent study of Andean religion, Sabine MacCormack's *Religion in the Andes*, accepts 1660 as a watershed and suitable termination date.[14] Yet the archives yield adequate, if not abundant, sources for a study of the Extirpation in the later period. It is my aim here to rectify this neglect and exploit the potential of the sources.[15]

The study of the Extirpation is also necessarily the study of the worldview that produced it. Spaniards had at their disposal a sophisticated conceptual apparatus, inherited from medieval scholasticism, that afforded traditional categories for interpreting manifestations of deviance from religious "truth." Much of the earlier part of this book will be devoted to exploring these categories, the most important of which were apostasy, idolatry, superstition, witchcraft (*brujería*), and sorcery (*hechicería*). Although these categories will be examined in depth later, it may be as well to provide brief definitions of them here. Apostasy was the sin of those who having been baptized into the Christian faith, chose to forsake it and return to the beliefs and rites of their former religions. Idolatry may be defined not only as the worship of idols, or false gods, but also, more properly, the offering to creatures (i.e., objects of creation) of worship due only to God the Creator. Superstition was understood as "religion carried to excess," either by worshiping God in an inappropriate fashion or by offering divine worship to something not deserving it. However, as I will demonstrate, the categories of idolatry and superstition became blurred by the seventeenth century. Finally, the distinction between hechicería and brujería is probably the most difficult to make. The *brujo*, or classic witch, was a true apostate who consciously renounced God and the Christian faith by means of a formal contract with the Devil, in return for special magical powers. *Brujos* were commonly believed to engage in devil worship. The *hechicero*, or sorcerer, by contrast, was a specialist in the manipulation of discrete magical objects and superstitious ceremonies who sought to achieve by these means some real effect in the material world, for example, to cause somebody to fall in love, get sick, or recover from an illness. The hechicero did not necessarily have an official compact with Satan or access to any special powers but rather practiced knowledge or techniques acquired from a human teacher.[16]

Although it is important to subject the Spanish conceptual apparatus—and the discourse within which Spaniards expressed their interpretation of native religion—to rigorous scrutiny, the history of the interaction of Christianity and native religion cannot be appreciated purely through the grid that Europeans attempted to impose on Andean realities, since these categories denied any active role to the phenomenon under observation. Perceiving Christianity as fundamentally active and dynamic and native religion as passive and unchanging, colonial Spaniards interpreted continued manifestations of the Andean sacred in terms of "persistence." But the trajectory of native religion in the colonial world cannot be understood merely in terms of what survived and what did not. Manifestations of enduring native beliefs and rites were not mere melancholy wreckage of the beached ship of Andean religion, or relics of a former time, left behind by the withdrawing tide of faith. Native religion was no inert repository of timeless beliefs and practices. It neither disappeared nor survived unaltered in the colonial period; instead, it underwent fundamental adaptations and transformations in a dynamic process of self-renewal. It continued to encapsulate the indigenous understanding of the world and to express its own objective reality.

As early as the 1560s, the Taki Onqoy movement bore witness to the adaptation of native religion in response to the Christian challenge as well as to cross-cultural exchange between Christianity and native religion. It is well known, for example, that the revitalized colonial huacas responded to the new religion by changing their form and altering their behavior. No longer were they confined to rocks, water, or hills; now they literally seized natives' bodies and caused them to shake, tremble, and dance insanely (Taki Onqoy means "dancing sickness"). Despite the movement's rejection of Christian influences, some female taquiongos took the names of Christian saints, such as Saint Mary and Saint Mary Magdalene, a phenomenon that Steve J. Stern has interpreted as native recognition of the power of the Christian pantheon and the expression of a desire at the core of the movement to ally with some elements of Hispanic supernatural power while simultaneously battling the European god.[17] In this way, Christian supernatural power could be turned against the Christian god and utilized to enact the subordination of the alien religion to the revitalized native religion. Thus "acculturation provided weapons for contesting Christianity."[18]

This phenomenon was only imperfectly perceived by contemporary Spaniards. The majority of the colonial clergy conceived contact between the two religions in terms of a fundamental dichotomy; the baptized native inhabitants of Peru were either true Christians or apostates. The two religions were seen as mutually exclusive alternatives, from which the Indians had to choose and between which they might switch back and forth. There were no intermediary stages.[19] Such an interpretation is flawed, first, because it fails to recognize the capacity of a religious system to adapt itself as a strategy of survival, and, second, because it ignores the real possibility of compromise and accommodation between two religious systems.

In recent years, the work of both Andean and Meso-

american historians and anthropologists has afforded
very sophisticated insights into the phenomenon of religious acculturation (the mutual interaction of elements
of two religious systems or the transfer of religious traits
from one culture to another). J. Jorge Klor de Alva's model
for colonial Mesoamerica replaces the old dichotomy of
"Christian"/"non-Christian" with one of "conflict"/"accommodation," wherein both positions encompass different patterns of interaction between the Catholic and
native religious systems.[20] Conflict, for example, may
take the form of outright apostasy (retention of native beliefs, participation in native rites, and abandonment of
Christian rites); or belief in native religion with participation in both sets of rites; or indifference to the beliefs
and rites of both religions. Thus, according to this model,
conflict does not necessarily signify overt acts of confrontation or defiance but may be characterized by passive
as well as active resistance to Christianity. Accommodation, by contrast, implies that some form of compromise
was achieved between the two religious systems. Klor de
Alva's model distinguishes three types of response: complete conversion, incomplete conversion, and overt conversion only. At one extreme, complete conversion means
that Christianity was both believed and understood
(probably the rarest of responses). At the other extreme,
overt conversion means that Indians neither believed nor
understood Christianity but, through obligation, participated in its rites nonetheless. Incomplete conversion
stands somewhere in between: Christianity was believed
but misunderstood. This, the most common native response, may itself be broken down into four distinct patterns: "external syncretism," in which belief in Christianity was founded on the premises of native religion with
active participation only in Christian rites; "internal syncretism," in which belief in Christianity was founded on
the premises of native religion with active participation

in both Christian and native rites; "compartmentalization," which is characterized by belief in both religions and active participation in the rites of both; and "nepantlism," which describes a very frequent phenomenon, noted by the Dominican missionary Diego Durán, whereby the native religion was lost or disfigured but, at the same time, Christianity was not assimilated or understood and participation in the rites of either or both was often characterized by a state of anomie or confusion.[21] These categories are not intended to be mutually exclusive; indeed, they blend easily into one another. In fact, accommodation cannot really be distinguished from conflict, since the two overlapped. Within a real lifetime, an individual might pass through any or all of these conditions in a continuous state of flux. The categories are, then, simply points of reference on a continuum, a collection of freeze-frames in a film that is the religious life experience of an individual.

Nepantlism—"a situation in which a person remains suspended in the middle between a lost or disfigured past and a present that has not been fully assimilated or understood"—is a useful category for interpreting religious interaction in the colonial Andes as it was probably the most common native Andean experience. It describes an uneasy no-man's-land, where, despite the dismantling of the structural basis of native faith, full conversion was impossible. The intense spiritual unease that it provoked was a highly unstable condition; although some individuals might remain *nepantli* all their lives, the tension had to be resolved at the communal level. Hence nepantlism was, of necessity, a transitory stage. The means by which native Andeans in general and their religious leaders and folk healers in particular sought to resolve this predicament is one of the subjects of this book.

The term "syncretism" is appropriate to the colonial Andes only in the broader sense of "synthesis" rather than the narrower sense of "fusion." Hugo G. Nutini, for example, refers to syncretism as "the fusion of the religious or non-religious traits, complexes of traits or institutions of two cultural traditions in the course of face-to-face interaction."[22] Fusion thus suggests that two discrete religious systems merge or blend to produce a single new one that may preserve elements of the originals to a greater or lesser degree. In the Andes, however, it is highly debatable whether the two religious systems merged in this way. Nathan Wachtel argues that there was less a fusion of the two religions than a juxtaposition (if the Indians admitted the existence of the Christian god, for example, they still denied him any influence over human affairs).[23] Michael T. Taussig also refers to the "blending" of Christianity with indigenous beliefs as "more a juxtaposition than a seamless fusion."[24] Rather than either juxtaposition or fusion, it may be more appropriate to speak of a "Catholic-Andean continuum with many intermediate stages," whereby the two religious systems became partially, but not fully, superimposed on one another.[25]

Syncretism may also be defined as "a type of acceptance characterized by the conscious adaptation of an alien form or idea in terms of some indigenous counterpart," or as "a synthesis growing out of the contact or collision of two complexes of elements or institutions (not necessarily religious) from different cultural traditions."[26] These definitions are closer to the truth for the Andes, the first, because it portrays the native religious matrix as the dynamic element to which alien elements are subordinated; the second, because it emphasizes mutual, though not necessarily equal, accommodation and the reconciliation of thesis and antithesis rather than simple fusion. It is in this sense only that a process of syncretism occurred in the colonial Andes.

When Christianity and native religion made contact, two interrelated phenomena were at work. First, as Manuel

Marzal has stressed, there was a slow process of religious acculturation whereby the majority of the native population of Peru came to accept its own reinterpreted form of the Catholic religious system. This was not a process of simple substitution but "part substitution, part addition, part synthesis" between the beliefs, rites, forms of organization, and ethical rules of the two systems. In the end, the Andean population accepted the Catholic religious system, but they reinterpreted Christian elements from within the native cultural matrix and introduced many indigenous elements.[27]

Religious rites (defined as fixed forms of communication with sacred beings, composed of words, gestures, and other symbolic elements that enjoy general cultural acceptance) were the key to this process. Rites serve as a point of contact and interchange between two religions and may act as a form of "transmission belt" of new significances. When one religious system comes into contact with another, the first may accept the rites of the second, attributing to them the meaning of its own equivalent rites; or, alternatively, it may conserve its own rites, conferring on them the significance of the equivalent new rites. Thus although the external appearance of a rite may alter little, at the same time, a reinterpretation of its meaning may occur. Melville J. Herskovits defines this principle of reinterpretation, which marks all aspects of cultural change, as "the process whereby old meanings are ascribed to new elements, or by which new values change the cultural significance of old forms."[28] This process can be both self-contained (or internal), spanning one generation to the next, and intercultural, integrating a borrowed element into a receiving culture.

The reinterpretation of Catholicism was accompanied by another process of adaptation and change within the native religious system. As the new Christian religious synthesis drew Indians into its orbit, the native system neither disappeared, nor persisted unaltered as an ever-shrinking redoubt, nor wholly fused with it. Instead, there was a redeployment of native practices and beliefs to respond to new circumstances. Rather than persist in splendid isolation, the native system grew, developed, and transformed itself in interaction with and in response to the new Christian synthesis. Its new form was greatly determined by the developing shape of that Christian synthesis. The native system was obliged, for example, to consider the relationship of the huacas with the Christian saints and, to some extent, redefine the significance of celebrations in their honor. These redefinitions should be interpreted, however, as acts of self-renewal, not as capitulation to the Christian system. Within a reduced sphere, the native system retained its own internal logic and understanding of reality. Hence the relationship between the two systems was neither fusion nor simple juxtaposition but mutual accommodation and *articulation* (in the sense that the ethnic polities of the pre-Hispanic Andean world had been articulated within the Inca Empire). The principal difference was that the Christian synthesis emanated from the apex of colonial society whereas the native synthesis was increasingly marginalized and confined to the base.

Both the new syntheses, the Christian and the native, were complex and multilayered, confronting each other as total systems and interacting at a variety of levels. They were characterized by what Serge Gruzinski, adapting a concept developed by Nathalie Zemon Davis, has labeled "cross-cultural exchange," what Nancy M. Farriss has called "a set of horizontal, mutual exchanges," and what Herskovits identified as "transculturation."[29] The two religious systems were like two streams, constantly converging, intermingling, and crisscrossing down to the present day, without ever flowing into one large river, the elements of each system folding over one another incessantly until there was no part of one that had not been touched by the other, in the manner of "a chamber of mirrors reflecting each stream's perception of the other."[30]

It should be stressed, then, that the concept of "separate spheres" does not diminish the importance of the interaction between the two belief systems, especially in the life experience of people moving within and between the spheres. The compartmentalization of beliefs exists today in the community of Kaata in the Qollahuaya region of Bolivia. Kaatans distinguish between rituals at shrines for the Catholic saints, which are performed by catechists and priests, and those at shrines for the mountain, the site of the graves of their ancestors, which are performed at a different time by different specialized ritualists. Kaatans never mix the two classes of shrines and their specific rituals.[31] Likewise, Robert Redfield commented on the compartmentalization of Christian and native cults in the Yucatán. Rites dedicated to Maya agricultural deities are performed by a shaman-priest called an *h-men*, whose prayers are said in the native tongue, whereas Catholic rites are performed by a native chanter who recites prayers from the Catholic liturgy addressed to God, Christ, and various saints. The offerings made to Christian divinities are different from those made to indigenous deities, and the rites of the two cults are usually performed in different places (although, in some communities, native and Christian rain ceremonies are performed simultaneously at separate altars in the same church). The distinction between the two cults is clear to the participants, who recognize two sets of deities who should be propitiated separately and in different ways. At the same time, there is no rigid separation of all Christian and indigenous elements; for example, Catholic saints have been added to the pantheon of nature gods, so that Saint Michael has become the chief rain deity. Both native and Christian cults ultimately serve the same purpose as their function is to secure supernatural aid in obtaining rain, growing crops, and restoring health. There is no conflict between the two cults; they are complementary ways of dealing with the supernatural.[32]

Thus it is possible within the religious life experience of individuals for two systems to remain to some extent separate but complementary. It is true, of course, that the separate spheres cannot be entirely autonomous. Atomized, isolated religious realms would be meaningless both for the collective perception of the divine and for the religious experience of individuals. If religion may be defined, according to Emile Durkheim, as "an integrated system of beliefs and practices regarding the sacred, shared by a community," then its component elements must be interrelated to be integrated.[33] If the central function of any religious perspective is to divine the immanent meaning in an incomprehensible universe, to convert chaos into "cosmos," then there must exist an overarching system of significance that reconciles opposites and contradictions. Meaning can only be conveyed within a holistic system that integrates all the parts. Thus the separation of certain realms of the supernatural must be subordinate to the fundamental unity of the overarching religious synthesis. Even though contemporary Kaatans distinguish between rites for the mountain shrines and those for the Catholic shrines, nonetheless, to them they are parts of one whole system of religious beliefs and practices.[34] Similarly, although seventeenth-century Nahuas "held certain realms [of the supernatural], distinguished by time and manner of genesis, carefully apart from each other," they "viewed the entire supernatural sphere as a unit at some level, meshing and serving ultimately the same purpose from the point of view of the individual and the corporation."[35] Therefore, it is not a contradiction to argue that in the colonial Andes one new overarching synthesis emerged, containing two interrelated and interdependent but separate spheres: nativized Catholicism and Christianized indigenous religion.

The crystallization of this synthesis may be clarified by following Farriss's differentiation between the public and the private spheres of religious activity. First, she distinguishes the level of the macrocosm (an all-encompassing concept of the divinity, the realm of transcendental theology) from the level of the microcosm (the lesser localized members of the cosmos attending to the more immediate concerns of human existence). Then, within the microcosm, she distinguishes two categories, the public sphere and the private sphere. The public sphere concerns the welfare and identity of the community and its corporate relationship with the supernatural. In relation to the native system, it is manifested in communal ceremonies of propitiation of the colonial huacas and of the modern *apus* (mountain spirits), as well as the nourishment of ancestors.[36] In terms of the Christian system, it encompasses the corporate or parochial cults of patron deities and saints. The parochial tier is microcosmic and particularistic, in that it serves the collective needs of a territorial grouping, but it has wider horizons than the private sphere, which is confined to the individual, his family, and his immediate surroundings. The private sphere is essentially the sphere of magic (which may be defined as the manipulation of highly discrete and localized supernatural forces for the benefit of individual clients). Whereas the public sphere is collective, inclusive, open, and declared, the private sphere is individual, exclusive, closed, and secret.[37]

The distinction between public and private religious practice is appropriate in differentiating between types of native religious specialists or shamans (native priests who communicate directly with spirits in the supernatural world), who, as I will show, were instrumental in the construction of the new religious synthesis, since they acted as mediators and conduits for acculturation and accommodation. Native religious specialists may be divided between those who catered to the collective needs of the community and those who served the personal needs of individuals (although both functions were often united in the same individual). In the first category were those who supervised the communal celebration of acts of worship of native deities and who were responsible for communication with, and propitiation of, huacas and ancestors. Conversing directly with the sacred spirits of the surrounding landscape, they acted as mediators between the community as an aggregate and its supernatural guardians. They included, for example, the *huacacamayoc*, or caretaker of deities, who was responsible for the physical maintenance of huacas and the provision of sacrifices, as well as the *huacapvillac*, who acted as an interpreter of the huacas' communications. In the second category were those, such as *curanderos* (folk healers) and diviners, who utilized some specialized knowledge and manipulated discrete magical items to cater to the personal needs of individuals and their families. These specialists dealt more in the realm of the "day-to-day miseries and preoccupations of village life."[38] They were consulted for the remedy of personal afflictions and ailments, the recovery of lost objects or animals, the resolution of broken love affairs and marriages or the obtaining of some desired person, and the prognostication of future events.

Practitioners of both types of cults were the victims of persecution, but the specialist in collective acts is less frequent among the idolatry trials than the practitioner catering to individual needs. This reflects a real decline in ceremonies of collective worship. The decreasing frequency of reports of native rites, particularly in the eighteenth century, may, in part, be attributed to the growing success of communities at concealing the extent of the practice of

Introduction 23

their own customs and beliefs.[39] Even so, although there
is evidence of the continuation of such ceremonies in
some areas well into the eighteenth century, they were already declining significantly in frequency in the seventeenth century, as enforced clandestinity made the public
sphere of native religion increasingly dysfunctional. The
Indians could not abandon Christian worship for fear of
punishment by the priest; but neither could they neglect
their traditional deities, whose wrath held them in terror.
Thus a split was effected within the public or corporate
sphere between open observance of Christian ritual and
clandestine adherence to the old religion. Native ritual
was driven underground, so that deities were worshiped
and fed in secret. But these furtive rites were not a satisfactory substitute for the old religion. In the more remote
areas, as idolatry investigations of the eighteenth century
reveal, all or a large part of the community could still participate. But, increasingly, clandestine rites ceased to be a
regular community activity and became instead a more
or less secret offering made by individuals, families, or
small groups in some out-of-the-way sacred spot. But
whereas hidden worship could sustain a personal relationship with a supreme deity, secret gifts to the corporate gods that no one else knew about or shared in could
not express and sustain an entire community's links with
the sacred. The principal characteristic of religion is, after
all, its collective aspect. Thus, at the corporate or parochial level, the native system was entirely replaced by
its Catholic competitor. The Christian saints, themselves
reinterpreted to conform to Andean realities, became the
focus of corporate identity for native communities. By contrast, the magical sphere of native religion survived conquest and evangelization, modified by horizontal exchanges
between itself and the Spanish magical tradition.[40]

Thus it was the private sphere of magic that succeeded
in adapting and developing its own synthesis in response

to the challenge of the Christian religion. Although it is
impossible to determine if magical activity in the colonial
period increased by comparison with pre-Hispanic times,
at least it remained frequent. If the Jesuit chronicler Bernabé Cobo was right when he asserted that sorcerers were
punished by death in Inca times, such severity probably
reflected the widespread existence of witchcraft.[41] The
insecurity of life for the ordinary Indian was only aggra-
vated under the colonial regime, and the need to seek relief, or the means to control new dangers, only encouraged resort to supernatural aid.[42] Indeed, much of the
business of colonial religious specialists was devoted to
counteracting the exactions of the Spanish priest, *corregidor* (chief judicial and administrative official), *fiscal* (native catechist and assistant), *alcalde* (Crown functionary
similar to a justice of the peace), and even Visitor-General.
It is possible that the trauma of conquest bred a proliferation of sorcerers practicing antisocial magic and that
witchcraft expanded with the impoverishment of natives
after the conquest.[43] Eric Wolf has argued that witchcraft
may function as a manifestation of "institutionalized
envy" by offering psychological sanctions against non-
traditional behavior.[44] Recent research has rightly questioned the appropriateness of Wolf's model of the "closed
corporate community."[45] Indian migration was much
greater than Wolf allowed for and, indeed, may be considered one of the fundamental determinants of colonial
society.[46] However, his observations on the function of
witchcraft are not necessarily invalidated. Indeed, the constant intrusion of persons and influences from the outside probably created a constant need for supplication of
supernatural powers to counteract dangerous new currents in native society. If Wolf was right that witchcraft
acts to maintain the individual in equilibrium with his
neighbors and to reduce the disruptive influences of outside society, then an increase in its activities would be ex-

pected when Spanish society introduced new opportunities for some (the political and economic benefits to be derived from cooperating with the conquering elite) and new forms of misery for others.

Native religion survived in the private sphere because it preserved its function and relevance. The conquest shattered the Andean social order and disrupted the bonds uniting the domestic group to the community. Faced with the breakdown of social consensus, native religion became even more relevant as one of the only responses available to make sense of this new "world turned upside down." In an incomprehensible and uncontrollable new order, the need to situate man in the universe became ever more pressing. If the aim of a religious system is to explain, even celebrate, the ambiguities, enigmas, and paradoxes of human existence, it was needed now more than ever.

The Spanish conquest, furthermore, brought unprecedented chaos into the native spiritual world because it confronted the accepted indigenous reality with a new spiritual reality. By refusing to accept the validity of the native reality, the Spanish conquest differed from any previous conquest to which the Andean peoples had been subjected. The Incas had attempted to establish one religion for the whole of Tawantinsuyu by diffusing the solar cult and bringing to Cuzco, the universal shrine of the entire realm, the various regional huacas.[47] But the ascendancy of the Inca solar god had represented merely a form of spiritual suzerainty or overlordship commensurate with the political hegemony that their human descendants had established. It did not signify the annihilation of the lesser local deities of the ethnic polities of the empire, nor did it disrupt the relationship of local cultures to their reality; rather, it signified a superimposition of a new set of practices and customs that themselves continued to emanate from the same cultural ensemble and foundations. Christianity differed because it sought, not the subordination of these native deities, but their utter destruction. It claimed a monopoly of the sacred and of the definition of reality.[48]

It was this challenge, above all others, that an adapted native religion had to meet. Its strength lay in its flexibility. It did not remain set in its mold and thus crack in the heat of Christian persecution. The initial response was one of conflict; battle was to be joined in a cataclysmic struggle to defeat the alien religion. But the crushing of Taki Onqoy proved that the Christian god had come to stay and that therefore some accommodation had to be reached. Since indigenous religion had a tradition of accepting the symbols of the dominant political authority, it did not remain impermeable to the ideology of the Spanish conquerors. But it refused to be overwhelmed by that ideology. Christian elements were not passively or uncritically accepted; they were screened, modified, and sifted through local traditions before reemerging newly processed.

It is little surprise that modern anthropological research has revealed fundamental transformations in native religion since the conquest and the colonial period. If ancestor worship, for example, still characterizes Andean communities, it has been dramatically transformed since colonial or pre-Hispanic times.[49] Although the concepts of huaca and apu have survived, their range of meaning has been narrowly circumscribed. MacCormack points out that whereas in the sixteenth and seventeenth centuries, most holy places had not yet been Christianized, in the contemporary Andes, most shrines are Christian, at least in name, and so are the sacred representations dwelling in them.[50]

One of the limitations of the sources on which this study is based is that, inevitably, they reflect an incomplete picture of this phenomenon. Many of these changes have taken place since the eighteenth century, when this study draws to a close. Both the native and the Christian syntheses have developed over the last two hundred years, before producing the current configuration. Many of the phenomena observed by modern anthropologists (the myth of Inkarrí, the association of apus and saints) are not reflected in the depositions of colonial idolatry trials. A further limitation of the sources is that these trials only reveal insights into the most marginalized communities of the archbishopric, where, by definition, the Christian synthesis had not yet taken hold. Its inexorable advance elsewhere in the viceroyalty during the period discussed here cannot be charted by these documents. Thus the sources are characterized by an irredeemable bias toward the thesis of continuity and self-renewal.

It is equally clear, however, that such a bias is entirely valid. While many transformations have been effected in native religion, at the same time, an element of continuity with pre-Columbian religion may also be discerned. Although the policy of extirpation destroyed objects of worship, removed religious leaders from their communities, and imposed penalties for the practice of native rites, many of the underlying principles of pre-Hispanic religion, particularly in the spheres of the agricultural and stock-rearing activities of country people and of folk healing, continue to be expressed by contemporary Andeans.[51] The sources testify to strong cultural survival, which, as Farriss observes for the Yucatec Maya, represents "not the preservation of an unmodified cultural system under the veneer of Spanish customs, but the preservation of a central core of concepts and principles, serving as a framework within which modifications could be made and providing a distinctive shape to the new patterns that emerged."[52] Thus, adapting Farriss's observations on the Maya, if the Andean cultural configuration became transformed under Spanish influence, it was along

Andean lines and in accordance with Andean principles. The ultimate hegemony of Christianity, especially in the public sphere, was incontrovertible. But within the "half-moon" that Christianity failed to conquer, Catholic elements were subordinated to the native system, becoming part of its own synthesis.[53] Thus the achievement of the native synthesis was not that it defeated Christianity but that, within its own reduced sphere, its distinctive logic and conception of reality were renewed.

One: THE EXTIRPATION AS REPRESSION

9

HICHE3EROS DE3VENOS
LLVITA'AICAVMV

"False Sorcerers."

I

THE EXTIRPATION WAS PRINCIPALLY AN INSTRUMENT OF repression. It was characterized by denunciations, accusations, investigations, interrogations, judgments, sentences, and punishments.[1] It was juridical rather than pastoral, condemnatory rather than forgiving, destructive rather than constructive. It smashed representations of sacred entities and rent asunder the reputations of native religious specialists and the timeless hallowed bond between the human inhabitants of this world and their supernatural tutelary deities. But its repressiveness was also its greatest weakness, for it was thereby rendered the object of never-ending controversy.

A debate had always raged within the Spanish colonial world as to whether repression was an appropriate response to the perceived "persistence" of native Andean religion. The Dominican friar Bartolomé de Las Casas insisted that the suppression of idols should be achieved through love, not fear, and the Jesuit José de Acosta warned that there was no greater opponent of faith than force and violence. Tearing idols from the hands of Indians against their will would only strengthen their hold over the native soul. The eradication of idolatry by compulsion, before the Christian message had been understood, was tantamount to slamming the door on the gospel rather than opening it. He agreed with Saint Augustine that nobody could become Christian by force and that idols must be removed first from hearts, not from altars. However, Acosta's observations were made with explicit reference only to those Indians who had not heard, or who had not been well taught, the Christian message. For the baptized Indians, a policy of severity was tolerable. This caveat left a large measure of ambiguity. Was force an appropriate measure, then, for baptized Indians who had not been well taught the Christian message? This was a question Acosta left unanswered.[2]

Despite the scruples of some theologians, the forcible repression of native religion was as old as the Spanish conquest itself. The spiritual conquest of Mexico had begun with the burning at the hands of the inquisitor-archbishop, Juan de Zumárraga, not only of native codices but also of native lords, of whom the most notorious was Don Carlos Ometochtzin of Texcoco, consigned to the flames in 1539. The Maya regions of the Yucatán had been subjected between 1559 and 1562 to the notoriously bloodletting idolatry investigations of the Franciscan provincial Fray Diego de Landa, who had tortured and killed numerous Indians to elicit confessions of native religious practices. In Peru, the rise of the native revivalist movement Taki Onqoy in 1564–65 unleashed the precursor of the seventeenth-century Extirpation, the idolatry trials conducted by Cristóbal de Albornoz. These investigations identified practitioners of native religious rites with "idolaters" and "apostates" in the minds of the civil and ecclesiastical authorities. As a result, the Second and Third Councils of Lima (1567 and 1583) established severe penalties of imprisonment and physical punishment for native religious specialists. The general visitation (1570–75) of Viceroy Francisco de Toledo (1569–81) confirmed that a judicial and punitive response was the most appropriate for those guilty of indigenous religious practices. Specialists were to be imprisoned during intensive instruction. Those identified as apostates were to be handed over to ecclesiastical justice to be punished according to the practices of the Inquisition. *Dogmatizadores* ("dogmatists" or propagandists of native beliefs) who had been baptized were to be "relaxed" to the secular authorities for application of the death penalty. Those dogmatists who hindered Christian preaching could be condemned to death directly by the secular arm, which had to inform the ecclesiastical authorities of its decision. It is true that those found to possess poor faculties of understanding or defects of catechism were to be treated leniently. However, no criteria were established for defining "poor faculties" or "defects." Thus an unresolved ambiguity remained as, in reality, most Indians, as *gente sin razón*, could be considered to suffer from poor capacity of understanding.[3]

The availability of repressive measures depended on the jurisdiction to which consideration of native religious practices was to be entrusted. Toledo advocated the submission of native specialists to the jurisdiction of the Inquisition. This was the logical conclusion of treating the Indians as apostates. But the Spanish Crown always refused to subject the neophyte Indians to the rigors and terrors of the Holy Office on the grounds of their "simplicity and poor understanding" and too recent instruction

in the faith.[4] If the traditional guardian of orthodoxy was
ruled out, the most effective substitute was the submission of native specialists to civil as well as ecclesiastical
tribunals, which would allow the application of the death
penalty. This too was refused by the Crown. A royal decree of 1575 established that idolatry trials that were not
criminal belonged to the jurisdiction of ecclesiastical, not
civil, authorities; only those whose practices led to death
would be judged by the civil authorities. This effectively
ruled out the ultimate sanction. As far as can be ascertained, the death penalty was never officially applied.[5]

Albornoz's idolatry trials of the 1560s were the paradigm for the future forcible eradication of Andean religion and confirmed that the Extirpation was to be a
fundamentally retributive enterprise. The repressive apparatus that was to characterize the later Extirpation was
first refined during this period. Since the trials identified
their victims as idolaters and apostates, it was logical that
they drew on the procedural methods of the Inquisition,
which was a model for the suppression of heterodoxy.
Thus if the Holy Office was not to be directly applied to
the Indians, at least its methods could be adapted. Albornoz borrowed from the Tribunal the device of the *auto de
fe*, which became the culmination of the idolatry trial,
providing a ritual context for the destruction of the
portable huacas, the abjuration of offenders, and the punishment of the *camayos* (religious leaders). The penalties
inflicted on the guilty also echoed those of the Inquisition. There were punishments of reform, including, for
example, service in the local church. There were punishments of separation and isolation, such as long-term or
perpetual confinement to a house of correction, or exile
from the community for many years. But those that most
clearly drew on the inquisitorial tradition were the punishments of infamy and shame, by means of public
humiliation and ridicule: dressing in the robes and head-

dress of the penitent, whipping, cropping of the hair, and passage through the streets half-naked on the back of a llama. These penalties were to remain typical of the later Extirpation and reflected its punitive objectives.

The emphasis on repression encouraged a quantitative rather than qualitative approach that was to characterize the later Extirpation. Albornoz's *Informaciones de servicios* (1570, 1577, and 1584) gave pride of place to the statistical balance, the names and numbers of idolaters identified, of religious specialists punished, and of huacas destroyed. Detailed knowledge of native religion, essential for its effective suppression, was furnished by Albornoz's *Instrucción para descubrir* (1583), a primitive forerunner of the extirpator's handbook. Here the most common native beliefs and types of huacas were enumerated.[6]

The techniques of repression inaugurated by Albornoz reached their maturity by the second decade of the seventeenth century. The campaigns of extirpation of 1609 to 1622 were a considerably more ambitious undertaking than Albornoz's in terms of both scale and duration. The principal addition to the repressive apparatus was the creation of the office of *juez visitador* or *visitador general de las idolatrías* (Visitor-General of Idolatry).[7] The title was first conferred on the priest Francisco de Avila in 1610 and subsequently extended in 1612 to two of his colleagues, Diego Ramírez and Hernando de Avendaño.[8] Thus whereas Albornoz had conducted his investigations merely in his capacity as an ordinary ecclesiastical Visitor, the Visitors-General of 1610 to 1622 were granted all the powers of the archbishop: jurisdiction over ecclesiastical judges, the right to visit all doctrinas, whether religious or secular, the power to check the level of linguistic knowledge of priests, and the power to remove *doctrineros* (parish priests of indigenous communities) from their offices. This was the first step in a significant professionalization of idolatry trials that made these campaigns qualitatively different from their sixteenth-century predecessors.[9]

The new Visitor-General disposed of a specialized team that was modeled on that of the Inquisition. It consisted of, as a core group, the Visitor himself (the equivalent of the inquisitorial judge), the fiscal (public prosecutor), and a notary or scribe. Sometimes the Visitor could be recruited from the ordinary ecclesiastical Visitors and might occupy the two offices simultaneously; but generally the priests of the Indian doctrinas were preferred for their experience and linguistic knowledge. It was the Visitor's responsibility not only to direct the inquiry and question witnesses and suspects but also to pass judgment and execute the sentence. The fiscal was in charge of communication with the Indians and the arrest of the guilty; he might also act as an interpreter. The notary recorded every declaration. Because at least the fiction of legal process was maintained, the Indian accused was entitled to a defense. This role did not necessarily merit a specialist and in many cases was a mere token gesture. The post could be filled by a member of the team's entourage or a local person of standing, such as the priest, an educated Spaniard, or even a *ladino* Indian. This clear demarcation of responsibilities was a further indication of the professionalization of the Extirpation.[10]

The extirpators' manual, *La extirpación de la idolatría del Perú* (1621), written by the Jesuit provincial Pablo José de Arriaga, surpassed Albornoz's in codifying the procedures of the idolatry visitation. A principal innovation was the issue of an "edict of grace" by the Visitor on his arrival in a native village, allowing three days during which individuals could denounce themselves or their fellows. This measure was derived from the inquisitorial practice of according absolution in exchange for a spontaneous confession or denunciation within a fixed period of time.[11] A second major innovation was the widespread practice of removing religious specialists from their communities for confinement in a specially constructed house of correction, the House of Santa Cruz at El Cercado (established in 1617). In 1621, there were about forty prisoners there.[12] The methods of investigation employed by the Extirpation in these years followed those of Albornoz. An inventory was made of huacas, *mallquis* (mummified corpses, bones, or other remains of ancestors), and religious specialists. Public sessions of abjuration and absolution ensued in the traditional auto de fe: the administration of punishment, the burning of the objects of worship, and the destruction of sacred sites. The stages of the idolatry visitation had already been formally codified at the synod of 1613, called in large measure to deal with the idolatry problem.[13]

The Extirpation not only modeled its methods and practices on the Inquisition but also shared its goal of enforcing orthodoxy through institutionalized terror. Duviols has called the Extirpation "the Bastard Child of the Inquisition," arguing that it constituted a true "Inquisition of the Indians."[14] The first edition of Arriaga's extirpation manual drew on the *Directorium inquisitorum* (1376), or inquisitors' manual, of the Catalan inquisitor Nicolás Eymerich, which assimilated idolatry to heresy and argued that all heretics should be under the jurisdiction of the Inquisition.[15] If Arriaga himself did not call on the Crown to revoke its decision and allow the subjection of the Indians to the Holy Office, he may have been prevented only by the traditional distrust between the Jesuits and the Tribunal. Although the Jesuit generals had always opposed the Tribunal's persecution of *conversos*, the open hostility between the Society of Jesus and the Inquisition dated from the trial of the Jesuit Luis López in 1578. Since that time, no Jesuit in Lima had been allowed to take part in inquisitorial activities without the authorization of the Superior. The creation of a parallel tribunal for the repression of native religion was an effective means of side-stepping both this controversy and the king's decrees on the Indians and the Inquisition. At the same time, an alternative tribunal entirely under archiepiscopal control must have seemed the most attractive option to the sponsor of the Extirpation, Archbishop Bartolomé Lobo Guerrero (1608–22). Inquisitorial jurisdiction would have impinged on the archbishop's own freedom of action. However, later advocates of the Extirpation urged the king to confer jurisdiction over the Indians to the Holy Office. In 1626, the archbishop of Lima, Gonzalo de Campo (1625–26), advised the king to place Indian idolatries under the jurisdiction of the Inquisition. If he recognized that the Tribunal's procedures and punishments in Indian cases would naturally vary from those in Spanish cases, he still considered it appropriate to inspire in the Indians "fear and terror." Indeed, this was the only method by which the "plague of idolatry" would be extinguished.[16] Avendaño wrote to the king in 1651 and again in 1653 asserting that the most effective method of extirpation would be to subject the Indian *kurakas* (chieftains or headmen) to inquisitorial supervision. He insisted that his purpose was not to deprive the bishops of their jurisdiction but to persuade them to share it with the Holy Office.[17] Although the Crown did not approve his request, Avendaño established a link between the two guardians of orthodoxy by fulfilling in his own person both the role of Visitor-General and *calificador* (judge responsible for "qualifying" or categorizing the offenses of the accused) of the Inquisition. This accumulation of functions became increasingly frequent in the later seventeenth century and early eighteenth century.[18]

Unlike the Inquisition, the Extirpation fulfilled a dual function, both judicial and pastoral. The campaigns of 1609 to 1622 were accompanied by a well- organized pedagogic policy, with preaching in the vernacular and persuasive pastoral activity. The Visitors-General were always accompanied by two or three Jesuit priests, and the ecclesiastical trials were preceded by a popular mission consisting of twelve sermons on the principal themes of Christianity.[19] However, the campaigns of 1649 to 1670 seem to have been characterized by a decline in missionary activity, with reduced participation of Jesuit missionaries, and an increased emphasis on the judicial function. The instigator of these latter campaigns, Archbishop Pedro de Villagómez (1641–71), revealed in his own writings the unresolved contradiction between these two aspects of the Extirpation. In his *Carta pastoral* of 1649, he observed that the visitations were more about "hearts" than "bodies," more about "hard work" than "force," more about "pity" than "justice." Thus it would be better to replace the use of "judicial apparatus and authority" with teaching, sermons, and confessions. In this way the Visitors could act as "fathers and teachers" rather than "judges or investigators."[20] Yet in 1654, in a letter to the king, he explained that the function of the Visitors was not to be "preachers" but "principally to be judges" and that "they should proceed in the manner of the Holy Office, publishing their edicts, carrying out their enquiries, compiling their cases, listening to declarants, and pronouncing and executing their sentences."[21] As long as the aim of the judicial process remained the physical and, as far as possible, the spiritual destruction of huacas, the priority lay with repression rather than pedagogy. Since these two goals were fundamentally incompatible, the pedagogy inevitably became "a pedagogy of fear." Despite its pastoral pretensions, the Extirpation lay closer to the Inquisition than to missionary activity.[22]

However much the Extirpation modeled its methods and procedures on the Holy Office and however much its ideology derived from the Tribunal's example, the "Bastard Child" failed to replicate the most important achievement of the Inquisition: it failed to institutionalize itself. Lacking a firm bureaucratic base, it never achieved the self-perpetuating power of the Inquisition. Precisely because it remained forever under the jurisdiction of the bishops, it failed to develop a body of committed careerists who would have conferred an independent existence. It lacked a permanent council comparable to the *suprema* (Supreme Council) of the Inquisition. It had no local bodies to represent it in the provinces. It had no permanent staff of officials. Above all, it had no financial base whatsoever. The Visitors-General remained dependent on the resources that the archbishop could make available to them. Thus if the Extirpation was ideologically precocious, it was institutionally immature. Its undoubted professionalization in terms of repressive methods was matched by an amateurish approach to its organization.

If the Extirpation never became an institution of colonial life, it was because its existence depended too much on the will of powerful individuals. In Peru, the eradication of native religion was always an affair of state. It relied excessively on the initiative of individual archbishops or viceroys. The campaigns of 1609 to 1622 were the result of an exceptional coordination between church and state authorities. The *audiencia* (supreme judicial and administrative authority), for example, collaborated with the campaigns, especially in the person of the auditor, the Jesuit Alberto de Acuña.[23] Such circumstances could not necessarily be repeated. In this excessive dependence on favorable patrons lay the explanation for the most curious characteristic of the campaigns of extirpation: their intermittent nature.

It is important to recognize that their intermittence did not necessarily reflect the "objective" frequency of native religious practices. It is not true to say that the campaigns against idolatry occurred between 1609 and 1622 and between 1649 and 1670 because these years witnessed an empirical and measurable recrudescence of native beliefs, independent of the actions of the colonial authorities. There is no reason to believe that the year 1609 was especially significant for native Andeans. The timing of the campaigns depended on developments within the Church hierarchy in Lima.[24]

It is clear that native religious practices were a constant of life in the provincial doctrinas. Parish priests regularly encountered "persistent idolatries" and reported them to the archbishopric. Such reports continued throughout the seventeenth century and into the eighteenth century. If they peaked during campaigns against idolatry, this was probably a result rather than a cause. But if there could be no campaigns without the alerting of authorities by local priests, equally such reports had no consequences unless there was a resolve in Lima to launch a campaign in response. This is illustrated by the notorious example of Francisco de Avila, the priest of San Damián de Checa de Huarochirí, who discovered in 1609 that the native celebration of the feast of the Assumption of the Virgin Mary in his doctrina also served as a rite of worship for Pariacaca, one of the local mountain deities. Avila's "discovery" of these practices provided the impetus for the campaigns of 1609 to 1622. But his efforts would never have spread beyond the confines of his own doctrina without the active support of higher authorities. It was the archbishop of Lima, with the approval of the viceroy, Juan de Mendoza y Luna, Marquis of Montesclaros (1607–15), who granted Avila the title of Visitor-General in 1610. It was also the archbishop who secured the appointment to the same office of other aspiring candidates, including Diego Ramírez, Alonso Osorio, Juan Delgado, Luis de Mora y Aguilar, Alonso García Cuadrado, Bartolomé de Dueñas, Rodrigo Hernández Príncipe, and Hernando de Avendaño, all of whom were, like Avila, priests of Indian doctrinas. Avila's discovery was only significant because higher authorities were disposed to exploit it for the launching of a centrally organized, coordinated, and concerted enterprise encompassing several provinces.[25]

This set a pattern that was to be repeated throughout the history of the Extirpation. The principal source of information about native religion was almost always the local priest. An enterprising doctrinero usually began an inquiry on his own initiative, or at the behest of the civil authorities, such as the kuraka, the alcalde, or village fiscal. Often he exercised full authority over the investigation, determining the sentence and punishment himself and merely sending a report to Lima for control purposes. Such investigations could operate independently of the existence of campaigns of extirpation. Indeed, they were the most common form of idolatry investigation during the seventeenth century. Thus although they might sporadically feed into more extensive campaigns, they could also operate autonomously and exist in isolation.

When campaigns *were* initiated, however, the control exercised by the center was tightened. Initially, the priest was allowed responsibility only for the preliminary investigation, during which he took the depositions of witnesses and possibly a confession of the accused, before remitting the case to the capital. Then one of two courses of action was taken. The priest himself could be appointed the official Visitor-General, not only for the doctrina and trial that he had first drawn to the attention of his superiors but also for the entire province, or even several provinces. This was the common practice during the campaigns of the 1650s and 1660s. There is no doubt that promotion to the office of Visitor-General, with its attendant powers, constituted a great incentive for the initiation of prosecutions by local priests. Alternatively, the trial could be transferred to Lima for consideration by the archbishopric's own lawyers and officials. This became increasingly frequent as the seventeenth century matured, reaching a peak during the eighteenth century. Whatever the response, it is clear that the instigation of idolatry trials depended on the close interaction of center and locality and the actualization by the central authorities of the permanently existing "potential" for campaigns against idolatry.

Although the discovery of native practices by local priests was by no means an exceptional event, not all local idolatry investigations resulted in campaigns of extirpation. The opportunities for "discovery" of idolatry were apparently infinite, yet the campaigns were restricted to certain decades of the century. This apparent paradox can be resolved by recognizing that only the personal decision of the archbishop of Lima could unleash a series of campaigns. The center was the most significant part of the equation.

The campaigns of extirpation bear an unequivocal personal imprint. Those of the seventeenth century were the work of three archbishops of Lima: Bartolomé Lobo Guerrero (1608–22), Gonzalo de Campo (1625–26), and Pedro de Villagómez (1641–71). It is not a coincidence that the first campaigns of the seventeenth century lasted coterminously with the tenure of Archbishop Lobo Guerrero. They began immediately after his succession to the see at Lima, and their abrupt termination followed swiftly on his death in 1622.[26] With the death in the same year of Arriaga, the supervisor of the latter years of the campaigns, and the recall of Viceroy Francisco de Borja, Príncipe de Esquilache (1615–21), the previous year, the presiding triumvirate had vanished and the circumstances favorable to the campaigns had come to an end. The hiatus was filled in 1625 by the new archbishop, Campo. He renewed the campaigns, with the significant innovation that his own episcopal pastoral visit was transformed into an idolatry visitation with himself as Visitor-General. This office had always been delegated by Lobo Guerrero. But the Extirpation was cut short once again by Campo's sudden death in 1626. Thus this wave of extirpation, which could have developed into a second series of campaigns against idolatry, was rendered little more than an epilogue to the first series of 1609 to 1622.[27]

The dependence of the Extirpation on the personal initiative of the chief prelate is clear from the absence of campaigns under Archbishop Hernando Arias de Ugarte (1630–38). His correspondence with the king indicates that he believed that idolatry was more a myth than a reality and that the Indians were exempt from it.[28] Born in the same land as the Indians and the first Creole to occupy the archbishopric, Arias may not have perceived native religious practices as so fundamentally alien and antithetical to Christianity. His views were certainly not based on ignorance as he had already held four successive bishoprics in America (including his native Santa Fe where Lobo Guerrero had "discovered" idolatries).[29] A personal tour of his new jurisdiction, Lima, confirmed his strong conviction. Arias's constitutions at the synod of 1636 made virtually no allusion to the problem of idolatry and no reference back to the constitutions of Lobo Guerrero on this matter. There was only one article on idolatry, which required priests to be especially vigilant that the Indians did not disinter the dead from Catholic cemeteries, and even this abuse was attributed only to the kurakas. As a result, he did not encourage idolatry visitations and certainly appointed no special Visitors-General of Idolatry. The surviving advocates of extirpation, principally Avendaño and Avila, suffered an eclipse, and the revival of the campaigns of extirpation had to await the succession of a new prelate.[30]

The second wave of campaigns of extirpation of the seventeenth century (1649–70) were summoned into existence, like their forerunners, on the initiative of the archbishop of Lima. The participation of Avila and Avendaño conferred a continuity of personnel on the enterprise, but their support for extirpation would have been fruitless without archiepiscopal authorization. Like Arias, Villagómez could draw on extensive experience as a prelate in America, but unlike his predecessor, he concluded that native religious practices were endemic. He had already conducted idolatry investigations in Arequipa, where he had been bishop between 1635 and 1640, and the constitutions of his synod of 1639 had devoted a great deal of attention to the question. A three-month personal visit to the province of Chancay in 1646 was the preliminary to the renewal of campaigns of extirpation in 1649. That year Villagómez published his *Carta pastoral de exhortación e instrucción*, which served as a new handbook for the Visitors he was to appoint. The work was clearly inspired by Arriaga's work of 1621.[31] The same year, Villagómez appointed seven Visitors-General of Idolatry: Avendaño (for Lima and El Cercado), Osorio (for Arequipa, Huamanga, and Huarochirí), Francisco Gamarra (for Canta, Tarma, Chinchaycocha, and Huánuco), Pablo Recio de Castilla (for Checras and Cajatambo), Felipe de Medina (for Yauyos, Jauja, Chancay, and Huaylas), and Bartolomé Jurado (for Conchucos and Huamalíes). Thereafter the campaigns proliferated, and a number of local priests were subsequently appointed as Visitors-General during the 1650s, including Diego Tello, the priest of Huaraz, Pedro Quijano Bevellos, the priest of Canta, and Bernardo de Noboa, the priest of Ticllo. The instigation and extension of these campaigns originated directly from the efforts of the archbishop himself.[32]

The 1660s have been seen, with justification, as the beginning of a decline in the campaigns of extirpation. Although idolatry investigations at a local level continued throughout the rest of the seventeenth century, there was no revival of centrally coordinated campaigns. Those of 1649 to 1670 were the last of the century. It is customary to date the beginnings of this decline to a 1658 letter of Villagómez to the king in which the archbishop complained of his difficulties in finding Visitors and missionaries for idolatry investigations.[33] The enterprise had been particularly prejudiced by the Jesuits, who had decided to withdraw their cooperation. The principal motive was the Company's fear that the Indians' respect for them would be lost and their pastoral work would be undermined if they continued to assist the Visitors in their work. It would be too easy for the Indians to conclude that the Fathers were passing on to the ecclesiastical judges the knowledge of native religious practices that had been revealed to them in the sanctity of the confession box. Participation in idolatry trials that were fundamentally punitive rather than instructive threatened to jeopardize their evangelizing missions. It is certainly true that the participation of the Jesuits had been essential to the campaigns of extirpation, but it is not clear that this letter should be taken at face value. First, such objections were not a novelty. Arriaga had reported the same scruples about participation in idolatry visitations among some of his fellows, yet this had not prevented them from accompanying the Visitors on the campaigns of 1609 to 1622. Second, this was not the first time that Villagómez had complained of his difficulties with the Jesuits. A 1654 letter to the king had already explained the reluctance of the Jesuits to participate. Yet this does not seem to have diminished the campaigns after that date. Finally, although their numbers may well have decreased, it is clear from their own documentation that Jesuit priests did continue to accompany Visitors during the campaigns of the 1660s. There does not seem to be any reason to attach any great significance to the letter of 1658, especially since the visitations continued unabated into the 1660s. The actual decline came after 1671, with the death of Villagómez.[34]

Another reason that has been advanced for the decline in the campaigns is the failure of the central authorities to contribute, as they had in the campaigns of 1609 to 1622, to the Visitors' expenses.[35] On more than one occasion, Villagómez asked the king to reverse his decision and allow the Visitors to draw on the Indians' communal resources for their support during visitations. The failure of the king to follow the archbishop's advice obliged the Visitors to find their own sources of financial support. It is arguable, however, whether such an obligation would have acted as a disincentive to participation in the campaigns. The leadership of idolatry investigations remained attractive to parish priests, who wished to draw attention to themselves and acquire significant powers. Despite his protestations to the king, which should probably be interpreted as an exaggeration to elicit further royal support, Villagómez was able to find fresh candidates for the visitations that continued well into the 1660s, especially under the indefatigable Juan Sarmiento de Vivero. In any case, it is clear that the Visitors simply employed their powers to enforce financial contributions from the communities subjected to investigation. The frequent denunciation of the excesses of the Visitors testifies to their willingness to recover their costs and make their efforts financially rewarding at the expense of the Indians. The extirpation *was* weakened by the lack of central financing, but this was *not* because of priests' reluctance to participate; rather, it was caused by the increasing corruption of the campaigns as the Visitors cajoled the Indians into surrendering financial resources. The accusations of seizure of Indian property and the use of torture may have been the real reason the Jesuits became more reluctant to participate. More important, the exactions of the Visitors resulted in the ever more frequent presentation of lawsuits by the Indians against their exploiters. The resort by native communities to litigation against their oppressors dealt the campaigns a fatal blow by paralyzing them in the red tape of bureaucracy.

It is clear that the decline of the campaigns cannot be attributed to loss of interest on the part of the ecclesiastical authorities in prosecuting native religious deviance. Not only did idolatry trials continue to take place throughout the later years of the seventeenth century, but they were also characterized by an increasing professionalization. In the 1690s, under Archbishop Melchor Liñán de Cisneros (1678–1708), many idolatry trials were summoned to Lima for resolution. This development was accompanied by another significant phenomenon, the increasing importance of the native defense, which assumed a prominent role for the first time. Whereas before the role of defense had not merited its own specialists, by the end of the century the office had acquired an element of continuity and was often occupied by the same individual during several distinct trials. Both these developments constitute a significant break with past practices of the Extirpation. Although there is no explicit documentary confirmation, it seems likely that this break reflected a conscious preference for methods different from those that had increasingly become discredited under Villagómez. In particular, the growing corruption and increasingly frequent counterlitigation, which the campaigns of the 1660s had provoked, may have persuaded the ecclesiastical authorities that locally based campaigns were no longer the most effective approach to the problem of native religious deviance. Thus the summoning of trials to Lima represented a substitute for the campaigns of extirpation, explaining why no Visitors-General of Idolatry were appointed under Liñán de Cisneros.

The determination to eradicate persistent indigenous religious practices survived undiminished into the third decade of the eighteenth century. The concern of the ecclesiastical authorities remained so great that the 1720s

witnessed a renewed attempt, albeit stillborn, to revive
the classic campaign of extirpation, as the title of Visitor-
General of Idolatry was revived for the first time in over
half a century. Although the evidence of this period has
been almost completely ignored by historians,[36] it reveals
a remarkable consistency of purpose among these latter-
day advocates of the traditional Extirpation and belies
the idea that by the eighteenth century indigenous religious practices had become more "acceptable." It is undeniable, however, that the investigations of the 1720s
never approached the scale of the mid-seventeenth century. If the surviving documentation is complete (which
is unlikely as very few cases survive from the eighteenth
century), only one priest, Pedro de Celís, received the
commission of Visitor-General. But his existence testifies
to the continuity of the ideology and methods of the Extirpation, even a century and a quarter after its inception.
Like the earlier campaigns, this late revival was dependent on the personal initiative of the archbishop of Lima,
Diego Morcillo Rubio de Auñon (1724–30).

It is clear from this brief account that the deployment of
campaigns of extirpation was an extraordinary, not a regular or commonplace, phenomenon. The exceptionality
of the Peruvian Extirpation is illustrated by comparison
with the viceroyalty of Mexico, which, after the early activities of Landa, never experienced waves of repressive
eradication of native religion.[37] The significant difference
between the two viceroyalties lay in the precocity of evangelization in Mexico, the revulsion at the harsh and repressive methods of Zumárraga and Landa, and the absence of any declared indigenous resistance (in the way
that Taki Onqoy was perceived, almost certainly errone-
ously, to be connected to the neo-Inca state of Vilca-
bamba). In Mexico, the seventeenth-century Extirpation
remained an individual, isolated enterprise, unable to excite the enthusiasm of either the ecclesiastical or the civil

authorities.[38] Most of the writings of the Mexican extirpators, such as Jacinto de la Serna, Pedro Ponce, Hernando Ruiz de Alarcón, and Pedro Sánchez de Aguilar, were not even published until the end of the nineteenth century. The pursuit of extirpation in Peru derived from the peculiar circumstances of the later, more disrupted evangelization, the geographic factors that favored the survival of isolated pockets distant from Christian influences, and, above all, the support of the Jesuits.

It is important to recognize that the pursuit of extirpation was not a norm, from which any subsequent departure must be justified as an inexplicable deviation. Rather, the experience of Mexico and that of Peru outside the years 1609–22, 1649–70, and 1725, would suggest that it was the Extirpation itself that was the aberration. If the Extirpation enjoyed the support of powerful advocates, it also endured the opposition of equally powerful antagonists. Indeed, the latter were so numerous that it is clear that the advocates of extirpation were not the upholders of the accepted orthodoxy but the defendants of a minority faction. The intermittent occurrence of the campaigns of extirpation was determined to a great extent by the permanent conflict between these two groups, a conflict that was especially fervent in that it derived from ideological disagreements about nothing less than what it signified to be a Christian. It is to this debate that we must now turn our attention.

II

When Spaniards of the sixteenth century encountered native Andean religion, they responded by inventing "idolatry." This is not to say that the concept of idolatry was a new one. On the contrary, it formed an integral part of the Spanish cultural heritage, determined by the classification of ancient paganism by the early Church fathers and modified by medieval Scholasticism. Clearly the Spanish mind was not a tabula rasa, nor a mirror that could reflect the "true" empirical phenomenon of indigenous religion. Thus the Spanish response to American religion may be called an invention because it projected onto the empirical experience of the New World an alien system of religious categories.[39]

Andean religion was interpreted according to the dichotomy between "idolatry" and "superstition." These categories had been clearly distinguished by classical Christian writers. According to Thomas Aquinas, superstition was "religion carried to excess." This excess lay, not in giving too much worship to God, but in offering worship to Him in some manner that was unfitting or, alternatively, in offering divine worship to something not deserving it. This latter category of superstition could take the form, first, of false observances, which were the expression of the belief that divine powers were found in certain creatures; second, of divination, which was the attribution of divine powers to demons; and third, idolatry, or the rendering unto *creatures* of worship due to God alone. Idolatry denoted, then, not only the worship of idols proper, as its etymology (*idolo-latria*) would suggest, but also the worship of any "creature" or object of creation, which, by definition, could not be divine and hence could not figure as an appropriate recipient of worship. Idolatry was explicitly defined as a subdivision of the broader category of superstition, any form of undue or excessive worship. The relationship of idolatry to superstition was, then, that of the part to the whole.[40]

By the sixteenth century, this classical distinction between idolatry and superstition had largely been lost among those writers whose works were to exercise a profound influence on the fight against native religion in Peru. Instead, the two categories had become closely assimilated. This relative departure from classical positions derived from the early modern identification of both idolatry and superstition with devil worship. For Aquinas, only the sin of divination had been explicitly associated with diabolical intervention. The sin of idolatry derived principally from the ignorance and vanity of humankind rather than from the evil machinations of demonic spirits. Humankind's propensity for idolatry arose, in the first instance, from their disposition (especially from their "misdirected affection" that led them to venerate beyond reason), their natural delight in representation, and their ignorance of the true God. The attempts of demonic powers to confuse humankind, by speaking through idols and performing wondrous acts, were only a complementary cause.[41]

Sixteenth-century writers, however, reversed the relative importance of these two principal causes. Diabolical intervention was no longer merely contributory but became *the* essential cause. Pedro Ciruelo, the canon of Salamanca Cathedral, whose work *Reprobación de supersticiones y hechicerías* (1530) became the standard reference on the subject in sixteenth-century Spain, wrote, "The very great sin of idolatry . . . is abominable in the sight of God because idolatry takes away from God the honor and obedience that is due to him and gives it to his principal enemy who is the Devil." Idolatry, the sin against *latria*, was no longer simply the worship of creatures; it was an act of pure treachery against God by offering his worship to the enemy, Satan himself. Idolatry had become synonymous with devil worship.[42]

Because the roots of both offenses lay in diabolical intervention, superstition was no longer distinguishable from idolatry. If all superstitions and false observances had been taught to men by the Devil, then all those who practiced them must be his disciples. Whereas Aquinas had defined idolatry as one form of superstition, Ciruelo reversed the equation and reclassified superstition as a subdivision of idolatry. Enumerating four types of idolatry, all originating from the Devil, he distinguished between, on the one hand, the clear and manifest idolatry of necromancers who spoke with the Devil and, on the other, the three other types represented by superstitions, false observances, and *hechicerías*. Diabolically inspired idolatry had been raised to a category in its own right.[43]

The assimilation of both idolatry and superstition to devil worship characterized the works of the Jesuit writers who were to provide the ideological basis for the Extirpation. The Jesuit provincial and missionary in Peru, José de Acosta, followed Ciruelo when he identified idolatry with devil worship and hence attributed a diabolical origin to native Andean religious practices. The first chapter of the fifth book of his *Historia natural y moral de las Indias* was entitled "That the cause of idolatry has been the pride and envy of the Devil"; elsewhere he wrote that honoring idols was the same as honoring the Devil. The huacas were mere mouthpieces for Satan, and their rites and ceremonies were simply a diabolical parody of the true faith.[44]

Acosta did draw a sharp theoretical distinction between idolatry and superstition. Whereas idolatry embraced mistaken beliefs and objects of mistaken worship (whether natural phenomena or man-made inventions), superstitions embraced mistaken practices (rites, ceremonies, and sacrifices).[45] Whereas excessive honoring of the dead, which amounted to worship, was a form of idolatry, the making of sacrifices and the gifts of food and clothing for those same dead were superstitions.[46]

In practice, however, Acosta used the terms almost interchangeably. He frequently assimilated superstition and the worship of huacas, referring, for example, to "the superstitious cult of their idols" or "all the images and huacas and other representations of the superstitions of the Indians" or the widespread "superstition" of "different classes of sacrifices and huacas." Acosta observed that those Indian nations characterized by superior power and organizing capacity had more numerous and more serious classes of "diabolical superstitions," whereas among those who had achieved less progress, "idolatry" was much rarer. The diligent catechist, he wrote, must not only fight the "vanity of idols" in general but must also refute the "particular gods and huacas and other superstitions that are special to their people." This "almost infinite variety of superstitions" derived directly from the worship of idols. Thus superstitions became indistinguishable from idolatry because the former were themselves fragmented derivatives of the latter. It followed that as residual vestiges of the ebbing tide of idolatrous beliefs, superstitious ceremonies and rites were as sinful as the true idolatrous reverence of creatures, since both arose from the same diabolical origin. Idolatry was the trunk from which grew the branches of superstition, and both were rooted in diabolical inspiration.[47]

The writings of the principal ideologue of the Extirpation, Arriaga, were largely derived from Acosta. Although Arriaga's manual only contained a few explicit references to Acosta's *De procuranda* (pp. 224 and 257), the entire work was founded on the latter's principles. For example, Arriaga's dictum that the "traces of idolatry" that remained in Peru had been "imbibed with the [mother's] milk and inherited from parents to children" echoed Acosta's famous reference to the "hereditary illness of idolatry" that had been "contracted in the very mother's breast and suckled by her milk." Like Acosta, Arriaga distinguished in theory between true idolatry, the attribution of divinity to creatures expressed in the worship of huacas and mallquis, and superstition, which included ceremonies, rites, and customs. For example, he acknowledged that *zaramamas* (two corncobs that emerged joined together) were not accorded the worship rendered to a huaca or *conopa* (a small stone, in which household,

family, or personal deities were said to reside, used to promote fertility of crops and livestock) but were "supersti-
tiously held as a sacred object." Even so, like Acosta, the
worship of huacas was often described indistinguishably
as idolatry or superstition. He referred to huacas as "idolatries" (e.g. "their huacas and conopas and the other
instruments of their idolatries"); yet, elsewhere, he
grouped huacas with superstition ("the huacas and other
superstitions"). Like Acosta, he believed that Indian superstitions sprang from the trunk of idolatry: "all are
branches and leaves born of the trunk of their gentility
and idolatry."[48]

This assimilation of idolatry and superstition to devil
worship was the fundamental principle of the ideology
of the Extirpation. Its most important consequence was
to confer the status of apostates, even heretics, on the Indians. As early as 1609, Avila had accused the Indians of
his doctrina of apostasy in continuing to celebrate native
rites.[49] Similarly, in 1614, Visitor Luis de Mora y Aguilar
absolved the inhabitants of the village of Concepción de
Chupas of the sins of "idolatry and apostasy."[50] This condition was understood to be endemic throughout the entire viceroyalty. Archbishop Lobo Guerrero informed the
king in 1611 that "all the Indians of my archbishopric, and
similarly those of the other bishoprics, are today as much
infidels and idolaters as when they were first conquered."[51] The constitutions of the synod of Lima of 1613
made constant references to the Indians as idolaters and
apostates.[52] Archbishop Campo informed the king in 1626
that he had found many parts of his archbishopric contaminated with "idolatries and heresies," for which reason
he recommended that trials of Indians for such offenses
should be placed under the jurisdiction of the Inquisition.
For the extirpators and their supporters, "idolatry" was
a choice rather than the product of deep-rooted habits.[53]

Thus idolatry, superstition, heresy, and apostasy had

all been assimilated until it seemed that the Indians were hardly Christians at all. But such an ideology was not monolithic, and the close identification of these sins was seriously questioned. Not all writers had agreed with Acosta's association of Andean religion with devil worship. The most famous opponent of the diabolical interpretation of native religion was the Dominican friar Bartolomé de Las Casas. Las Casas followed Aquinas in attributing to the Devil a complementary role in idolatry. For the Dominican, the origin of idolatry lay in the perversion of man's natural religiosity. When the guidance of grace and instruction was lacking, the worship due to God could become misdirected by the very strength of humankind's religious appetite; hence latria became idolatry. It was true that Satan was able to take advantage of the misplacement of humanity's religious urge to prevent recognition of the true God and to have himself worshiped instead; but the original source of idolatry sprang from humankind's innate blindness in the absence of the teachings of Christ and not from the all-pervading power and malevolence of Satan. The intervention of the Devil was limited to the initiation of magical practices among the Indians, which were clearly distinguished as superstitions (the sinful attempt to learn of future contingencies from other than natural or divine sources) and not idolatry.[54]

Like Las Casas, some experts in Andean religious practices were concerned to save the autochthonous religious tradition from obloquy. By sharply differentiating superstition from idolatry, an explicit intention to give worship to creatures in every native rite could be denied. Whereas Arriaga found idolatry in every aspect of daily life, the chronicler Cristóbal de Molina refused to consider that ceremonies linked to the family rites of the cycle of life were idolatrous but rather defined them simply as expressions of communal solidarity. The native rites of

name giving and the ritual cutting of hair were ceremonies performed "without the slightest trace of idolatry." Such interpretations were not confined to Peru. In
Mexico, the Dominican friar Diego Durán distinguished
between true idolatry and superstitious customs. He tolerated the use of floral ornaments on Christian festivals
that coincided with those of Tezcatlipoca as there was
"no trace of idolatry in it": they merely expressed "an ancient custom." Custom was here distinguished from idolatry by the fact that it was automatic and deprived of all
conscious foundation. Since the institutional framework
for native religion had collapsed, any survivals, deprived
of the fundamental coherence that formerly unified all
acts of life, could only be classed as superstition. It was
this distinction that dominated the debate between the
advocates of extirpation and their opponents.[55]

It is clear that the debate sharply divided ecclesiastical
opinion. One of the principal purposes of Arriaga's manual was to "satisfy learned and serious people" of the truth
of what "they have doubted and even contradicted on
many occasions, . . . that there are idolatries among the
Indians [whereas they have said] all are good Christians."[56] The issue caused such great disagreement
among the great clerical minds of the era that when Archbishop Campo first arrived in Lima, he was so impressed
by the passion on all sides that he decided to conduct a
personal visit to his archdiocese to verify for himself the
existence of native religious practices. He wrote,

I found such a great variety of opinions about this when I arrived in Lima. . . . [M]ost of those who told me that there was a
great deal of idolatry were theologians, preachers and others
with great zeal for saving souls; others told me that it was an
invention of the Visitors who under this pretext tried to make
money, and that the Indians were victims of a grave injustice
when they were thus accused; others said that they believed
there was some idolatry but not as much as was claimed.[57]

Thus there was at least a three-way divide on the issue, with two factions opposing the advocates of the Extirpation.

It was at this time, between 1622 and 1626, when the first wave of campaigns had ended and the triumvirate responsible for their execution had disappeared, that much of the hitherto repressed resistance to the Extirpation was expressed. Among the first to voice their opposition were the mendicant orders. In 1622, the provincial of the Augustinians, Francisco de la Serna, informed the king that "not even a trace" of idolatry was to be found among the Indians in their doctrinas. He pointed out that the investigations of Luis Cornejo, the Dominican provincial who had been appointed by the archbishop himself to investigate native practices throughout the archdiocese, had concluded that the Indians were not guilty of the worship of idols but rather only of "abuses and rites" that they observed "in imitation of their ancestors." De la Serna was drawing on arguments familiar to Molina so as to absolve the Indians of the charge of idolatry. To settle the matter, the Augustinian provincial declared his intention to conduct visitations to all the villages of the archbishopric of Lima and the bishopric of Trujillo, since he was extremely skeptical of the account given by the Jesuit Arriaga. This open challenge to the ideology of the Extirpation reflected in part the old hostility of the mendicant orders toward the Jesuits; but it also expressed an interpretation of native religious practices fundamentally at odds with that of the advocates of Extirpation. The provincial of the Mercedarians clearly shared this alternative interpretation when he informed the king in 1626 that few Indians were idolaters, unless the term was to be extended to their "false superstitions," in which case there would be few who would not be included. The accusation of idolatry was invalid, not because elements of native religion did not survive, but because Indian rites were only a vestige of the past, a reflex action, a mimicry of their ancestors without the true content of belief.[58]

The Extirpation was also attacked by persons within the religious and political administrations of the archbishopric. In 1622, after the death of Lobo Guerrero but before the arrival of the new archbishop, the *cabildo eclesiástico* (cathedral chapter) of Lima suspended the idolatry visitations, allegedly on the grounds of excesses that had been denounced by the Indians, and began a secret investigation against the Visitors.[59] When Campo renewed the campaigns in 1625, the audiencia of Lima called into question not only the seriousness of native religious practices but also the procedures of the idolatry campaigns and their apparent excesses. They alleged that the Visitors and the Jesuits were exaggerating the extent of idolatry to justify the importance of their work. If the Indians confessed to idolatry, it was because they were "simple people" who told the Visitors what they wanted to hear in return for rewards or in order to please them and free themselves from their inquiries. If they did not confess, the Visitors took away their livestock on the pretext that it was destined for sacrifice to the huacas. Thus not only were the charges false, but the investigations subjected the Indians to serious abuses and exactions.[60]

The sophisticated argument that the Visitors were "inventing" idolatry to justify their work subverted the very foundations of the Extirpation. It is clear that hostility was inspired in part by questions of encroachment on jurisdiction and of infringement of rights. The Extirpation provided the opportunity for an enormous extension of the archbishop's (and the Jesuits') powers. The audiencia was angered by the archbishop's high-handed treatment of its own fiscal and of the *procurador de los Naturales* (attorney for the natives) when they had attempted to intervene to secure justice for some Indians who had been incarcerated at El Cercado. But opposition to the principles and methods of the Extirpation was not merely an expression of petty infighting within the archbishopric since it extended beyond mere political convenience. There were many prelates in other dioceses of the viceroyalty who shared reservations about the necessity of campaigns of extirpation. These reservations rested on deep ideological disagreements with the Extirpation.

Some bishops rejected the central contention of the Extirpation by denying the existence of any form of native religious practices. The bishop of Cuzco, Lorenzo Perez de Grado (1619–27), wrote to the king that he had found his diocese "clean of idolatries, abuses and ancient rites." The bishop of Trujillo, Francisco de Cabrera (1616–19), contested the need for campaigns of extirpation in his diocese since not only were the Indians "as free of these and other similar errors as Burgos and Toledo" but their devotion to Christianity was so strong that he was "envious of it for the Spaniards." This view was expressed to oppose the encroachments of the Jesuits on his jurisdiction and to resist the plans of the viceroy and archbishop of Lima to give the Company the doctrina of Lambayeque, which fell within his diocese.[61]

Other prelates opposed the Extirpation in the absence of considerations of rival jurisdictions. Few of them denied all trace of ancient belief or custom. But if the Indians did indeed preserve vestiges of their former religion, these were not to be interpreted as "idolatry," nor were they to be remedied by trials and severe punishments. The bishop of Arequipa, Pedro de Perea (1619–30), admitted the existence of "the relics of idolatries and superstitions" among the Indians but advanced instruction in Spanish as the most potent antidote. Those who maintained these customs were the *hatunrunas*, unacculturated Andeans who lived in villages with little contact with Spaniards; the acculturated ladinos, who lived in Spanish towns, were innocent of these practices. Hence the remedy was greater acculturation, to which end he advocated forbidding the use of the native tongue among the Indians. Instead, they should converse in Spanish, which could be imparted to them by village fiscales and *caciques* specially trained in local seminaries, modeled on the school for Indian chieftains in Lima and replicated in every bishopric. The ultimate goal was the union of both *naciones*, Indians and Spaniards, in one republic. This alternative interpretation of the significance of persisting native customs implicitly denied the foundations on which the campaigns of extirpation were based. For despite the fact that the bishop wrote at the height of the trials, he omitted to advance persecution as a suitable remedy. His failure to respond to Esquilache's call of the previous year for all prelates to launch idolatry campaigns in their own dioceses must be understood in this context.[62]

Perea was not the only prelate to propose alternative remedies for the "persistence" of native practices. The constitutions of the diocesan synod for Trujillo, drawn up by Bishop Carlos Marcelo Corne (1619–29) in 1623, denied the existence of "idolatries" among the Indians and lamented only their "fraudulent superstitions and abuses." But to satisfy the demands for further investigations on the part of those who "claimed" that idolatry was "universal" throughout the viceroyalty, the bishop appointed, not specialized extirpators of idolatry, but the ordinary ecclesiastical Visitors, to make inquiries into whether any "heathen rites" were still performed or any "superstitions, spells, or other tricks" practiced. If they found evidence of pagan practices, they were to correct the Indians principally through preaching; rigorous punishment would be necessary only for those who were stubbornly rebellious. The term *extirpación* itself was employed only with reference to "superstitions" and "magic," not with reference to "idolatry."[63]

If Corne and Perea offered tacit and indirect opposition to the techniques of the Extirpation, the bishop of Huamanga, Francisco Verdugo (1621–37), used his authority directly to prevent the extension of its activities to his diocese. In 1621, he suspended the Visitors because of the distress they had caused among the Indians, substituting their work with his own personal visits to the Indians in the company of Jesuit missionaries. Like his colleagues in Trujillo and Arequipa, Verdugo was convinced that there were no grounds for accusing the Indians of idolatries. The advocates of extirpation, motivated by private interests and ambitions rather than by zeal for souls, had not told the king the truth. They blamed the poor spiritual condition of the Indians on their innate incapacity and propensity for vice, when in reality it was they themselves who were guilty of failure to instruct the Indians adequately. The Indians were clearly not "a barbarous people," incapable of understanding the mysteries of the faith. Their instruction had been prevented by the burdens of excessive work, which caused them to flee from the doctrina, making it impossible for priests to teach them. After all, if even the Spaniards themselves, despite their indoctrination from a very early age, were sometimes corrupted and went astray from the faith, was it surprising that the Indians, who had been so inadequately instructed, were still infirm in the faith? They were not idolaters but poor Christians.[64]

Although the documentation for the political organization of the campaigns of the 1650s under Villagómez is sparse, there is evidence that the tradition of opposition to the Extirpation had not faded. As Duviols has indicated, the first part of Villagómez's *Carta pastoral* is devoted to refuting the arguments of those who denied the need for idolatry visitations. These views must have been significant to elicit such a response. The letters included at the back of the work indicate the continuation of a vehement polemic over the existence and significance of native religious practices. The bishop of Cuzco, Juan Alonso Ocón (1643–51), lamented the widespread persistence of idolatry in his diocese and attacked those "priests and other ecclesiastics" who made cause with "Behemoth" by denying this ugly truth. The Jesuit Francisco Patiño denounced those who dismissed the existence of idolatry as a wild fantasy or excused it as a vestige of the past. Those priests who failed to perceive or to act against the idolatry taking place under their noses were themselves guilty of "interpretive idolatry." This debate was not silenced by Villagómez's *Carta pastoral*, and Duviols is not correct when he writes that there were no more manifestations of opposition after 1650.[65]

At least one bishop, Francisco de Godoy, the prelate of Huamanga (1652–59), opposed the principles of the renewed campaigns. Godoy did not deny the existence of idolatry; on the contrary, he claimed he had found significant traces of native religious practices. He was even prepared to threaten individual Indians with the traditional punishment for "apostates of the faith," burning at the stake, to terrify them into disclosing their religious practices.[66] But these "idolatries" or "superstitions" were to be understood as "traces" or "vestiges" of ancient religious practices rather than as real apostasy. Such errors were not exclusive to Indians but were shared by blacks. If the Indians were still practicing their old beliefs, it was not because they were inherently wicked but because the Spaniards had failed in their duty to instruct them adequately. The Indian potential for assimilation of the true faith was boundless since "among all nations there has never been any which has received the ceremony of our religion as this one has." The Indians were the chief attendants at divine worship in Huamanga and received the bishop and his priests with love and devotion. It was this optimism about the Indian character, sharply at variance with the assessment of the advocates of extirpation, that convinced him that with culture and education the Indians could become good Christians.[67] Improved preaching would be one principal method. In a letter of 1652, he wrote, "With ordinary preaching and education, many idolatries which have remained from their ancestors will be eliminated, since there is no means to eliminate them other than preaching." Another method was the administration of the sacrament of Communion. In subsequent letters of 1656 and 1657, the bishop claimed that "the principal remedy against their idolatries" was the participation of the Indians in "the mystery of the Incarnation of the Son of God." All Indians should be prepared to receive the sacrament "since while they do not take Communion, they will not be true Christians." These were sufficient for the dissemination of true belief among the Indians and for an end to their native practices. Campaigns of extirpation played no part in the bishop's scheme.[68]

For Godoy, the devotion of the Indians to Catholic worship was genuine and confirmed them as true Christians. The survival of native religious practices could not disqualify their devotion. The issue was how to make them better Christians.

The interpretation of the advocates of extirpation was irreconcilably opposed. Ocón alleged that, far from being exaggerated, the stranglehold of idolatry in Peru was greater than had previously been realized, to the extent that Christianity only existed "in embryo." And Patiño wrote that by returning to their heathen ways after hearing the true faith, the Indians were "damned twice over," not only by comparison with their former ignorant state but also by comparison with the Spaniards; for if Spaniards were poor practicants of Christianity, at least they believed, whereas the Indians were guilty of insincere belief. Thus if the Spaniards were "bad Christians," they were still "good Catholics"; the Indians, however, were "Christians in name only" and "apostates and idolaters" in reality.[69] Whereas for the opponents of extirpation the majority of Indians were *passive* idolaters, content to imitate what they saw others do without contemplating the nature of the gestures and the acts performed, for its advocates they were *active* idolaters, guilty not merely of *material* idolatry (through ignorance or confusion) but also of profound, interiorized *formal* idolatry (through pertinacity).[70]

It was the interplay between these two currents of thought that determined the intermittent occurrence of campaigns of extirpation within the archdiocese of Lima as well as the infrequent extension of these campaigns beyond its confines. Both Lobo Guerrero and Villagómez intended to extend the trials to all the dioceses of the viceroyalty, but both achieved only partial success. In 1619, Viceroy Esquilache ordered visitations to be initiated by the bishops of Huamanga, Cuzco, Arequipa, La Paz, La Plata, and Santa Cruz de la Sierra.[71] It is clear that there were idolatry trials in Huamanga in the second decade of the seventeenth century, since Patiño's letter indicates that Bishop Agustín de Caravajal (1613–18) presided over investigations in his diocese.[72] There were also trials in Arequipa under Villagómez himself between 1635 and 1640. Ocón's letter refers to idolatry visits in his diocese of Cuzco in the 1640s: "I left a judge of idolatry in these provinces, who has been sending me cases of dogmatizadores."[73] Similarly, Manuel de Mollinedo, bishop of Cuzco from 1673 to 1699, gave an account in 1674 of idolatry trials in Pucara in his diocese.[74]

But most dioceses did not witness campaigns of extirpation. This was *not* because the bishops were too self-interested, apathetic, or lacking in zeal to lend their support. Instead, as a matter of principle, few agreed with the strategy of the central authorities. If this opposition did not take the form of an overt critique of the policy of extirpation as such (there is no documentary evidence to indicate such an approach), it consisted instead of the advocacy of alternative policies, in the service of a different priority: not to "extirpate" idolatry but to make good Christians out of *plantas tiernas,* "tender plants." The dispute remained one between those who believed that they were punishing apostates through a combination of persecution and instruction and those who believed that by persuasion and patience, they were gradually transforming the Indians from poor Christians into good Christians.

The widespread acceptance of the antiextirpation current among both secular and religious authorities is the chief explanation for the failure of the campaigns to be promulgated more widely. The crusaders of extirpation could not take advantage of the authority conferred by orthodoxy but were forced to present their case and win their battles in every generation. The initiation of a particular campaign of extirpation represented only a temporary victory for their promoters in a long-standing conflict. Against such a background, the intermittence of the campaigns becomes understandable.

The potent and compelling ideology of the Extirpation survived the absence of permanent institutions and periods of disfavor, remaining the root cause of the profound gulf between the advocates and the opponents of the persecution of native religion. The principal issue of contention was the assimilation of indigenous religious practices to the synonymous categories of idolatry, apostasy, and devil worship. The key to this assimilation lay in the identification of the "idolater" with that master of religious deviance haunting the Spanish imagination, the hechicero or sorcerer. Not only the theory but also the practice of the Extirpation was to be dominated by this crucial identification.

Two: THE IDOLATER AS *HECHICERO*

POИTÍFÍSES·VALLAVÍƷA
LAÍCAVMVHÍCHEƷE

el gzan hichessero Andia

los

"A great sorcerer."

The person of the hechicero, . . . *incarnated in the eyes of Christians as the instrument of the Devil, became the perfect model of the idolater, born from the debris of idolatry.*
—Bernand and Gruzinski, *De l'idolâtrie* (1988)

It is a great hechicería . . . *to give worship to objects which is only due to the true God.*
—Testimony of the witness Felipe Guaman, *Idolatrías* (1647)

I

IN 1646, DON GERÓNIMO AUQUINIVIN, GOVERNOR OF THE villages of Pampas and Colcabamba in the province of Huaylas, denounced himself before the archbishop of Lima, Pedro de Villagómez, as an *hechicero idólatra* (idolatrous sorcerer). He was charged with having invoked the huacas of his ancestors and having offered *chicha* (maize beer) to some skittles in order to win a game. Observing that the Indians of his village had been trying to lift a *huanca*, a very heavy stone, with little result but exhaustion from their efforts, Auquinivin had called for some chicha in which to wash his hands so that he could raise the boulder more easily.[1] When some drops of the maize beer had inadvertently fallen onto the stone, his nephew, Alonso García, had asked him if he had intended to offer chicha to the huanca. Realizing that his nephew suspected "some superstition," the governor had replied that the stone could not drink. Two days later, having beaten García in a game, he had given the victorious skittles some chicha to drink in celebration. His nephew had challenged him again, to which he had replied, "How could they drink, having no mouth?"[2]

In the accusation, the two sins, *hechicería* and *idolatría*, were indistinguishable. Although in the strict sense the cacique's actions constituted idolatry, or the rendering of worship to creatures, the evidence was couched more in the language of sorcery. The witness Felipe Guaman accused his native lord of very great "hechicería" by offering the boulder chicha to drink according to the pagan custom. His libation to the skittles after his victory was another great "hechicería" because "this is to give worship to objects which is only due to the true god . . . and all the Indians of the doctrina consider Don Gerónimo to be a great idolater."[3]

Another witness, Pablo Alfonso Mallqui, echoed Guaman in equating idolatría and hechicería. He confirmed that Don Gerónimo had invoked the aid of the stone as his father and that the Indians present had been shocked at such idolatry and superstition, all supposing him to be "a great idolater and hechicero." García agreed that the cacique had invoked the stone with the following words: "Ah villcarumi jampas upiay anaymanmi churasayki,"

"O huanca, my mother, you drink too and I will put you in your correct place." These were words used only by "hechiceros" and "idólatras" when they worshiped their huacas. After spilling chicha on the stone, he had consumed what remained in the cup with great reverence, "as if the stone was his very God and Creator." The sin of rendering worship unto a creature, the classic definition of idolatry, was here represented as the sin of hechicería.[4]

As a result of these declarations, Auquinivin was closely questioned about his "intention": had he meant to worship the stone and the skittles, or had he expected to derive any benefits from his actions? This he emphatically denied and said his only intention had been to amuse himself; if he had intended some malice by it, would he have done it so openly in front of all the Indians? In this way he sought to allay the accusation of idolatry by denying any genuine desire to render worship or any belief in the efficacy of what he did.

This case serves as a preface to the frenzied extirpation of the 1650s and 1660s and as a paradigm for the ideology of extirpation. The assimilation of idolater to sorcerer was to be characteristic of the onslaught on native religious practices.

It is important to recognize that this fusion of idolater and hechicero was central to the Spanish mind. Although the Indian witnesses employed the vocabulary of hechicería, they did so only in an attempt to conform to the worldview of the extirpators, not because this was a genuine reflection of native perceptions. There is no evidence that the Indians had interiorized these categories in the sense that Spaniards understood them. The witnesses' depositions were recorded not by themselves but by a notary who may have interpreted their words in his own fashion. Even if the statements were reported accurately, it is impossible to know if the accounts were offered spontaneously or uttered in response to suggestive questioning by the Visitor-General. The most likely explanation is that the witnesses couched their accusations in the language best designed to secure their purposes. The accusers of Auquinivin were his enemies, and their aim was to present the sort of evidence best calculated to destroy him. They understood that the accusation of native religious practices would entangle him in the Spanish legal net. It was the most effective disqualification. But there is no reason to suppose that they invoked the words *idólatra* and *hechicero* as anything more than useful labels with which to stigmatize their intended victim. The assimilation of idolater to hechicero evident in these depositions reveals little of the mentality of the Indian protagonists but testifies to the imposition of Spanish mental constructs on indigenous experience.

II

The sin of hechicería, with which idolatry had become identified among the advocates of the Peruvian Extirpation, had a long history in metropolitan Spain. For the peninsular, the popular conception of the term "hechicero" was not the same as it was for the learned jurist or theologian. For the peasant community of Galicia, the hechicero or hechicera was closely related to the brujo or bruja.[5] Both terms were employed more commonly in the feminine than in the masculine. "Bruja" generally denoted (and still denotes) a person who consciously and malevolently caused harm by hidden means to people, their animals, or their interests. The reputation of the bruja was based on threats that served a dual purpose: to imply the effective possession of certain powers and thereby to secure what she wanted from her neighbors. "Hechicera," in contrast, traditionally denoted a person who cured and gave remedies for illnesses (in which case she was synonymous with the curandera), who manufactured love filters and protective potions, and who identified the bruja who had caused harm and challenged and undid her work. More than anything, she was a counteragent. Nevertheless, the dividing line was not impervious, since a person who possessed powers to dispel magic might logically be assumed to be able to inflict it as well. The step from hechicera to bruja was a short one, and any hechicera who refused to help a client was vulnerable to denunciation as a bruja.[6]

Of course, our understanding of the peasant conception originates in the writings of those jurists and theologians who formed the Tribunal of the Inquisition. As a result, it is refracted through the prism of a rather different imagination. Whereas the community distinguished an hechicera from a bruja according to the supposed action and result, the inquisitorial mind discriminated less between one type of practitioner and the other and more between various categories of offense (such as superstition or false observances). The learned mind was most preoccupied, not with the accused's *acts* but with her *intention* and *belief* about those acts and, even more important, the *origins* of her alleged powers. For the inquisitor, the issue was whether the suspect had indeed achieved some genuine effect in the real world through the manipulation of hidden powers, or whether she had merely practiced deception. The dichotomy was one of hechicera/bruja/*supersticiosa* against *embustera*, or trickster.

At the same time, the word *bruja* was recognized to carry special connotations that distinguished it from *hechicera*. The bruja was one who had made a formal express pact with the Devil by means of a contract, in which she renounced God, swore allegiance to the Enemy, and agreed to sexual intercourse with him and collective worship at mass meetings in secret places (*aquelarres*).[7] The term "hechicera" included a broader category of superstitious practitioner. An hechicera might have either an implicit or an explicit pact with the Devil, but she was not in possession of any special powers. Rather she enjoyed the use of some simple knowledge or technique that had been passed on to her by a human teacher. She was usually guilty of mixing Christian prayers and invocations in her practices. Unlike the brujas, who gathered in covens, hechiceras invariably worked alone. The bruja was technically an idolater since she worshiped Satan and her life was devoted to his work; the hechicera merely sought to achieve her desires through supernatural means.[8]

In practice, the distinction between "bruja" and "hechicera" was rarely made. The two terms were used interchangeably since their practices shared the inspiration of the Devil. That the term "bruja" was used to refer to what was essentially an hechicera is clear from the absence in almost all parts of Spain of references to mass attendance at aquelarres or explicit pacts with Satan, which would constitute true *brujería* (witchcraft).[9]

The categories of hechicero/brujo or embustero, as employed by the Inquisition, bore little relation to empirical observation of the real actions of those so accused. Instead they formed part of a Devil-witch mythology that was the independent and abstract creation of learned minds, an elaboration on the part of those whom Carmelo Lisón Tolosana has called "malefiz-meister," or experts in *maleficio*, eager to construct a metaphysical system with which to make sense of religious deviance. The categories were fixed and rigid, admitting of only two possibilities: fraud or brujo/hechicero. No alternative reality was admissible. The mythologers were the definers of reality and suppliers of truth. In their inability to conceive of an alternative reality, thinking minds had been constricted by the myth.[10]

The cornerstone of this mythology was the accusation of a pact with the Devil. Such a pact, which could be express or tacit, was held by all commentators to be the fundamental basis of all magic.[11] The express pact was of two types: one made with the Devil himself, who appeared in physical form, in which the participant renounced the faith and rendered total obedience in body and soul; the other made not with the Devil himself but with an intermediary, who was one of his ministers (*encantadores* [enchanters], hechiceros, or brujos).[12] The implicit pact was also of two types. The first was one made by those who, although they did not renege on their faith, believed in and performed diabolical ceremonies and invocations; it was considered a pact because the practicants believed in the efficacy of the ceremonies (these people were commonly called hechiceros). The second, considered a less serious offense, was one made by those who did not believe in such ceremonies but on a given occasion allowed them to take place for whatever they might be worth (e.g., to restore bodily health).

Those guilty of either an explicit or an implicit pact were heretical idolaters and would be punished as such. But it was very important to establish the precise nature of the words with which the invocation was made. If they were expressed as a command, there was no heresy; if they were imploring or pleading, they constituted respect or worship for demons and were true idolatry.[13]

Experts on magic maintained an ambiguous position concerning the reality of the acts alleged to have been committed by the makers of these pacts. The great theologian Francisco de Vitoria argued that although some of the works of magicians were illusory and a fiction of the senses, others were real; therefore, what was said about brujas, although generally imaginary, could sometimes genuinely occur.[14] This dichotomy was recognized by other commentators. The Franciscan friar Martín de Castañega, author of one of the most authoritative works on magic in sixteenth-century Spain, affirmed the reality of the diabolical pact. He believed that brujos could fly through the air, since the Devil's power was sufficient if

God allowed it. But he also believed that the Devil could disturb the senses of his adepts and make them hallucinate that they were flying to the aquelarres.[15] Castañega tended to explain phenomena not by diabolical intervention but by the laws of nature, thus encouraging the rationalist tradition, even as he avowed the reality of the pact.

This ambiguity represented an uneasy marriage of two traditions of thought regarding the reality of the deeds of hechiceros or brujos which had their origins in the early Christian period. One tradition, which might be designated the "credulous" school, believed in the reality of the phenomenon and condemned, above all, the act itself; the other, the "skeptical" or "experimentalist" school, denied the reality of the hechicero's claims and censured not the alleged act itself but the intention behind it.[16] The classic works of the credulous school included not only the famous *Malleus maleficarum* (1486), the European encyclopedia of demonology, but also, from Spain itself, the highly influential treatises of Pedro Ciruelo (1530) and, to a lesser extent, Castañega (1529) and Vitoria (1540). Although these authors were not convinced of the reality of every manifestation of hechicería, they certainly accepted the reality of the vast majority of instances. The concepts expressed in these works derived from the Scholastic doctrines of the thirteenth century, as outlined by thinkers such as Johannes Nyder and summarized in the *Directorium inquisitorum* of Eymerich (1376). The later sixteenth century saw an escalation in works conforming to the credulous tradition, for example, those of Jean Bodin, Pierre Grégoire, Nicholas Rémy, Henri Boguet, Pierre de Lancre, P. Binsfeld, and, in Spain, Martín del Río's *Disquisitionum magicarum libri sex* (1599).[17]

The ideas of the skeptical tradition originated in the writings of the school of Lope de Barrientos, the fifteenth-century bishop of Cuenca, and were represented in the first half of the sixteenth century by the important current of rationalistic demythologizing thought of Pietro Pomponazzi, Gian Francesco Ponzinibio, Samuel de Cassinis, and Paulus Grillandus.[18] This school of thought found expression in Spain in the work of Martín de Arles (or de Andosilla), for example, his influential *De superstitionibus* (1510), the pioneering work of Spanish antisuperstitious literature, which denied the "false beliefs" about women who cast malevolent spells.[19] This work, the popularity of which resulted in the publication of five editions in the sixteenth century, was the antithesis of the *Malleus*.[20] The work of Benito Pererio (1603) on magic denied the reality of almost all the acts attributed to brujos. In 1631, the Jesuit Friedrich von Spée argued in his *Cautio criminalis circa processus contra sagas* that given the lack of evidence of real acts, brujos were effectively being condemned for their intention and consequently the punishments inflicted on them were too severe.[21] This skeptical attitude toward the reality of hechicería was not a radical departure from previous orthodoxy; such ideas had not been uninfluential in the past. Saint Augustine himself had attributed the supposed ability of witches to metamorphose themselves to "imaginative fantasy" or visual illusion created by the Devil. The notion was to carry great authority in the Western Church throughout the first half of the Middle Ages. But from the thirteenth century, as the thought of Aquinas superseded that of Augustine, the official position became increasingly one of absolute belief in the reality of hechicería, with the brujo no longer being seen as the victim of fantasy but as an adept in diabolical arts. Still, although this became the orthodoxy, Europe remained divided between what Julio Caro Baroja calls the "Augustinians" and "non-Augustinians," those attributing the phenomenon to imagination and those believing in its reality.[22]

The works of the credulous school, although central in

the development of a theory of demonology and hechicería, had very little impact at the level of individual
prosecutions.[23] The work of del Río, for example, seems
to have influenced very little the treatment of hechiceros
by the Inquisition.[24] Accusations of demonic pacts were
very rare. The Supreme Council of the Inquisition exhibited a skepticism characteristic of the experimentalist
school and a consequent benign cautiousness in its prosecution and sentencing of supposed offenders. Thus
while as a matter of theology inquisitors might accept the
Devil's role in the work of hechiceros, when confronted
with flesh-and-blood offenders, they expressed serious
doubts.[25] Even when defendants were found guilty of the
actions attributed to them, they received remarkably light
punishments in relation to the crimes of which they were
accused. This leniency, in such stark contrast with the fe-
rociousness shown to Protestants and Judaizers, was the
rule in the peninsular Inquisition throughout the sixteenth and seventeenth centuries. Such relatively light
punishments imposed on those accused of brujería demonstrate that the Inquisition implicitly denied the reality
of many of the accusations. Otherwise how else could a
person who had worshiped the Devil, had carnal intercourse with him, and produced deaths and catastrophes
be punished less severely than a Protestant or Judaizer?
There is no explanation unless the inquisitors accepted
that these accounts of relations with the Devil were ficti-
tious. Caro Baroja identifies the backgrounds of the inquisitors as the determinants of their skepticism. Their
training in canon law rather than in pure theology made
rationalism rather than speculation their strength. This
important fact saved Spain from the huge witch mas-
sacres so characteristic of northern Europe.[26]

A notorious example of inquisitorial disbelief was the
report produced by Alonso de Salazar y Frías after the
Zugarramurdi witch trials in 1614.[27] This was not an iso-

lated instance but the culminating point of a long process. In 1526, the *consejo* (council) voted by a narrow majority that although witches did actually travel to the sabbat, the effects of their *maleficio* were largely illusory.[28] In 1538, it decided that the aquelarre was a figment of the imagination. The people were to be reminded that the loss of harvests was not always to be attributed to the actions of brujos but rather to the will of God and that not everything written in the *Malleus* was to be believed since the work was based on hearsay and its author might have been deceived.[29] In 1555, the Supreme Council rejected a demand by the people of Guipúzcoa for the persecution of witches and decided that there was insufficient evidence to arrest the accused.[30]

This phenomenon was common to many parts of Spain. In Galicia, too, the Tribunal functioned as a brake on witch-hunting activities. The Supreme Council showed itself to be very attentive to local tribunals that had uncritically accepted evidence for hechicería and on several occasions ordered the suspension of cases initiated at the local level.[31] A famous memorial of 1538 by the bishop of Mondoñedo, answering questions raised about brujería, ordered inquisitors to verify if witches had really done the things to which they had confessed. However, the same memorial also stipulated that even if their deeds were purely imaginary, they were still to be punished as here-tics since the offense lay in their belief in what they had confessed. A confession was not in itself enough to prove such events had actually occurred; but it was sufficient to prove that the accused had imagined it to be so, and herein lay the heresy. Thus skepticism about the real actions of the accused focused attention on beliefs rather than deeds.[32]

Ridicule and scorn characterized the Tribunal's dealings with hechiceras. The high incidence of female offenders, who greatly outnumbered their male counterparts, was significant. Those who had not meddled in matters of faith but had only claimed to possess knowledge of certain herbs or practices of healing (which the inquisitors called *hechicería herética*) were treated largely as examples of a new facet of feminine stupidity. To concede these women any importance would have been to recognize them and make them more dangerous. No diabolical intervention was conceivable in the actions of those who lacked any true scientific understanding of their purported actions. The punishments were light except when their magical beliefs brought confusion into matters of faith, for example, by claiming that the Holy Spirit had given them the power to cure with herbs. Inquisitorial contempt for the female sex ensured that their claims could not be taken seriously.[33]

Indeed, universally, the hechicero was portrayed as an embustero.[34] In Murcia, the bruja was regarded as nothing more than a swindler of unfortunate victims.[35] In Galicia, brujos were condemned as embusteros and were given light punishments. The fraudulent character of their activities was reinforced by the willingness of the accused to abide by this classification to escape severe punishment. Nearly all prisoners admitted that even if they used specialist books to obtain a better result, they did not genuinely believe that they could manipulate special powers; on the contrary, they confessed that they deceived the people for their own benefit.[36]

This understanding of the nature of the hechicero emigrated with theologians and jurists to the New World. The Inquisition was established in the viceroyalty of Peru to safeguard religious orthodoxy among the settlers of European and African origin. As is well known, its jurisdiction did not extend to the *república de los indios*. However, since the Extirpation was inspired by the ideology of the Inquisition, it is important to understand the workings of the Holy Office in Peru and, in particular, its treatment of hechiceros. It will be instructive to turn to some exemplary cases that came before the Inquisition during the seventeenth century when the extirpation trials were at their height.

Many of those brought before the Tribunal for hechicerías were *mulatas* (women of mixed African/European descent) who acted as intercessors in the magical world. The magic of colonial Peru was extremely rich and varied since, like its human inhabitants, it drew on three continents. *Mestizas* (women of mixed Native/European descent) and *mulatas*, as the heirs of two distinct races, were well placed to operate as magical specialists for both; and their repertoire could include practices from European, African, and native magical traditions. They were prime candidates for heterodoxy.

As in metropolitan Spain, the inquisitors of the viceroyalty of Peru displayed a strong skepticism toward the powers that the hechicera attributed to herself. The account of trials by the Tribunal for the years 1647 and 1648 refers to "frivolous superstitions and hechicerías that tend more to be feminine tricks and deceptions to cheat people out of their money and do not infer any suspicion of heresy or pact with the Devil."[37] This inquisitorial incredulity explains why the punishments, although harsh in human terms, were light in relation to the alleged offenses of idolatry, worship of the Devil, and even murder of a priest through maleficio. Since the penalties administered were frequently the same as for those who chewed coca, it is clear that the inquisitors did not take these alleged deeds seriously. As in the peninsular, the focus fell on the question of intention and belief since the heresy lay in the state of mind of the defendant.

Even those accused of idolatry and diabolical pacts were able to exonerate themselves by denying true belief in the efficacy of their actions. The occasional application of torture by the Tribunal only encouraged the defendants to

disavow any intention to invoke or communicate with the
Devil. Petrona de Saavedra was accused of idolatrous love
magic and an express pact with the Devil, whom she had
invoked as "most illustrious and all-powerful." When casting spells, she had venerated two small Indian figures
and had called on "Lusbel," or Lucifer, to grant the desires of her clients. In her first confession, she insisted that
the invocation of Lusbel had been a trick to earn money
and that, in reality, she knew nothing of diabolical arts. If
some of her magic had been successful, it was only by coincidence, and if she had experienced visions of an old
man in the mirror while she was chewing coca, it was a
trick of the light or the result of her drunken imagination.
In her heart, she did not believe that her Indian figures
had any virtue whatsoever, since they were only made of
stone. Under torture, she adapted her testimony, confessing that she had advised her client to call upon the Devil;
but she insisted that she had not expected him to hear her,
since she did not believe that she had the power to speak
with him. Once her interrogators were convinced of the
sincerity of her denials, they were prepared to relax the
punishment. The sentence against her was lenient in relation to the seriousness of her offenses. Even though she
had been accused of idolatry, she was required only to abjure *de levi* (and not *de vehementi*, which was reserved for
the most serious crimes), to suffer two hundred lashes,
and to remain in exile from the city for four years. Remarkably, this punishment was lighter than that administered to other defendants who were guilty of the less
grave offense of superstition. It is clear that the inquisitors, although determined to put a stop to her deviant actions, were convinced neither of the reality of diabolical
intervention nor of her genuine intent to invoke such assistance.[38]

Similarly, the defendant Melchor de Aranibar, also accused of an explicit pact with the Devil, was allowed to

exculpate himself by denying the reality of his communications with an old man who had given him herbs with which to cure. Under threat of torture, Aranibar retracted his earlier confessions, disclaiming the existence of both the old man and the herbs. All the magical acts he had performed had been his own sleight of hand, which he offered to demonstrate to the inquisitors. As a result, the sentence of torture was revoked and his punishment was set at banishment for four years and one hundred lashes. The admission of fraud was what the inquisitors were expecting, and they were prepared to reward it with a reduction in the severity of punishment. Small wonder the prisoners complied.[39]

The same strategy was employed by many other defendants. Ana María de Contreras successfully excused herself from the accusation of making a pact with the Devil when she denied any intention of worshiping idols or belief in the efficacy of what she had done and attributed her practices to the need to earn a living. Luisa de Vargas also denied any belief in what she did and claimed that her only intention had been to defraud others of their money. Francisca de Bustos admitted that she had jealously guarded her reputation as an hechicera but that, in reality, she had no idea how to cast spells and had only pretended to possess supernatural powers to trick people into giving her coca, chicha, and clothing. Francisca de Benavides confessed that she had acquired her fame as a bruja and hechicera after the Inquisition publicly punished her for the offense; as a result, she had decided to specialize in frivolous remedies, which had no substance but which alleviated her poverty. Clearly, the work of the Tribunal could, on occasions, be completely counterproductive.[40]

The "qualification" of an offense as, for example, an explicit or implicit pact bore little relation to the punishment inflicted. It could hardly be otherwise since the calificadores frequently disputed the character of offenses. Of the five calificadores sitting in judgment on the case of Josepha de Baides (charged with chewing coca and predicting the future), one concluded that she was guilty of an explicit pact since she had invoked the Devil, another believed that her actions were so clearly fraudulent that she could only be accused of an implicit pact, and the other three compromised on a judgment of an implicit pact, with suspicions of an explicit pact. Whereas two of the calificadores in the case against Juana de Morales, who had chewed coca and invoked the Devil, rejected out of hand the accusation of an explicit pact, the other five proposed that she had made an implicit pact, with suspicion of the former. The arbitrariness of these categories is revealed by the fact that Juliana Gutiérrez, who had also chewed coca and invoked the Devil, was accused of an implicit pact and suspicion of an explicit pact, whereas the following year Ana de Arala was condemned for an explicit pact for the same offenses.[41] Even when the full express pact was recognized, the sentence might be extremely light. Juan Romero confessed to seeing devils in his house but was only obliged to abjure de vehementi and to attend a Jesuit college. He was excused from a whipping because of his advanced age.[42]

The "qualification" of types of pact was a theoretical distinction of no great consistency. It remained an abstract phenomenon and functioned principally as an intellectual framework within which to set the behavior of religious deviants. It was not the measure against which such behavior would be corrected. Because the defendants were universally perceived as fraudulent tricksters, the inquisitors did not seek proof of genuine diabolical intervention. The punishment inflicted was not determined by the category of the offense but by the need to deter future deviant behavior. Irrespective of the type of pact of which the defendant was accused, a prisoner who demonstrated sincere contrition received a lighter penalty than one who was stubborn and uncooperative under interrogation. The inquisitors' priority was to convince the defendants of the foolishness of their hubris, persuade them to recognize their own impotence, and administer punishment that was sufficient to dissuade them from repeating their deviant actions.[43]

The tradition of incredulity and skepticism about the self-proclaimed powers of hechiceros in the peninsular Inquisition was transferred not only to the activities of the Inquisition among the Spaniards, blacks, mestizos, and mulattos of Peru but also to those of the Extirpation among the indigenous Andean inhabitants. This ideological obsession determined the Spanish response to the native Andean religious specialist, in whom the fusion of idolater, apostate, and devilworshiper took on human form. The archidolater, the Andean hechicero, was nothing more than a fraud.[44]

III

The association of the native Andean religious specialist with the category of the hechicero antedated the campaigns of extirpation. The earliest pronouncements of the ecclesiastical authorities in Peru recognized the pivotal role of the hechicero in native religious practice. Constitution 26 of the First Council of Lima (1551) asserted that those who did the most damage to the baptized and unbaptized Indians alike were the *sacerdotes* (priests) and hechiceros and that it was at their instigation that many Indians returned to their ancient practices. As a result, any Christian Indian found exercising this office would be punished on the first offense with fifty lashes and on the second offense with ten days in prison and one hundred lashes; on the third offense, he would be sent as an incorrigible to the bishop's judges for punishment. The same fate would befall any unbaptized hechicero or any

Indian who consulted an hechicero. Constitution 60 laid down additional penalties for those who employed the services of hechiceros for the purpose of maleficio, including excommunication and a fine of fifty pesos.[45]

Under the influence of the discovery of Taki Onqoy in 1564–65, the Second Council of Lima (1567) distinguished for the first time between Indians in general and hechiceros and dogmatizadores. The two latter groups would be subject to penalties of isolation and separation so that, whether they were baptized or unbaptized, those hechiceros, confessors, and diviners who had perverted the Indians could be confined in a place near the church. Those who had sinned lightly would be released after suitable admonishment, but the more culpable would be maintained in imprisonment and receive instruction. Any relapsed idolater or dogmatizador was subject to punishment by the bishopric and the "full vigors of the law," implying that certain prisoners could be handed over to civil justice. However, a royal decree of 1575 laid down that noncriminal trials for idolatry should be under the jurisdiction of the ecclesiastical authorities, and only hechiceros whose practices had caused deaths would be judged by the civil authorities. Since there was great skepticism about the ability of hechiceros to cause real deaths, most offenses of idolatry and hechicería, already closely linked, would depend on ecclesiastical justice.[46]

The first extirpator in Peru, Albornoz, reinforced the equation of the religious specialist and the hechicero. His *Instrucción para descubrir todas las huacas del Perú y sus camayos y haciendas* (1583, 1584) attributed the responsibility for the preservation and evangelization of native religion to the eponymous camayos or *hechiceros huacamayos*, those individuals charged by their communities with the upkeep of the huacas. These hechiceros were characterized both as servants of the Devil, whom they invoked in their superstitions, and as liars who deceived the Indians with their false preaching. Similarly, the many different types of doctors ministering to the Indians' medical needs were all hechiceros and supplicated the Devil before practicing.[47]

The seeking out of idolatry and the destruction of huacas was distinguished from the attack on the sect of Taki Onqoy, which, as is clear from the *Informaciones de servicios* of 1570, 1577, and 1584, Albornoz preferred to classify as apostasy.[48] Its advocates, for example, the famous Juan Chono or Chocna, were *predicadores* (preachers) or dogmatizadores rather than hechiceros.[49] Hechiceros were usually grouped together with those guilty of superstitious observances; or were identified with huacacamayos, ministers of idols.[50] In the evidence of Cristóbal de Molina in the *Información* of 1577, the priests and ministers of huacas were described as hechiceros while the ringleaders of Taki Onqoy were dogmatizadores.[51]

The distinction was not absolutely clear, however. Elsewhere Albornoz referred to "preachers and other hechiceros" who spoke with huacas and even used the term *predicadores hechiceros*.[52] Furthermore, the punishment meted out to hechiceros and dogmatizadores was comparable. Some hechiceros were merely entrusted to their local priests for instruction, but generally they were subjected to the same quasi-inquisitorial rituals of public humiliation as the dogmatizadores: degrading clothing, whipping, and cropping of the hair. They shared the same long-term punishments of perpetual service in the local place of worship, or possibly confinement in special houses adjacent to the church, a measure that foreshadowed the Casa de Santa Cruz del Cercado, the Jesuit house of correction on the outskirts of Lima.[53] Implicitly the crimes of hechicero and dogmatizador were bracketed together as two types of specialists in idolatry or apostasy.

The identification of hechicería and idolatría was already clear from the evidence of the witness Cristóbal de Molina who testified that Albornoz had spoken of the creation of a *red barredera*, a sweeping net that would leave no hechicería and idolatría untouched. Molina left an invaluable account of native rites and beliefs in his *Relación de las fábulas y ritos de los Incas* (1574). Despite cataloging a variety of native terms to describe the religious specialist, he identified the ministers of indigenous ritual as hechiceros.[54]

The native chronicler Felipe Guaman Poma de Ayala followed Albornoz and Molina in assimilating the indigenous religious specialists to the category of hechicero and characterizing them as *hechiceros mentirosos*, or false hechiceros. He admitted that his experience of hechiceros derived from his service to Albornoz, the Visitor-General who had "consumed all the huacas, idols, and hechicerías of the realm" and in whose company he had witnessed with his own eyes the destruction of many *"ídolos* [idols] *y hechicerías,"* especially the false hechiceros of Taki Onqoy. Those specialists who divined from dreams or fire and those who claimed to rid the body of disease by removing stones, toads, or maize from it (*hechiceros que chupan*) lied to the Indians in order to earn a living. Those who served as priests of huacas and gave confession deceived the Indians by telling them that they ate, drank, and spoke with the huacas when they did not. All were lying "hechicerías idólatras."[55]

The writings of the Jesuit José de Acosta identified the hechicero as the individual most responsible for the preservation of the "sacrilegious and diabolical superstitions" of the Indians. Nothing had caused greater difficulty in the propagation of the gospel than the work of these hechiceros, among whom he included the *pontífices de ídolos*, who offered propitiatory sacrifices, and those "confessors" who comforted the sick by hearing their "sins" as well as the infinite number of "diviners, sorcer-

ers, augurers, and other false prophets" the majority of
whom continued to practice. He wrote that the hechiceros, embaucadores (impostors), and *maestros de idolatrías*, called *humos* or *laiccas* in Peru, would have to be
"fought tooth and nail and their deceptions unmasked,
their ignorance demonstrated, their nonsense ridiculed,
and their guile refuted." Those who refused to reform
should be separated and punished severely. He also drew
attention to the significance for evangelization of the
public self-denunciation of repentant hechiceros who
could be obliged to preach to the Indians, retracting their
errors and vilifying their own tricks and lies; such a spectacle was to become a salient feature of both the Extirpation and the work of Jesuit missionaries. More than previous commentators, Acosta dwelled on the role of the
Devil as the puppet master manipulating the hechicero,
emphasizing not only that the ministers of huacas spoke
with demons but also that they had received instruction
from Satan himself. Of course, the hechicero had long
been understood to be the instrument of Satan, but in
Acosta one can feel the heat of the fire, smell the smoke,
and savor the brimstone.[56]

But the most detailed examination of native religious
specialists in colonial Peru and the most unequivocal in
identifying them with the hechicero was written by the
mastermind of the Extirpation, the Jesuit Arriaga. The
whole of the third chapter of his manual of extirpation
was devoted to "the ministers of idolatry . . . commonly
called hechiceros." Like Molina, Guaman Poma, and
Acosta before him, Arriaga was aware of the complexity
of functions of the religious specialist, each of which possessed its own terminological referent in the vernacular.
He implicitly recognized the inappropriateness of the
term "hechicero" to describe these practitioners since he
acknowledged that those who killed through *hechizos*
(spells) were extremely rare. But although he went on to

provide an exhaustive catalog of the different types of religious specialist, like his predecessors he continued to use "hechicero" as a general category under which to group them all. Arriaga still presented his specialists as mere subdivisions of a universal genre of European origin.[57]

Arriaga began by recording the native generic term for religious specialist, *umu* or *laicca*, or in some parts of Peru, *chacha, auqui,* or *auquilla,* all of which meant "father" or "old man." Then he listed the terms for every specialty. The most senior was the huacapvillac, or "he who speaks with the huaca," whose responsibility was to take care of the huaca and transmit its communications to the village. Arriaga's interpretation, typical of educated seventeenth-century clerics, was that these messages were generally inventions by the huacapvillac; however, he acknowledged that on some occasions it was possible that the Devil did in reality speak through the huaca.[58] This ambiguity had characterized earlier commentators.

Other specialists identified by Arriaga were the *mallquipvillac*, who performed the same function in relation to the mallquis as did the huacapvillac in relation to the huacas; the *libiaopvillac* and the *punchaupvillac*, who spoke with Lightning and the Sun, respectively; and tne *yanapac*, who was an assistant to the different types of *villac* and was vulgarly known as the *sacristán* (sexton). Aside from those responsible for native deities, there were the curanderos, known as *macsa* or *viha*, who cured using fraudulent and superstitious means. These practitioners earned the name of hechicero less for their curing activities than for the mixture of superstitious observances. The specialists who gave confession were known as *aucachic*, though this office always had to be combined with that of villac or macsa. The *azuac* were those who prepared the chicha for the huacas' feasts. The nomenclature of diviners was related to the material they employed: the *socyac* used maize; the *rapiac,* human limbs; the *pacharicue,* the legs of spiders; the *cuyricuc, cuyes* (Andean guinea pigs); and the *moscoc,* dreams to predict the future.[59]

Apart from all these hechiceros, those who, according to Arriaga, most properly deserved the name were the *cauchus* or *runapmicuc,* meaning "those who devour people." What earned them the title of hechicero, or even more correctly, brujo, was the fact that they had killed people through maleficio and so conformed more truly to the European concept of brujería than those who made offerings to creatures or healed using superstitious means. Arriaga thus implied that the term "hechicero" was inappropriate for the other religious specialists he had just described.

Yet he still insisted throughout the manual on using "hechicero" as a generic term for all the varieties of religious specialist. The twenty-third question of his fifteenth chapter on how to interrogate subjects insisted that the hechicero should be asked which of all these offices outlined above he exercised, as well as if he had spoken with the Devil and in what form the latter had appeared. His edict against idolatry identified hechiceros as ministers of idolatry who interceded with the huacas for the Indians, took confession of their sins, and sacrificed cuyes in order to divine the future. The constitutions of the visitations leave no doubt about the equation of the hechicero and the *ministro de idolatría,* which encompassed curanderos and native confessors. Elsewhere he records that the Visitors preached against "huacas and hechiceros"; that when a woman was about to give birth the Indians called the hechicero to make a sacrifice; that it was the hechiceros who taught the Indians that the Christian god was only for Spaniards and that the saints were the huacas of the Viracochas; that it was the hechicero who ordered the Indians to throw white maize on the highway so that passersby would take the sickness of the village away with them, and who climbed to the summit of mountains to plead with the deity to put an end to the affliction; that it was the hechicero who made sacrifices to idols of stone on high mountains; that those curanderos known as *ambicamayos* were a type of hechicero, as were those who gave confession; and that those who instructed the young in idolatries and superstitions were hechiceros.[60]

Because the religious specialist was an hechicero, he was also an embustero, a trickster. In his role as interpreter of the huacas, he was seen as little more than a crude ventriloquist. During interrogation, he would be asked in what manner he pretended that the huaca spoke to him and what replies he conveyed to the Indians; if he said that while speaking with the huacas he went into a frenzy, he was asked if he believed it was through the action of the Devil or on account of the chicha he had drunk. Hence if he wished to insist on the reality of the huaca's communication, he had to accept the premise that the Devil had inspired him; or, to avoid the seriousness of this charge, he had to deny the reality of his powers by blaming his own drunkenness. Small wonder most subjects were goaded by this double-edged sword into denouncing themselves as frauds.[61]

The Jesuits provided the central intellectual thrust behind the Extirpation through the works of Acosta and, especially, Arriaga, whose writings dominated the idolatry trials not only of the early seventeenth century but also those initiated by Pedro de Villagómez and even his eighteenth-century successors. The Company of Jesus produced, apart from Acosta and Arriaga, one other great commentator on native religion, Father Bernabé Cobo. Like his forerunners, Cobo perpetuated the identification of religious specialist and hechicero. In his *Historia del nuevo mundo* (1653), he followed Arriaga's classifications of native specialists, translating, for example, *villac-umu*, or high priest of Coricancha, as "the diviner or hechicero who speaks" and repeating the assimilation of confessors and superstitious healers to hechiceros. Following Acosta, the hechicero was explicitly defined as an agent of the Devil: "Under the name of hechicero are included all those who use superstitions and illicit arts to achieve objects that surpass human faculties through the invocation and aid of the Devil, with whom an explicit or implicit pact is the basis of such power and knowledge."[62]

Cobo distinguished four types of diabolical superstition: "magic arts," or the attempt to achieve some miraculous effect; "divination," or the unnatural knowledge of hidden events; maleficio or hechicería proper, which did harm to others; and "false observances," or the use of objects for purposes for which they were not naturally appropriate. The experts in all four types of superstition were indiscriminately designated hechiceros.

Cobo perceived the true presence of the Devil in the work of those hechiceros called umu, who had genuinely acceded to a contract with the Devil. As a sign of vassalage to Satan, they would carry a representation of him made out of a hollow bone and black wax. When they called on their master to answer their questions, he replied in a hoarse voice that was heard by the other Indians. The powers of the umu lay in the field of divination. They were consulted to locate lost or stolen objects and to learn of the future. They were uncannily accurate, often perceiving events in distant places that could not have been ascertained by natural means.

However, like his predecessors, Cobo did not accept the reality of the powers of the majority of hechiceros. While it was possible that some might have had an understanding with the Devil, most operated without any communication or pact. This included the majority of diviners or *sortílegos* of the second category, those who merely prognosticated from grains of maize or spiders' legs or who chewed coca. Those hechiceros who were curanderos were accused of hoodwinking the Indians with ridiculous and useless methods that failed to achieve their ends. It was true that some of these practitioners knew something about plants and occasionally could cure; but those they wished to make better just as frequently died. The majority of these curanderos merely uttered superstitious words and indulged in futile sacrifices. No true diabolical intervention could be discerned in their fraudulent work.

Cobo was extremely skeptical of the powers of the curanderos known as *camasca* or *soncoyoc*. He dismissed their claims that they learned the faculty of healing from a spiritual visitor in their dreams. Their initiation most commonly arose, he argued, from their rapid recovery from an ailment for which they subsequently became the curandero. He was sure that many had pretended to suffer from such an affliction in order to be able to boast of a remarkable recovery. Those who claimed to be able to suck the origin of their patients' illnesses out of the body in the form of toads or worms took these objects with them and placed them in their mouths at the moment of sucking. The operation whereby they removed snakes from the patient's belly was "an illusion and hoax of the Devil." Thus if the Devil was at work, it was only to produce the illusion of power and not genuine effects. By acknowledging a real demonic presence in the work of only a minority of hechiceros, Cobo followed his forerunners in perpetuating the notion that the vast majority of practitioners were merely ineffective charlatans.[63]

IV

All commentators were agreed that the sin of idolatry was synonymous with that of hechicería and that the Andean religious specialists were hechiceros. The lack of distinction between the idolater and the hechicero was one of the principal characteristics of the idolatry trials launched by the Extirpation. The confusion was most evident in the charges brought against individual offenders. Strictly, hechicería was sorcery, or the superstitious manipulation of occult forces to attain ends incommensurate with the means, especially for the purposes of maleficio. As such it was theoretically distinct from the sin of idolatry. But evidence of sorcery, such as bundles of llama fat, wax figures, and coca, was frequently used as proof of idolatry; conversely, the worship of huacas and the possession of representations of native divinities or idols were sufficient to substantiate a charge of hechicero.

Although accusations of hechicero or idolater were made separately, the most common was a joint charge of hechicero idólatra, as in the case of Don Gerónimo Auquinivin. The evidence most frequently presented to substantiate this latter charge was not that of sorcery proper but that of the worship of native deities or sacred objects. The accusation of hechicero idólatra was made against Auquinivin on the basis of his libation of some skittles and his offering of chicha to a large stone. No evidence of genuine hechizos was offered.[64] Another cacique denounced as an hechicero idólatra, Tomás de Acosta, was accused of sacrificing to a huaca kept in his house and making offerings of chicha and coca to the mortal remains of his ancestors so that they would give him a good harvest from his land. The worship of ancestors and huacas was construed to constitute sufficient proof of hechicería.[65] Another kuraka, Leandro Pomachagua, was accused of idolatries and hechicerías because he had protected village huacas from the investigations of the priest.[66] There were innumerable additional examples.[67]

It is clear that the incriminating act of the hechicero idólatra was not sorcery or the making of spells but the act of sacrificing to huacas or worshiping other creatures. Suspects and witnesses were explicitly encouraged by the Visitors to offer this type of evidence. Juan Sarmiento de Vivero began his interrogations by reminding witnesses of the seriousness of the sin committed by those hechiceros idólatras who believed in superstitions and hechizos, worshiping huacas and making sacrifices to them, and denying God the worship he was due as the true God. The equation of idolatry and hechicería was explicit.[68]

The intellectual assimilation of the native religious specialist to the category of hechicero had two important consequences. The first was the confusion of the different functions of the Andean religious practitioner. "Hechicero" became a generic term for a variety of specialisms, covering activities as diverse as shamanism, divination, communication with spirits, astrology, and therapeutic technologies.[69] Hechiceros included those responsible for ministering to the needs of the huacas and for interpreting their communications (the huacarimac or huacapvillac).[70] At the same time, they also included those who sought to propitiate the *apus* (the spirits inhabiting the mountain-tops) to secure good health, good harvests, or fertility in livestock.[71] Thus ordinary Indians who continued to worship ancestral deities could be accused alongside the huacapvillac himself; and the client who invoked the apus for the remedy of an illness could be as guilty as the healer himself. This diversity of practice was disguised by the nomenclature imposed by the extirpators.

The second consequence was that native specialists were defined as lying tricksters. The profound skepticism about the reality of the powers of the peninsular hechicero was transferred to the native practitioner. In Peru, the attempt to replace the native religious system with Christianity intensified the need to devalue the religious specialist to undermine his psychological hold over the Indians. If the Indians believed in the literal reality of his powers, it would be very difficult to overcome the fear and respect he commanded. The exigencies of evangelization encouraged the representation of the hechicero as a charlatan and excluded his manipulation of genuine supernatural powers. The result was an enormous undervaluing of the significance of the indigenous religious specialist for his community. By refusing to accept the native religious specialist on his own terms, the extirpators signaled the limits of their attempts to understand indigenous society from within.

As Carmen Bernand and Serge Gruzinski have observed, "the person of the hechicero, . . . incarnated in the eyes of Christians as the instrument of the Devil, became the perfect model of the idolater, born from the debris of idolatry."[72] This identification of hechicero and native religious specialist was not confined to theory but was the most important determinant of the manner in which offenders were treated. The contemporary Inquisition was characterized by its relatively "humane" conduct toward the hechicero, in stark contrast to the treatment meted out to Protestants and Judaizers. If the Andean idolater was equated with the hechicero by the Inquisition's "Bastard Child," it is logical that, in practice, he was not punished as a dangerous heretic but rather as a deceitful fraud.[73] In this way, the concept of the hechicero subverted the notion of the idolater as heretic and created a fundamental contradiction within the ideology that sustained the Extirpation. For this reason, the concept of hechicería was more significant in determining the practice of Extirpation than the concept of idolatry.

Three: THE IDOLATER AS SHAMAN

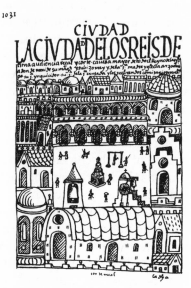

The city of Lima.

Aboriginal medicine-men, so far from being rogues, charlatans or ignoramuses, are men of high degree; that is, men who have taken a degree in the secret life beyond that taken by most adult males. . . . [T]hey are of immense social significance, the psychological health of the group largely depending on faith in their powers.
—A. P. Elkin, *Aboriginal Men of High Degree* (1945)

I

THE MAJORITY OF DEFENDANTS IN THE IDOLATRY TRIALS OF the mid-seventeenth century were specialists in the techniques of magical healing. Their practices that fell under the scrutiny of the Extirpation were essentially curative rites. Andean societies understood extrasomatic influences as the determinants of illness. Ill health could be caused by supernatural beings angered by human sins or by neglect of their worship; by the dead who cursed their living relatives; by sorcerers on behalf of enemies; or by the introduction of a pathogen or loss of "soul" as a consequence of sudden fear.[1] These extrasomatic influences could only be controlled by consulting a specialist who was well versed in the techniques of manipulating, channeling, and counteracting them. The methods of these seventeenth-century specialists may be better understood by drawing comparisons with those of modern *curanderos*, or experts in healing.

The religious specialists of modern South American tribal communities exhibit practices and patterns of behavior that are typical of shamans. *Shaman* derives from the word *saman* of the Tungus people of Siberia, meaning "one who is excited, moved, or raised"; it has been applied by extension to religious specialists around the world.[2] Shamans are specialists in direct confrontation with the supernatural world; they are the intermediaries of the seen and unseen worlds, the guardians of the psychic equilibrium of their society. They bear a unique claim to direct experiential knowledge of the divine and, hence, the authority to act as privileged channels of communication between humans and the supernatural. By the evocation of an altered state of consciousness or state of ecstasy, they gain access to an ordinarily hidden reality where they may interact with spirits who are at their command and who carry out their bidding for good or evil. With the aid of these spirits, which constitute the fundamental source of their power, shamans are able to inflict or counteract witchcraft. Since South American tribal societies perceive a causal relationship between illness and witchcraft, the curing of the former requires the detection of the latter.[3]

Shamanism is an ecstatic healing tradition. Nevertheless, not all treatment of illness necessarily involves the shamanic journey to the Lower or Upper World (or from

one cosmic region to another). Healing is typically performed in two ways; either something that is lacking
must be put back into the body of the person who is ill or
something that does not belong in the body must be removed. The latter kind of healing does not involve the
shamanic journey but consists of working here in the
Middle World, using divination techniques and moving
backward and forward between ordinary and nonordi-
nary reality in order to see the illness and remove it.
Restoring something that is lost or lacking (often the vital
soul of the individual) does involve the journey. Thus
whereas all native curanderos are shamans in that they
heal illnesses by gaining access to alternate realities and
forming relationships with spirits, not all healing requires
the shamanic journey of ascent or descent into other
worlds.[4]

The typical characteristics of modern shamans in the
Peruvian Andes are described by the anthropologists Juvenal Casaverde Rojas and Juan Victor Nuñez del Prado
Béjar in their respective studies of the communities of
Kuyo Grande in the district of Pisaq in the Cuzco area
and of Qotobamba, also near Cuzco.[5] In both communities several categories of religious specialist are distinguished whose practices and method of selection are typical of shamans. The specialist who stands at the apex of
the religious hierarchy in both communities is the *alto
mesayoq*. The feature that characterizes one most clearly as
a shaman is one's selection by the deity Ruwal (synonymous with the apus, or mountain spirits) by means of a
lightning bolt. This is the preferred method for conferring powers on the human representative of the apus. The
origin of the word *mesayoq* lies in the *mesa*, or strange-
shaped stone of special powers, with which the shaman
is left as proof of his or her selection after awaking from
unconsciousness. After such an initiation the shaman is
able to communicate directly with Ruwal, Pachamama

(the deity personifying the earth), and the great regional apus, as well as with the spirits of the dead. By conjuring them up in audible form, the shaman can convey their advice and warnings to the community and in this way is responsible for maintaining the close relations between the village and its protective deities. His other talents include the ability to rescue lost or stolen objects, to indicate the whereabouts of a thief, to discover the hidden cause of an illness, to predict the future, and to perform magic spells. His power is a benevolent one. He can cure illnesses caused by all the evil spirits and is consulted in the most serious cases.

Another specialist in healing is the *hanpeq* (in Kuyo Grande) or *runa hanpeq* (in Qotobamba). His cures may be effected with traditional medicine, without the intervention of supernatural spirits, or through his own magical powers. The magical force of the curandero is required to activate the healing power of certain rites or medicines. His powers are inferior to those of the alto mesayoq. He has the power to convoke only the local apus and may consult them about problems within their jurisdiction. He makes offerings to Ruwal and Pachamama, but he cannot convoke them. He can cure illnesses only of middle importance. He can also divine in consultation with the apus. Among the Incas, this figure was known as the *hanpeqcamayoq*, or expert in medicine, and was given to the practice of both black and white medicine. He could also have combined his specialism with service as the *huacacamayoq*, or minister to the huacas.

The *pampa mesayoq* also specializes in curing various types of illness but is inferior in status to the previous two curanderos, being able to converse only with the *aukis*, or spirits inhabiting smaller mountains, and performing similar functions but with less efficacy. Some devote themselves to healing those who are suffering from contact with specters or corpses, for which purpose they must possess the *uraña mesa*, or stone with special power to cure these illnesses. The pampa mesayoq can practice black magic or fight it, cure illnesses, localize stolen objects, and divine.

The *watoq* in Kuyo Grande is the diviner who uses his powers to diagnose illnesses, determine the truth of a confession, find lost objects, identify hostile hechiceros, and establish acceptable sacrifices for a deity. This is not an exclusive office since divination is performed by the alto mesayoq, the pampa mesayoq, and others who learn the techniques. In Qotobamba this role is performed by the *wishch'uq*, and there is also an herbalist curandero called the *maych'a*.

In both communities the specialist in the practice of black magic is the *layqa* or brujo. By applying the principles of imitative or contagious magic, he can cause deterioration in the health of victims or death. The layqa is considered the pupil of Supay, the evil-doing spirit to which the Christian Devil has been assimilated and who will claim both the layqa's body and soul at death and take them to Hell. His powers derive from a pact with Supay or from Qhaqya, a malevolent spirit of lightning. In either case, the layqa's initiation is through the power of lightning. In this way lightning can be an instrument used in a malevolent form by Supay or in a benevolent form by the apus. The layqa is able to make use at will of the malevolent spirits *soq'a* and *pachatira*. However, he is still inferior to the pampa mesayoq and has no access to the great deities of the native system.

The generic term for all these magical specialists in both communities is *paqo*. It appears that one individual may occupy more than one category at the same time but not within the same community. So, for example, one religious specialist recognized by the community of Sonqo as an alto mesayoq is regarded by the villagers of Q'ero as a hanpeq. Interestingly, almost all these specialists are believed to be incompetent but are consulted because there are no better ones. Paqos from other places are accepted more readily than those from the community.[6]

The shamanic characteristics of these modern practitioners were typical of the victims of seventeenth-century idolatry trials. Since these individuals required knowldge of witchcraft to cure illness, it is not entirely surprising that they were accused of hechicería. The association derived not merely from Spanish classificatory systems but also from the real activity of the offenders. Beneath the superstratum of theological preconceptions imposed by Spaniards, it is possible to discern, through the records, a substratum of typically indigenous modes of thought and methods of practice. The vast majority of offenders were practitioners of native rites performed to restore the physical health of individuals through the propitiation of apus or native deities; or they were the clients of curanderos mistaken for such practitioners themselves on account of the consultations they had made.

If the hechiceros of idolatry trials were native curanderos assimilated to European elite categories, they themselves did not necessarily accept their fate as meek and passive victims. The vast majority resisted the attempt to classify them as practitioners of evil magic, which is what the label "hechicero" implied. An examination of the reaction of the defendants to the accusations against them provides important details of their activities and allows the reconstruction of their own self-perceptions.

II

The reaction of defendants on being accused of hechicería depended on their understanding of the meaning of the term. Some freely admitted to it. Pedro Guamboy was prepared to accept the label of "hechicero", readily acknowledging that he had cured wounds with herbs and

that his reputation as an hechicero derived from his healing activities.[7]

Most defendants, however, seem to have understood
the dangers of admitting to the charge and employed a
variety of strategies to avoid stigmatizing themselves with
the designation. A few professed incomprehension; either they were unaware or they chose to feign unaware-
ness of what it meant to be an hechicero. María Ticlla denied that she was an hechicera because she did not know
what the word meant. When it was pointed out to her
that she had already been punished for the offense by a
previous Visitor, she excused herself on the grounds of
confusion. Pedro Villanga confessed that he was undeni-
ably an hechicero. But he must have been unaware of the
meaning of the word, because when questioned on the
specific magic he had practiced, he assured his interrogators that he had done no such thing. Juana Conoa acknowledged that she had appeared before the Visitor Alvaro de Lugares on a charge of hechicería and agreed that
she had acquired a reputation as a healer on account of
her talents at massaging pregnant women with grains of
maize when they were about to give birth and her treatment of spider bites with herbs. When challenged about
how she could say she was not an hechicera if she had indulged in these practices, she said that an old Indian
woman had taught her and she did not know if it was
magic or not.[8]

One tactic employed by many defendants was to argue
they had done nothing more than consult a curandero,
which was the lesser sin of being a *mingador*, or one who
has recourse to hechiceros. In such an instance, they
might accept the term "hechicero," but only as applied to
the other party; their own reputation as a practitioner
was wholly unjustified. María Llano admitted seeking
advice from an hechicero to cure herself of an illness but
emphasized that she was only a mingadora, not an

hechicera herself.[9] Santiago Poma emphatically denied being an hechicero idólatra but agreed that he had consulted hechiceros, in particular, one Domingo Yanqau who had sucked small stones and pieces of wood from the arms and chest of his dying son. Sebastian Quito admitted that when he had been ill he had been attended by María Ñata, an hechicera, who had removed the head of a mouse from his stomach as well as three *yungas* needles, tied up with cotton and fat, from his kidneys, leaving not one scar.[10] Juana Aycro testified that she had been branded an hechicera and punished by Lugares for calling on an hechicero, Juan Anchaicachanqui, to cure her.[11] Inés Carpa acknowledged that she had consulted an Indian woman for the health of her child, for which she too had been punished as an hechicera by Lugares. The woman had asked her for llama fat with which she had rubbed the girl's body before throwing it into the fire.[12] Pablo Ato denied the accusation of hechicero, attesting that he had simply allowed himself to be treated by a wise Indian who had diagnosed his trouble as bewitchment and had given him some herbs to drink. A second hechicero had perceived in a dream the identity of the malefactor and had treated him by rubbing his throat and chest with white maize and coca and then throwing it in the fire.[13] María Ticlla disagreed with her interrogators that she was an hechicera; she had merely followed the advice of one who told her that her livestock were dying because she did not know how to make offerings to the mountain spirits.[14]

Sometimes this argument disintegrated under closer examination and the defendants were obliged to admit reluctantly that they had indeed practiced cures. In these cases, they would generally still deny the epithet "hechicero," preferring to present their actions in the most innocuous fashion possible. María Arriera denied being an idolater or hechicera and attributed her reputation to her consultation of a woman called Angelina who had cured her by rubbing her body with a cuy. In the hope of minimizing her guilt, she added that she had paid her nothing and that the woman had come to her to offer her services. She admitted buying orange earth from an Indian woman but denied it was destined to hechicerías; rather, she understood it would bring her good luck. Presented with evidence against her, she confessed she had performed simple cures with a certain white liquid, *yurac iacu*, and a plant, *ancori*, endowed with the quality of curing colds and fevers. Asked why, if she was not an hechicera, she went looking for such dubious substances, she said it was because she had been told by the girls who had dealings with Spaniards that their use would bring her good luck, which was not a sin. In this way she sought an authoritative endorsement for her activities. But the strategy of concealment was a dangerous one for it was an offense as serious as that of hechicería itself.[15]

Other defendants freely admitted their healing activities but rejected the charge of being hechiceras. Clearly they understood the implications of supernatural or malevolent influences inherent in the label. Such a defense rested on the insistence that their activities had involved no magic or superstition, only the time-honored methods passed on to them by their forefathers, which, what was more, they had seen Spaniards put to use themselves. María Inés spurned the accusation of being an hechicera despite her punishment for the offense twenty years before by the Visitor Felipe de Medina. She confessed she had returned to the practices for which she had been castigated but insisted that these had never been anything more than the duties of a midwife and healing with herbs she had seen Spaniards use, such as *chuquilla* and *ñunuño*. The suspect Domingo Guaman admitted that he knew how to cure scrofula and rashes with herbal concoctions but protested at the accusation of being an idolater or an hechicero, asserting that he had never made use of magic to cure. He had neither done harm nor consulted any supernatural powers; rather, he had put into practice for the benefit of members of his own family the specialist knowledge he had acquired by natural means. Alonso Martín assured the Visitor that he was not an idolater or an hechicero, and if this was his fame, it was because he knew how to cure spider bites using burned *ají* (chili pepper), as taught by his mother. Juan Caxa was convinced that people believed him to be an hechicero because he cured stomach pains by administering liquid *quinchimali* and *chamana* and by applying the leaves to the offending area of the body. Luis de Aguilar echoed the same predicament when he attested that if he was said to be an hechicero idólatra, it was because he cured the sick by bleeding them and administering drinks made from the herbs *viravira*, *chichamani*, and *pincopinco*. Such undertakings had in his view received the sanction of the Christian church since his knowledge had been imparted to him by Father Lázaro Sánchez, who had encouraged him to search for these herbs when he had been his sexton. Such appeals to the endorsement of the Church were not received with sympathy and did nothing to alleviate his punishment.[16]

Those who based their defense on the absence of magic or superstition from their activities were wise and understood the primary preoccupation of their interrogators. For it was not the act of healing in itself that provoked the anxiety of the authorities. Indeed, numerous authors had written on the subject of the lore of plants and concluded that its use *per se* did not necessarily involve superstition. Vitoria considered many cures made with special herbs to be efficacious on the basis of their natural virtues. If they appeared miraculous to the common people, it was because they did not understand the nature of the plants. Such knowledge was not in itself proof of diabolism. The crux of the matter lay in the origin of such knowledge. It could be acquired through the tradition of learned authorities such as Pythagoras; or it could be imparted by the Devil. Furthermore, once acquired, such knowledge could be used in a natural way without aid from either good or bad spirits. These conclusions thus allowed the curative use of herbs in certain circumstances. But such a position was ambivalent and left open to debate how in any particular instance the source of knowledge could be determined.[17]

Vitoria's tolerance was reflected in the resolutions of the Council of Lima of 1567 (ratified by the Council of Lima of 1583). Constitution 110 stipulated that those curanderos whose healing derived from "empirical" experience were to be provided with written permission to practice. The only condition was that it should be verified that they did not employ "superstitious" words or ceremonies.[18] It is difficult to determine whether such licenses to practice were in fact granted, but many other commentators were similarly indulgent of nonsuperstitious healing. Guaman Poma distinguished between common hechiceros and the curanderos whom he called serojanos barberos. Because of their skill with plants, the latter were able to practice as effectively as doctors of medicine. Although it was common for the priest or corregidor to bring proceedings against them, calling them hechiceros, in fact they were only Christians, and it would be far better that they should be given a license to practice.[19] According to Arriaga, the sin of the native curanderos lay not in the cures they aimed to effect but in the superstitious or idolatrous methods they employed. Indeed, such was his respect for their knowledge of native herbs that he proposed that priests should provide practitioners with instruction and thus remove any suspicion of superstition. In this way full advantage could be taken of their abilities without the danger of sin.[20] This stance was adopted by Archbishop Villagómez. In his instructions to his Visitors-General, he wrote that whereas the Indian hechiceros and ministers of idolatry should by no means be allowed to cure the sick, the healing activities of other Indians, whose practice rested on expert knowledge of the virtues of plants, should be approved. Such approval would always be conditional on an investigation by the village priest of the methods of curing so as to ensure the absence of all superstition.[21]

This relatively tolerant attitude toward the practice of healing with herbs explains why a cooperative and contrite offender would not necessarily receive a severe punishment. The harshest condemnations were reserved for those who had performed cures in the context of strictly idolatrous invocations of native deities, such as mountain spirits, or who had combined healing with maleficio or superstitious observances, especially the mixture of sacred elements, such as the use of Christian prayers or the invocation of Christ, the Virgin, or the saints. Each of these will be considered in turn.

The association between healing and the continued worship of native deities was the clearest justification for the term "hechicero idólatra," because it was based on the pre-Hispanic philosophy that the health and physical well-being of both the community and the individual depended on the maintenance of harmonious and balanced reciprocal relations between humans and their tutelary deities who were resident in the natural phenomena around them. Typically then, the offense of which the defendants were accused took the form of offerings to mountains, springs, stones, and rock faces, either by the curandero himself or by his client, in order to restore the health of the sufferer.

Such offenses were viewed with far greater alarm than the mere practice of cures. Vicente Napuri confessed to having cured one woman of a fever, using an herb called *sucosuco*. This offense was insignificant, however, by comparison with his prayers to a mountain called Sailla for the recovery of his wife's health, or his cooperation for this purpose with the hechicero Juan Anchaicachanqui, offering llama fat to the mountain by throwing it into his fire.[22] The defendant Diego Pacha was tried as an hechicero, not for attempting to cure his daughter, but for making placatory offerings to a rock.[23] Magdalena Callao was charged less on the basis of her cures than on the evidence that she had made offerings to a rock for the health of a client. Furthermore, as part of the cure, she had spread ashes in the streets in the pagan fashion and had called on the sick girl's relatives to participate in the ceremony. The professed purpose of the ceremony had been to prevent the girl's ancestors from taking her, clearly the perpetuation of a pre-Hispanic philosophy of illness as the collective responsibility of the family and the result of neglect of its duties to the dead. The act of healing, innocuous enough in itself, was rendered idolatrous by its context. To make matters worse, Callao was also accused of the bewitchment of a child she had allegedly refused to cure; thus it was maleficio and the use of native ceremonies that had condemned her.[24]

Similarly, those hechiceras who were basically midwives were prosecuted not for their rudimentary medical talents but for their sacrifices to mountain spirits to ensure the health of mother and child. Magdalena Sacsacarva had served as a midwife, facilitating births by rubbing her patients' bodies with ground white maize. But the real basis for the charge that she was an hechicera was her sacrifice of white *sango* (maize gruel) to the mountain Sunivilca. Her colleague Magdalena Cusituna, also accused of being an hechicera, had sought to benefit pregnant women by sacrificing to Sunivilca, which she had invoked as her creator.[25] Francisca Mayguay had likewise made sacrifices of maize and chicha to a mountain called Maguaca Coto to ease the delivery of children.[26]

Some curanderos were apparently guilty of consulting a wide variety of native deities. Fernando Carvachin had supplicated the huanca of his village to restore the health of one young woman, offering it coca and a dead llama kid and invoking it thus: "My Father and God, you who have taken the health of this poor girl, give her life and banish her affliction." He had also been known to prevail on the ancient deities of the sun and the sea for similar purposes.[27] Nor was he exceptional in this. Juana Conoa had taken part in sacrifices to the sea to ensure a safe passage and good health for those traveling to the *mita*. María Quillay admitted she had worshiped the sea and the earth to effect her cures.[28] Francisco Malqui confessed he had worshiped the rising sun and performed propitiatory rituals with various colored earths to gain this deity's favor so that the sick who consulted him would regain their health.[29]

What further incriminated these curanderos as hechiceros was the fact that their competence strayed outside the field of healing. Their dabbling in what Spaniards construed to be divination, or superstitious attempts to manipulate future events, added the crime of false observances to their sins. So Fernando Carvachin had sought the intercession of the sun not merely to effect cures but also to bring good fortune or to influence the behavior of third parties. For example, to secure the release of a client from prison, he had pleaded on his knees to the rising sun: "Lord and Father, Creator of this miserable Indian, release him from his danger." He had also sacrificed to the sea so that his kuraka would have a favorable outcome in a lawsuit for the *cacicazgo* (chieftainship), with the words "My mother, nourisher of all, let my kuraka return in good health and with victory in his case." Such activities carried the weight of a double charge: idolatrous invocations and superstitious observances.[30]

Divining and amorous magic were the classic examples

of the attempt to exercise undue influences through occult means. The defendant María Inés was questioned more closely on her supposed prediction of the whereabouts of a lost mule than on her alleged cures with herbs.[31] Francisca Mayguay stood accused not only of being a curandera but also of having consulted a stone to learn the identity of thieves who stole from the fields.[32] Juana de los Reyes was tried as an hechicera and idolater not just because she used the ritual death of white cuyes in the healing of patients but also because she bathed women in plants and yellow soil in order to attract men; in other words, she stood accused of the sin of superstitious love magic.[33] Similarly, Isabel Guanca had combined healing with the use of occult influences. Her consumption of ground-up shell to cure her knee pains and of the herbs *quina quina* and *espingo* to cleanse her body and her use of the plant *toradilla* for fevers aroused little comment from her interrogators; nor did they waste much time on her use of llama fat to soothe her aching feet. But she was questioned closely about her supposed maleficio with two wax figures, which she admitted were part of an attempt to force her daughter to show her more respect, and the superstitious utterances she may have made in their presence.[34] Likewise, the accusation of hechicería against Isabel Concepción rested less on her treatment of sick girls than on her unnatural methods of discovering the cause of the afflictions. On more than one occasion, for example, after diagnosing an illness to be the result of an intrusive element in the household, she had proceeded to locate, secreted about the dwelling, effigies of the victim wrapped in wool and hairs and run through with thorns. This clairvoyant ability and the woman's lack of any convincing explanation for it, rather than her curative abilities, were what troubled the prosecutors so much that they put her to the torture to elicit more information on its origin.[35]

Apart from the presence of maleficio or sorcery, the other intrusive element in the activities of curanderos that provoked the severe disapproval of the authorities was trespassing on Christian preserves. It has been seen that the scandalous notion of ecclesiastical blessing for his cures was what had caused Luis de Aguilar to incriminate himself more deeply as an hechicero, over and above the healing in itself. Far more weight was attached to the inclusion of Christian elements in the practices of curanderos than to their experiments with herbs. For example, María Sania was convicted not only of the use of dog excrement and cuyes' teeth for curative purposes but also, more seriously, of the superstitious abuse of an image of the Immaculate Conception for fortune-telling and the location of lost objects.[36] Pasquala de Salsedo was tried as an hechicera idólatra not just on the grounds of her cures with cuyes but principally because of her magical use of relics. Apart from administering the herbs *chinchimali* and *cuno cuno* for mule blows and fevers, respectively, she had taken a skull from a chapel devoted to Saint Anne and used it to divine the whereabouts of lost animals. She had also insisted that a man whom she diagnosed as bewitched could only be cured by imbibing at midnight the ground herbs *mollo spingo contrayerva* and Santa Marta. The specification of midnight was a false observance, far more serious than the administering of the herbs.[37] The offence of the curandero Sebastian Quito was not that he knew how to cure spider bites and snakebites with plants; rather, it lay in his failure to restrict his healing activities to the known virtues of herbs and his "dabbling with superstitions." His subsequent punishment by the succeeding Visitor arose less from repetitions of his cures than from denying that he had been punished as an hechicero and for his ignorance of the faith.[38]

In these trials, the focus on superstitious observances

was so pronounced that practitioners were occasionally dismissed with permission to administer cures provided that they did not mix indigenous or false Christian ceremonies. Some curanderos of the province of Chancay were absolved without punishment on the understanding they would avoid the use of all superstition in future and restrict themselves to the application of herbs according to their virtues and the qualities of the sickness.[39] Thus the official tolerance of healing with herbs was actively manifested in the idolatry trials.

If healing activities were not taken too seriously, it was largely because they were considered fraudulent and inefficacious. The principal accusation against the curandero Agustín Carbajal was not healing with herbs but "leading other Indians to believe" that he was a fortune-teller and a clairvoyant. If Carbajal had genuinely been able to discover treasures buried at huacas, it could only have been by means of a contract with the Devil. Thus, his defense accepted the accusation of fraud to save his client from the more serious accusation of a diabolical pact. He was not a genuine magician but a "ceremonial trickster." After all, his greatest crime had been to "let himself be deceived by his own greed for treasure," an act not deserving punishment. In any case, it was very frequent among the Indians that they cured and availed themselves of "other tricks" to alleviate their poverty. The sentence imposed confirmed that his offense had been mere lies with no pact with the Devil, and he was condemned to only six months service at the hospital of Huánuco and instructed not to indulge in such activities in future. If skepticism about the reality of diabolical contracts led Carbajal's interrogators to discount the likelihood of a pact, his actions could only be judged as hollow and inefficacious. His healing activities became simply one example of a monstrous fraud he had perpetrated on the Indians.[40]

This suspicion that native practitioners were frauds rather than genuine accomplices of the Devil was confirmed by many offenders' ignorance of the intellectual basis of the herbs they used. The art of the Devil implied a certain intelligence and willful knowledge that could hardly be discerned in these creatures, who had no intellectual comprehension of the workings of sympathetic healing or scientific understanding of the properties of herbs. Thus the hopeless ignorance and confusion of María Inés under the inquiry of her interrogators precluded any possibility of a pact and, in their eyes, only left the alternative of fraud. She failed to recall the name of a plant she had used in her cures and betrayed her ignorance of the science of healing when she declared that by warming it with a candle before anointing the patient, she had been able to use a "cold" plant to cure a "cold" illness. The sentence against her condemned her as a "backsliding deceiving hechicera," "leading the Indians to believe" she had done harm and located lost animals. Whereas attention was given to her maleficio and divination, her curing was not even considered worthy of note. Such activities only aroused the contempt and incredulity of the extirpators.[41]

The efficacy of practitioners' divination and love magic was met with equal skepticism. Juana de Mayo admitted bathing women in herbs to bring them good luck in their amorous adventures with men but insisted that she was ignorant of the arts of magic. Her inability to cast spells had left her unable to perform magic with a magnet that one client had supplied. If she had given her clients ground avocado pear stone and ground *mollo* shell, it had been an act of deception in return for money. If she had told clients that she kept a snake, it had only been to impress and frighten them. Her prosecutors implicitly accepted her disavowals when they identified her most serious offense as that of denying her own guilt in chewing coca.

Her frank confession of the foolishness of her deeds and her show of contrition earned her the benevolence of her interrogators, who readily accepted her professions of ignorance.[42] Thus faced with a lack of official interest in their powers, the defendants found that the course of least resistance was to confess to fraud, especially as a means of escaping severer punishment. The contempt of the extirpators for the real abilities of the curanderos originated from their identifying them as hechiceros. By association with their supposed European counterpart, they inherited the status of charlatan. The consequence was a huge underestimation of their talents and their role on the part of Spaniards and an unshakable refusal to take seriously the powers they claimed for themselves. All this despite the undeniable fact that most of the defendants asserted their full confidence and trust in the methods they employed.

III

In the trials of its own hechiceros idólatras, the Extirpation reproduced the skepticism and incredulity that characterized the Inquisition's persecution of hechiceros in metropolitan Spain. The Visitors-General discounted the likelihood of a real demonic presence in the activities of Andean religious specialists. The defendants themselves, resisting the label "hechicero," were at pains to deny any evil intent or real manipulation of supernatural powers. Thus it is all the more surprising to find that in a number of cases a real demonic presence *was* perceived by the extirpators, and the existence of a pact between the practitioner and the Devil was upheld. In these cases, the role of Satan was not confined to the realms of abstract theory but was judged to be a physical reality. Not only did the defendants themselves confess to the diabolical contract but they also furnished detailed descriptions of the external appearance of their demons and of the relationship they maintained with them. A few even accused themselves of sexual intercourse with Satan's followers.

Inés Carva testified that she had spoken personally with the Devil on at least two occasions and was able to describe his physical appearance in some detail. Furthermore, she had received him into her bed "in the same manner as she would receive her husband." This had apparently been a genuine sensual experience since she was able to remember the impressive size of his sexual organ and the sensation of his hot sperm. Another defendant, Juana Icha, insisted that she had been taught her skills as a diviner and curandera by a demon who had visited her house at night on several occasions. She too had been seduced by him and had similar vivid memories of how his semen, freezing cold in this case, had invaded her body.[43]

The existence of such testimony raises several important questions. With regard to the attitude of the extirpators, it is necessary to consider why men whose characteristic traits were incredulity and skepticism pursued such testimony and elicited further details. Had they suspended the healthy disbelief typical of their colleagues both in the Extirpation and in the Inquisition? With regard to the defendants themselves, it should be considered if this testimony was evidence of the internalization of Christian concepts about the Devil. It is necessary to establish how far the defendants genuinely believed in what they confessed and how far such admissions may be attributed to a desire to conform to the expectations of their interrogators.

A closer examination of the testimony will indicate, first, that these cases were exceptional; confessions of diabolical intervention were typically *not* sought or obtained by the extirpators, who, on the whole, retained their skepticism. Second, if confessions of real demonic presence *were* on occasion elicited, they were not spontaneous but were extracted under duress; as such, they represent an attempt by the accused to give testimony that would conform to the preconceptions of the extirpators. Last, there is no evidence of internalization by the defendants of the Christian concept of the Devil or of any association between Satan and native deities. On the contrary, despite the intrusion of the language of European demonology, the contact of these defendants with the supernatural world still conformed to native rather than European paradigms. They had by no means adopted the worldview of the dominant elite represented by the extirpators. Indeed, the most noticeable characteristic of their testimony is the marked similarity between their activities and experiences and those of modern-day South American shamans.

It is entirely pertinent to examine the contention that the testimony of these defendants was molded to fit the expectations of their interrogators. Such a phenomenon would not be unique to colonial Peru. In the European context, the Italian historian Carlo Ginzburg has suggested a model for the assimilation of religious deviants to elite categories, in particular, that of witches.[44] His work on the self-styled Benandanti of sixteenth- and seventeenth-century Friuli examines how those who in the beginning portrayed themselves as the adversaries of witches, with whom they did battle for the fate of the season's crops, ended up accusing themselves of participation in diabolical sabbats. Such a transformation was effected in the process of the inquisitorial trials to which the accused were subjected. The confessions of participation in the sabbat were elicited by means of two devices: torture and suggestive questioning. For example, when one of the Benandanti cited the inspiration of "the angel of God," the inquisitor asked whether the angel had frightened him and had asked to be worshiped. Within a few days the witness had admitted he believed the angel was really the Devil tempting him. In this way the testimony was adapted to the inquisitors' own theological preconceptions, representing a "superimposition" of the inquisitorial schema onto a "pre-existing stratum of generic superstitions." Under inquisitorial pressure the cult of the Benandanti was transformed into something more distinctively characteristic of traditional witchcraft.

The impact of the trials was not limited to merely external professions of diabolism; a fundamental change was wrought within the Benandanti's own self-perceptions. In the 1570s, belief in the diabolical sabbat was foreign to the conception the Benandanti held of themselves and had to be elicited by the proddings of the inquisitors; but by the mid-seventeenth century confessions of attendance at nocturnal sabbats presided over by the Devil had become spontaneous and unsolicited. Whereas the earlier Benandanti had attended nocturnal gatherings in spirit form only, subsequently they acknowledged the physical reality of the sabbat. Their former concern with the protection of children and harvests had been replaced by an exclusive preoccupation with the making and unmaking of spells. The original myth of a battle in defense of the faith had been rejected in favor of the sworn pact with the Devil as the source of their powers. By the 1640s, then, the transformation into witches was accomplished at the popular level. Thus not only did the inquisitors succeed in eliciting admissions of diabolism from the accused, they also managed in some way, if not exactly to impose their worldview on the popular mind, at least to operate as the major influence in the creation of a fundamentally altered form of popular belief. Ginzburg points out that the transformation of Benandanti into witches was "spontaneous" in the sense that it was not determined by conscious calculation; but this "spontaneity" was channeled by the "opportune intervention" of the inquisitors. The admissions of making a pact with the Devil would probably never have occurred without the inquisitors' intervention.[45]

This model raises interesting questions of analogies in the Peruvian context and is useful for the interpretation of the cases of Inés Carva and Juana Icha. The confessions of these two curanderas to explicit pacts, even sexual intercourse with demons, were demonstrably extracted under duress. As with the Benandanti, the use or threatened use of physical force and the posing of suggestive questions were highly effective. It was the investigating priest, Antonio de Cáceres, who introduced the references to "demons" and the satanic pact. Both of the accused attempted to describe nothing more than their reciprocal relationship with tutelary mountain spirits called Apu Quircay and Apu Parato. It was Cáceres who interpreted these activities as diabolical.[46]

It is true that the first reference to satanic intervention in Juana Icha's case is found in the evidence of the key witness, Felipe Curichagua, who suggested that the successful outcome of Icha's predictions might have been due to a "pact with the Devil." Although it is impossible to know if this accusation was elicited by a leading question that has remained unrecorded, it seems safe to assume that, even as a spontaneous utterance, it was framed in a form intended to conform to what the priest expected to discover. Curichagua was Icha's mortal enemy. By presenting her activities as diabolically inspired maleficio, he could set in motion legal action against her that might culminate in her removal from the community. This would seem sufficient motive for the witness's charge, without assuming his internalization of the European concept of the Devil. Since the acceptance of this evidence was dependent on the Visitor seeking it out, the inference must be that the mention of the Devil was the result of pressure from above. It is a simple fact that witnesses speaking of pacts with the Devil are only to be found in cases in which the Visitor has evinced a particularly strong inclination to view them in such terms. As I will illustrate, other investigators showed little or no interest in uncovering demonic arts, and in these instances, the witnesses never mentioned the Devil.[47]

Cáceres's conduct of the interrogation bears out this interpretation. Juana Icha insisted on the purely beneficial intent of her healing activities. Her specialist knowledge originated from a natural source; it had been imparted to her by her Indian teacher and mentor ten years previously as a resource for survival. But no sooner had she offered this information than Cáceres prompted her to tell him if this Indian had spoken with any "demon" to effect his cures, at which she described a huaca of silver he had kept in his possession. Every subsequent question about this huaca was framed in the terminology of demons, which the defendant repeated in her responses. Asked, for example, if the "demon" had spoken with the Indian, she replied that he had told her that a certain rumbling noise they heard on making offerings signified that the "demon" was asking to be fed.[48]

Since the entire deposition was made through an interpreter, there is no reason to suppose that Icha ever employed the word "demon" herself, still less that she had internalized the Christian concept. It is more likely that she referred to her spirit as her apu, the word her interrogators themselves record as part of the "demon's" name, Apu Parato. It is true that she was reported to have invoked the spirit as Supay, which Spaniards understood to be the native word for the Devil. However, this offers no evidence of any internalization of the Christian concept. In the indigenous tradition, Supay designated, in typical Andean fashion, an ambivalent supernatural entity who could be either benevolent or malevolent according to how he was propitiated. Such a description fits Apu Parato, who alternated between bringing her presents and beating her. Supay did not mean the Devil; the language of discourse between interrogator and subject was clearly that of the former, and demons were a part of his mental construct, not hers.[49]

The confessions of sexual relations with the Devil were induced after the application of torture and by means of highly suggestive questioning. When Inés Carva admitted that she had offered lambs to Apu Quircay, Cáceres asked how many times she had seen and spoken with "the Devil." Her account of their reciprocal agreement, whereby she would "feed" the apu in return for his provision of maize and potatoes, provoked an interrogation on how many times she had slept with "the Devil." Her response, twice, encouraged the Visitor to pursue the question of how "the Devil" had conquered her and whether his semen had been hot or cold.[50]

The procedure with Icha was identical. No sooner had she revealed that Apu Parato had appeared to her demanding to be fed than the Visitor wanted to know how many times she had slept with him. She responded that he would often disappear for weeks at a time between visits, but when he finally came, he would abuse her after sleeping with her. Later, to satisfy the priest's insistent curiosity, she agreed that the Devil had inserted his member in her, ejaculating a cold yellow liquid. Whereas in her preliminary confession she had maintained the Devil had only visited her in dreams in the form of her dead husband, later she admitted that he came when she was awake, in the form of an Indian with a black cape. Pressed on why she not confessed the "explicit pact" in her first confession, she pleaded that the Devil had deceived her into not confessing truthfully. Besides, she had feared that if she confessed to having intercourse with the Devil, she would be burned. So whereas at first, she resisted complying with the Visitor's account of her story, once she was sure she would not be punished severely, she adapted her account to fit the demands of her interrogators.[51]

Yet even this pressure was not sufficient to make her concede that either she or her mentor had ever maintained a pact with Apu Parato when they went to feed him. To elicit this admission, Cáceres enlisted the aid of two experts in Indian languages who persuaded her to confess all her sins and, in particular, the pact with the Devil. Faced with this relentless insistence, she succumbed. She was then subjected to a further session to establish the origin of her rash statement that the images of Christ and the saints in the church were nothing but bits of wood. Her insistence that it was nothing more than her own poor understanding failed to convince Cáceres. Employing torture to loosen her imagination, he succeeded in extracting the desired admission that her "demon" Apu Parato had so instructed her but that now she recognized her error. The contrived nature of her declarations could not be more obvious.[52]

The threat of torture and the use of suggestive questioning were not confined to the cases of Icha and Carva. The curandero Pedro Guamboy confessed to cures with herbs but insisted that his reputation as an hechicero only derived from his success at healing. When introduced to the instruments of torture, his deposition began to conform more closely to the model of European demonology. He rapidly admitted that he had performed maleficio and regretted his deception by the Devil.[53] Francisco Malqui confessed to the use of colored earths with which he performed ritual offerings to the "Devil" to secure the health of clients. He had also allegedly worshiped the rising sun because "the Devil had deceived him that it was God." It is difficult to conclude with certainty the role of suggestive questioning in prompting these responses, since the questions are not always recorded. However, the Visitor was certainly attempting to put words into the defendant's mouth in the latter instance, by asking him if he had ever "worshiped the sun, holding it to be God."

No explicit suggestion of the role of the Devil by the Visitor is recorded; but even if the reference was a spontaneous one on behalf of the defendant, which is unlikely, it was no doubt triggered by a desire to tell the Visitor what he wished to hear. There is no evidence from this case of an internalization of the Christian concept of the Devil, still less of any Indian wish to worship the Devil.[54]

The role of force and suggestive questioning is hard to determine in cases in which testimony was recorded as a continuous summary of a witness's deposition. However, the determination of the Visitor to classify the relationship with a tutelary spirit as a demonic pact is often sufficient to evoke references to consultations and sexual intercourse with "demons." María Ticllaguacho obliged Visitor Pedro Quijano Bevellos by testifying that she had seen "the Devil" on no less than ten occasions, five times in the form of a lion and five times in the form of a fox. This "demon," who invariably spoke to her through the huaca Mallmainque, which was a standing stone on a lake, had persuaded her to serve him and forget she had ever known any other god. By consuming some black manure he had given her, she had acquired clairvoyant powers. Like Icha and Carva, this witness accused her "demon" of having shared her bed, in this case in the form of a lion. So vivid was the recollection elicited by the priest that she was able to describe the coldness of his semen and the depth of her revulsion. She recalled the details of a conversation with her demon in which he had challenged her that she did not love him; she had replied, how could she love him "if he was a lion and the very Devil?"[55]

The evident role of force and suggestive questioning in extracting these confessions has led one historian to conclude that the case of Juana Icha, in particular, is exemplary of the imposition on indigenous confessions of European expectations about witchcraft.[56] However, it is important to recognize that the cases of Icha, Carva, and

Ticllaguacho are atypical of the majority of idolatry trials. Confessions of sexual intercourse with demons are the exception and not the rule. Cáceres and Quijano were idiosyncratic in their obsession with eliciting the details of demonic pacts. Most Visitors showed scant interest in proving a real satanic presence. The insistence on interpreting native religion through the eyes of European demonology led, not to credulity, but to skepticism—the same skepticism that had been displayed toward the professed powers of curanderos.

Pedro Guamboy was threatened with torture by the Visitor Juan Sarmiento de Vivero to force him to admit that "the Devil" had deceived him into performing maleficio. Asked if the Devil had appeared to him or spoken with him, Guamboy confessed he had seen him at least ten times in the form of a huge shadow that seemed to reach up to the sky. He even admitted that he had flown through the air at night in the form of a large turkey. But in the sentence passed against him, he was condemned, not for any pact, but for the foolish things he had *believed*. He was admonished for his belief that his communications with a sacred rock had enabled him to fly through the air. He was also reprimanded for his *conviction* that he could deprive people of their lives by making magic with the earth where they had left their footprints. Finally, he was berated for "having led others to believe" that he was knowledgeable about certain herbs that could cause men and women to get married. The words *believe, convince,* and *understand* represented the nature of his sins. His codefendant María Inés was also censured for having "given the impression" that she was a diviner and "leading innocents to believe" that she had done them some harm by occult means. The characteristic skepticism of the extirpators manifested itself in an emphasis on the sinful beliefs of the defendants rather than on the alleged outcome of their acts.[57]

Other declarants were ridiculed by the incredulous Sarmiento. When Felipe Cupeda recounted how he had entered a huaca and had conversations with the spirits therein, he was instructed not to believe in foolish dreams that could only have originated from sunstroke. The Visitor was convinced of Cupeda's sincerity but discounted the possibility of real supernatural intervention. The only alternative was a sleeping fantasy induced by the hot sun, in which case the sin lay in the subject's belief in the reality of imaginary events rather than in any genuine contact with supernatural beings, demonic or otherwise.[58]

In such a climate of skepticism, it is not surprising that the question of the pact does not seem to have been the predominant influence on the determination of sentence. Pedro Guamboy, who was not accused of a pact, received a relatively harsh punishment of public humiliation, one hundred lashes, the stigma of a perpetual cross around his neck, and four years exile to the House of Santa Cruz at El Cercado. Other prisoners who were openly charged with maintaining a pact got off lightly. María Sania, accused of a tacit pact with the Devil because her divining of future events surpassed the limits of human powers, was ordered to pay the costs of the case, to serve two months in the village church, and to refrain from committing the same offense again on pain of punishment with the full rigor of the law. The sentences administered to such offenders implicitly belied the accusation that they had made a pact with the Devil.[59]

The same offense could generate different penalties, not according to the offense committed but with reference to an assessment of the character of the accused.[60] Fernando Carvachin and Catalina Llacsa were found guilty of idolatry and hechicerías and of having maintained overt and visible communication with the Devil. They were given a standard sentence of public humiliation and whipping, to be followed by exile from their village and service in a Lima hospital for the rest of their lives. However, the penalty was commuted to service in the local church in view of their "honest confession" and "the true signs of repentance" they had shown. By contrast, Leonor Rimay, for the same offense and for her explicit pact with the Devil, was to suffer public humiliation, whipping, and confinement to the Lima hospital for life, since she had shown herself to be "an impenitent and relapsed rebel with no hope of correction."

Other cases support this interpretation. Harsh sentences were imposed on María Arriera and Sebastian Quito, both accused of hechicerías. Like Guamboy, Arriera was condemned for her sins of deception, "leading others to believe" that certain liquids and plants had the virtue of bringing good fortune; but, above all, she was reproved for having been obstinate in not surrendering her idols. Quito was similarly reproached for stubbornly insisting that he had never been punished as an hechicero as well as for his ignorance of the faith. Despite the absence of the accusation of the pact, they were both sentenced to public humiliation, whipping, and two years banishment to Lima. Their fate had been sealed by their "attitude problem."[61] By contrast, Pablo Ato had his corporal punishment remitted on the grounds of his willing confession; he was condemned only to wearing a cross around his neck for one year, with the threat of one hundred lashes if he removed it. Juana Chapa also had her corporal punishment waived for the same reason.[62]

The punishment administered depended on the reaction of the accused to the authority of the interrogators. If he proved to be sullen, resistant to revealing information, or unrepentant of his deeds, he could expect severe treatment; if, however, he showed himself willing to submit to the Visitor's authority and manifest genuine contrition, he could benefit from relative leniency, no matter how serious the charge against him. The concern of the extirpators was not to pursue devil worship in the abstract or to apply inflexible automatic penalties for preestablished categories of offense; rather, they were interested simply in controlling Indian behavior and preventing relapses into deviance. The punishment would only be as severe as was necessary to secure this end. Hence the preference for harsh, suspended sentences, which hung over the head of the accused like the sword of Damocles and functioned as a deterrent to further transgressions.

The pact with the Devil had a relatively restricted role in the schema of the extirpators. Despite the cases of Icha, Carva, and Ticllaguacho, the Visitors displayed little desire to prove a real demonic presence that could be held responsible for magical acts. In such a climate of skepticism, there was little need to resort to the charge of a satanic pact. But why was the charge made at all? The existence of religious deviance in God's universe needed an abstract explanation to allay the philosophical unease such activities provoked. The schemings of the Devil were a convenient apology for the imperfections of those who could no longer plead ignorance of the true faith. But demonological theories were confined to the field of abstract speculation; they were not intended to be a guide to the concrete reality of the foolishness of individual Indians. It has already been demonstrated that the Supreme Council of the peninsular Inquisition had been at pains to make this point clear to its provincial employees in Spain. If the accusation of a satanic pact was certainly made against Indian practitioners, it featured more as an intellectual reflex to provide a metaphysical framework within which to situate the case rather than as a determinant of sentence and punishment.

It did serve another purpose, however. It functioned as an awesome threat for any defendant who refused to cooperate with the investigators and continued to insist on the reality of his powers. In the Spanish worldview, only one explanation could account for such real powers: the pact with Satan, the consequences of which could be terrible. Therefore, far better that the accused admit what his interrogators expected of him: that his practices had been nothing more than foolish deceptions, lies, and tricks. The extirpators themselves could not comprehend the possibility of demonic intervention in the actions of Indians for whom they felt nothing but contempt. It appeared more reasonable to dismiss native practices as so many tricks, especially when the suspects were clearly so witless and incompetent. The awesome presence of the Enemy could hardly be seriously detected in the foolish ramblings of these ignorant peasants, who by their own admission had merely sought to scratch out a living from the gullibility of their neighbors. The most plausible proposition was not the threatening and awesome satanic pact but simple human fraud. These were the only two alternatives available to the defendants. A third alternative, considering their claims as valid in their own terms, was not a possibility. It was precisely this option that the extirpators sought to eradicate, because, in their view, it allowed the offender to remain on ambiguous ground. Here there is an analogy with the prosecution of the Benandanti who were obliged either to admit that they were witches and practiced in the sabbat or to acknowledge that their accounts were pure fantasies. Just as the Benandanti were offered the simplistic and mutually exclusive options "witches or rascals," so too the native practitioners of Peru were urged to choose: were they hechiceros or tricksters?[63] The answer that was expected of them testifies to the skepticism, not credulity, of the extirpators.

The insistence on viewing native healing and divining as chicanery prevented the extirpators from any appreciation of the function of such practices within the indigenous world itself. However, the accounts they recorded allow an attempt to reconstruct the self-perceptions of the declarants. Although the defendants' accounts are presented in the language of European demonology, their content remains faithful to indigenous paradigms. There is no evidence to suppose that the schema of the extirpators had been interiorized by the accused. Indeed, as even the case of Icha has indicated, the defendants were remarkably persistent in proffering their own interpretations of what had occurred to them. There is little to suggest that any transformation occurred in native perceptions of their own practices, along the lines advanced by Ginzburg for the Benandanti. These defendants preserved their own interpretation of their relationship with the supernatural world.

The relationship between the practitioner and the tutelary lord (the "demon") was most commonly characterized as "feeding" the apu in return for the granting of special powers. Both Inés Carva and Juana Icha dwelled on their reciprocal relations with the tutelary mountain spirits Apu Quircay and Apu Parato. The demands of these spiritual visitors were for food and sustenance in the form of coca leaves or offerings of animal blood. In return for feeding the apu in this way, the defendant would be provided with maize and potatoes. This was a typical example of traditional Andean reciprocity.

The physical descriptions of these supernatural entities fit native forms of religious belief rather than European categories. Apu Parato and Apu Quircay took the form of Indians in native dress. Other declarants described contact with native American animals such as the jaguar, the condor, or the llama. Leonor Rimay described a black llama, Fernando Carvachin a condor, and María Ticllaguacho a lion. Since by "lion," these declarants presumably meant "jaguar," one of the archetypal forms of the spiritual representation of South American shamans, the indigenous content of these confessions was clear.[64]

But the feature that most clearly defined these defendants as forerunners of modern South American shamans was the spiritual initiation conferred on them by the tutelary spirit. It was this alone that, in the eyes of the community, consecrated them as diviners and curanderos. Even today such an experience is the necessary prelude to acting as a shaman among the indigenous peoples of South America. Although the practical aspects of healing may be easily taught by a master, the neophyte still requires an ecstatic experience in which the guardian spirits demonstrate his or her chosen condition as a healer. This experience, whether in dreams or in a waking state of altered consciousness, typically takes the form of conversations with spirits and the souls of dead shamans. "Primordial mythical revelations" are imparted to the subject which will serve as the fountainhead of his future powers.[65]

These defendants recounted initiation experiences in which the tutelary lord revealed to them hidden or future events and imparted privileged knowledge about the healing qualities of plants and other substances. Juana Icha's mentor, Catalina Suyo, confided to her that as a young girl tending her llamas she had been swallowed by a spring on the mountain Julcan, wherein she remained for several days in the company of a golden-haired man who invited her to feed him thereafter at that spot. This ecstatic experience had been the beginning of her life as an interpreter of the supernatural. Icha herself had received instruction from this woman as regards the curative properties of llama fat, maize, and coca and the manner of making offerings to sacred stones; but it was only her personal relationship with Apu Parato, conferred directly on her by the spirit in the same manner as with her mentor, that consummated her marriage to the supernatural world.[66]

The experience of being swallowed by the numen was

replicated by other declarants. Felipe Cupeda described how his soul abandoned his body and entered a huaca. It occurred one day when he went fishing. His body began to tremble and on offering up a prayer, he settled down to sleep beside some stones near the river. In his dreams, a black man and a mestizo took him to a huge table where many people were eating. When they tried to persuade him to remain with them, a Franciscan friar entered and told him to go home. The diners protested, but the friar silenced them, telling them to leave the Indian alone since he knew nothing. Cupeda's soul remained three days inside the huaca before returning to his body.[67]

Other declarants explained how their knowledge of healing had been imparted to them by means of a spiritual guardian. As a young girl, Leonor Rimay had fallen gravely ill after the apparition of a black llama that had followed her from the river to her home. Subsequently, an old *Padre* with a bushy beard came to her in dreams and taught her how to cure with plants and cuyes and how to divine using saliva in her palm. On other occasions he appeared as a lion and told her to worship Coriguanca, a white stone that stood near her house. When she brought offerings to this place, he furnished her with the necessary replies for the demands of her clients. Her method was to address the huaca as "her god" and "the god of her ancestors," who had chosen her for her office and bid her serve and worship him. She believed that the huaca could communicate to her the whereabouts of lost objects, sensing "in her heart" if the item was to be found or not. The infallibility of her prognostications brought her such fame that she was consulted by all the Indians of the valley.[68]

Carvachin had been initiated into the secrets of healing by an old Indian who had appeared to him. This Indian gave him a string of blue and black beads, telling him always to take them with him when he went to worship his huacas and to offer some of them to ensure the effectiveness of his cures. After accepting them, the witness lost consciousness. Two months later, an Indian shepherd, passing near a spring, was startled to witness the emergence of a rainbow and fell ill from fright. The defendant, remembering the Indian's exhortations, ground up some of the beads and sprinkled the powders at the spring, begging for the health of the shepherd. He informed the family that he had done what was necessary for the man's health, and after some weeks the shepherd completely recovered. Carvachin's reputation spread, and he let the other villagers know that they should prevail on him to communicate with the huacas for the satisfaction of their needs.[69]

The defendant Hernando Hacaspoma related how he entered a state of "ecstasy" in which he was deprived of his senses whenever he went to make offerings to his ancestral deities. The voice of his forebears informed him if there were to be epidemics and if the community would enjoy good or bad harvests. If the answer was favorable, he went to the village and told them to celebrate; if not, he ordered them to make new offerings. Thus, in an altered state of consciousness, he was in direct communication with the primordial ancestors, whose *camaquen* (or life force) entered his heart to convey messages to the villagers.[70]

Such relationships may be representative of an archetypal bond between shaman past and shaman present. But this bond was not immune to the processes of change. With the advent of Christianity, an alien supernatural system, there was serious malfunctioning and even breakdown in the union of tutelary spirit and his messenger to the community. The time-honored reciprocal relationship of practitioner and spirit had begun to fall victim to the inroads made by the new faith. What attests most clearly to this is the increasingly violent and unsatisfying relationships the declarants had begun to maintain with their apus. Fernando Carvachin protested that his spirit would materialize only to strike him and scold him for neglecting the magic which he had taught him. María Ticllaguacho grumbled that her "demon" had whipped and beaten her for believing in the Spanish god. And Juana Icha complained bitterly to her interrogator that her apu had never before mistreated her in the way that he was now accustomed to do.[71]

Such conflict, presented in external physical terms, represents the mental turmoil consequent on the invasion of the indigenous consciousness by Christian images and practices. The determining factor in Ticllaguacho's increasingly brutal relationship with her spirit was her defiance of the essential condition that she should forget she had ever known any other god. Her huaca would appear to her in the form of a ferocious lion with bulging, fiery eyes and scold her for believing in the Spanish god and praying to him. Whipping and beating her, he had left her half-dead. By continuing to pray to the Christian god, she provoked an outraged antagonism in her autochthonous guardian. The Christian insistence on its exclusive monopoly of the numinous world had apparently generated a corresponding demand among the indigenous deities. Given that the Andean tradition was one of the incorporation of new deities into the existing pantheon, this expressed a dramatic transformation wrought by the invading religious system.[72]

The predominant influence on Carvachin's relations with his spirit seems to have been the need to resist the strengthening grasp of Christianity. His tutelary spirit appeared to him in his fields and beat him, scolding him in his native tongue for neglecting the magic he had taught him. This crisis of confidence in his native deity was symbolically represented by a journey he made in his dreams. His guardian came to his house in the form of a donkey and told him to accompany it to Lima. Somehow he found himself transported to the capital where the creature took him to every church, bidding him enter alone while it remained outside. In this manner the spirit attempted to force into Carvachin's consciousness the subconscious struggle taking place between the two competing religious systems. A similar interpretation could be put on Cupeda's account of the descent of his soul into the huaca where the inhabiting spirits debated for it with a Franciscan friar.[73]

The increasingly vicious and unsatisfying nature of Icha's relationship with Apu Parato seems largely to have sprung from the conflicting demands on her religious loyalties. On the one hand, her apu appeared powerless to prevent her from attending Christian worship, ranting and raving outside the church in a futile fashion while she prayed inside and fleeing in terror at the mere mention of the name Jesus. On the other hand, he resorted more and more frequently to physical abuse, both as a punishment for succumbing to the pressure of the fiscales to go to church and to castigate her for her neglect to "feed" him sheep fat. At the same time, he failed in his reciprocal obligations by coming to her empty-handed, complaining that he had found nothing to give her, to the point where she admitted to her interrogator that ever since she had associated with this "demon," she had fallen into a wretched, poverty-stricken existence. In despair she had even offered him money to buy her clothes, but her "demon" had remained sadly silent. Asked why, if this was the case, she had not abandoned him, she said she had believed that he would solve everything for her.[74]

Yet the increasing diffidence of her apu was not reflected in a corresponding diminution of her supernatural talents. She was still able to convince her fellow villagers that she was the manipulator of sinister powers that had led to the deaths not only of animals and Indians but also of important figures of authority, such as the priest. The enmity such a reputation had earned her was the catalyst for her denunciation. The breakdown in the relationship seems to have been in her own mind, some crisis in her own psyche, presumably triggered by a realization that despite her influence, her material position was fast deteriorating. In short she was plagued by an ever more common curse among practitioners, self-doubt.

Whether these doubts and oscillations in spirit-shaman relations existed before the advent of Christianity is impossible to determine. Presumably there must always have been deities who failed in their reciprocal obligations just as there were humans who neglected their duties. The Andean deities had always been capricious and ambivalent. But in earlier times there had been no competing religious system that could both breed and profit from dissension in the indigenous religious world. What is evident in the colonial period is the significant role of the new faith in disrupting the age-old pattern of mutual commitments. The defendants may not have internalized the concepts of the Christian religion, but their self-perceptions were nonetheless altered by the intrusion of an alternative numinous world.

IV

The later seventeenth century witnessed an increasing professionalization in the procedure of idolatry trials. Whereas the defense of native religious practitioners had formerly lacked any consistent theoretical foundations, by the 1690s trained lawyers had begun to elaborate a more explicit, more unified, and more sharply defined justification for the use of herbal remedies. The assumption of the role of defense by one individual, the procurador de los naturales Joseph Mexia de Estela, contributed enormously to the greater coherence and continuity of the arguments advanced. It has already been demonstrated that the crucial issue was less the use of herbs in itself than the addition of clearly superstitious practices. The consequence of this emphasis was to encourage both prosecution and defense to examine yet more closely the *source* of the curandero's powers and the *manner* in which he had acquired knowledge of the curative properties of herbs. Whereas the prosecution continued to evoke the accusation of the diabolical pact, the defense elaborated arguments to demonstrate that indigenous healing remedies could be explained purely by reference to natural causes. Thus the debate became explicitly one of the natural or the supernatural origin and application of such knowledge.

The procurador attempted to demonstrate that those who employed natural remedies for licit ends were not guilty of the charges of superstition or hechicería. For example, his clients Francisca de Ribera and María de la Cruz had been falsely accused of murderous maleficio, since they had been engaged in nothing more sinful than an attempt to cure afflictions that had been ailing them. If they had drunk wine mixed with ground iron powders in the presence of a lodestone (*piedra imán*), it was in the belief that they could cure the *mal de madre* from which de la Cruz was suffering. The coca found in their possession had not been directed to superstitious ends but had been used as a remedy for de Ribera's toothache. The attempt to heal these ailments could not be construed as magic or superstition since it was a licit purpose for the objects they were using; the lodestone was a well-known remedy for the mal de madre and coca was effective for toothache.[75]

Accusations of hechicería could not rest on evidence of healing with herbs or the chewing of coca since neither was an offense of superstition. The former was a common custom among Indians on account of the impossibility of obtaining better medicine, and the latter was an everyday practice among Indians at work, from which no superstitious purpose should be inferred. These arguments, employed by Mexia de Estela in defense of his clients María de la Cruz and Augustina Barbola, was resisted by their kuraka, Don Carlos Apoalaya, who had brought the charge of hechicería. He objected that the frequency of the custom of chewing coca was an insufficient excuse as the habit was, after all, the very root cause of their superstitions. Why else would the Inquisition and the archbishop of Lima have forbidden its use? If the Indians chewed coca for purely innocent ends, why did they do it in the presence of heathen skulls, out in the pampas and depopulated regions? But Mexia de Estela insisted that the issue was not the use of herbs or of coca in itself but rather the properties of these herbs (whether they could produce the claimed effects) and the words of invocation used. Since his clients had employed no diabolical spells, they had practiced, not magic or superstition, but natural philosophy.[76]

The defense of some declarants was prejudiced by the attribution of their powers to the communications of a "guardian angel" (angelito). This incontestable supernatural origin of their specialist knowledge of herbs exposed them to the traditional accusation of making a demonic pact. Thus the role of this guardian in their spiritual initiation became the primary preoccupation of their interrogators. The activities of Juana Augustina as a renowned diviner and curandera, advising clients on the whereabouts of lost items and bathing women in herbs as a cure for their ailments, were of little interest to her accusers. Characteristically, her superstitious observances earned her greater censure. To aid her in her divination, she chewed tobacco and, invoking the apostles Saint Peter and Saint Paul, spat it out into her hand. Merely by moving the saliva with her fingers, she was able to deduce from the course it took across her hand whether the lost item would reappear or not. But her greatest sin had been her communication with a guardian angel who appeared to her whenever she prayed the Pater noster, the Ave María, and the Salve. She had been taught how to summon this spiritual guardian by her stepfather, and it had appeared to her several times after his death, usually whenever she was at a certain stream. It was from the angel that she had learned how to attract good fortune and the love of men, both for herself and her clients, by taking baths in herbs.[77]

Her alleged initiation by the spiritual guardian became the most serious charge against Juana Augustina and justified the accusation of making a demonic pact. To escape this charge, the initial strategy of the defense (on this occasion Felipe Carranza, not Estela) was to deny the reality of the angel. She had learned the use of herbs, not from any angel, which was a story she had invented, but from her stepfather, and although she had divined with tobacco and saliva, it had been mere trickery so as to earn a living. She humbly asked pardon of God and promised never to use such superstitions again. When it became clear that her accusers were not convinced, she returned to her original story. The angel with whom she communicated had been bequeathed to her by her stepfather, who had been a doctor and not a brujo, in order that she might earn her livelihood. Again she begged forgiveness for her deeds, abominating her pact with the angel and promising not to repeat her superstitions with herbs since they were "the work of the Devil." Like her predecessors, she had been obliged to accept the terminology of her accusers as a sign of her true contrition. But, more important, the central issue of the angel had determined the interpretation that the origin of her powers was supernatural rather than natural.[78]

The dispute concerning the natural or supernatural origins of herbal remedies was revived in the trial of Juan Vásques in 1710. The consideration of the issue in this case was the most detailed that may be found among the documentation of the idolatry trials. Like Augustina, Vásques confessed that a guardian spirit had initiated him into the secrets of the healing properties of herbs. Once, as a child, sleeping in a field, an old white man appeared to him and showed him a cross emblazoned on his hand. He was astonished to discover a similar sign on his own arm where four black marks like moles had formed, apparently in the shape of a cross. In this same dream, the old man taught him to recognize certain herbs that would be of great value for the curing of pains and illnesses, including the *yerva de la golondrina* for side pains, the *yerva de Santa Lucia* for purging the disposition, and the *yerva de San Juan* for problems of urine and sores. Sometime later, seeing a young Indian in great pain and remembering the vision, he went to look for the yerva de San Juan and gave some to the boy to drink, by which means alone he recovered. For some years after this he performed no more cures but came to Lima to earn his living. At confession one day, he told a priest of his knowledge and of his fear of using it. The cleric reprimanded him and refused to absolve him until he used his talent as a gift of charity for others. However, he failed to follow this advice until he himself fell ill with side pains. In a dream an "angel" appeared to him, telling him to look for the yerva de San Juan at the mountain of San Gerónimo, and there indeed he found it with a cross emblazoned on it. Imbibing a drink he prepared from it, he recovered, for which "he gave thanks to God."[79]

To justify his deeds before his accusers, Vásques was careful throughout his account to attribute his powers and his success to God, as if to suggest that they were performed under the auspices of Christianity. Any doubts he might have experienced were assuaged by the reassurances he received from Catholic priests. For if he was still reluctant to make use of his powers, the insistence of a *second* priest convinced him. One day in Lima, seized by a conviction that he should cure the sick with herbs, he went to confess to settle his conscience. The priest refused him absolution until he had provided the sick with the benefits of his abilities. Administering to a crippled Indian a drink prepared from the yerva de San Francisco, he enabled the man to walk again. He took no payment from the man since his confessor had insisted that his cures should not be performed for personal gain.

Suspecting the use of superstitious means, his interrogators questioned him closely about his cures of illnesses provoked by maleficio. Vásques explained how he could discern from a client's spittle and from his pulse the origin of his ailment, as clearly as if it had been reflected in a mirror.[80] In this way, he perceived not only the nature of the affliction but also which herb would be most appropriate for the cure. His healing was always preceded by praying the creed. The prosecution remained unconvinced that he had revealed the true origin of his powers. Although Vásques was an Indian ladino and could respond adequately to questions in Castilian, an experienced linguist, Vitorino de Soria, was summoned to repeat the questions to him in his native language. Responding to the persistence of his interrogators, he declared that "he had possessed this knowledge since he had experienced that vision in his dreams . . . but that he had had no master nor had he been taught any illicit methods nor communicated with or invoked the Devil, and had only used the method of the saliva and the creed."[81] Threatening him with torture, the prosecution insisted that he should confess "the truth," which was that he had made a pact with the Devil who had taught him his tricks through illicit means. He replied in Castilian that he had had no master other than the insight that had been communicated to him in his vision, that he had only used the herbs already declared, and that he could not be forced to say anything else. The supernatural origin of Vásques's powers encouraged the prosecution to situate these events within the framework of the diabolical pact.

Alarmed by the possible consequences of the communications with his spiritual guardian, Vásques attempted in a subsequent statement to disavow his earlier confession. Instead of attributing his extraordinary abilities to the old man of his dreams, he credited his grandfather with imparting to him the knowledge of which herbs to apply to which illnesses. He retracted his earlier account, claiming that he had only invented this story in the belief that it would help him escape punishment. He had had the moles on his arm since he was a child; they were natural and were not formed in a vision as he had previously said. His ability to see the nature of afflictions as clearly as if human bodies were open to the eye was innate and could only be the will of God. He denied that in performing one of his cures he had summoned the old man of his dreams, extinguishing the candle since his guardian would refuse to enter while there was light. Confronted with the testimony of witnesses, he admitted that in the darkness he had changed the pitch of his voice and pretended to be the old man, but he insisted that it was only a trick that he had been taught to earn money. He also denied having said he had eighteen devils, who appeared at graves and at huacas, to help him with his cures; nor was it true that he had performed cures by offering blood to the sun or to the Devil. He emphatically denied any type of diabolical pact.[82]

The accusation of the diabolical pact had forced Vásques to adapt his account until it adhered to a model acceptable to his interrogators. In this respect his experience resembled that of Juana Icha. But whereas the imposition of the framework of demonology obliged Icha to elaborate on the demonic character of her apu, Vásques was goaded into minimizing the significance of his old man figure. If the former was drawn reluctantly into a confession of the pact, the latter, by contrast, was enticed into a retreat from it. The testimony of both Icha and Vásques adapted under interrogation, but the *direction* in which each moved was completely opposite. Despite the questions put to Vásques about his communication with "the Devil," he was not pressured into confessing the origin of his acts in the pact; rather, he was allowed to disavow his spirit and withdraw into confessions of trickery. The search for a genuine demonic presence had not been typical even in the mid-seventeenth century; by 1710, it was totally absent. Despite the importance attached to the old man figure, the concept of diabolical intervention remained a theory. The issue in dispute was not whether this spiritual guardian actually existed, nor was it whether communication with such a supernatural entity was possible; the issue was Vásques's sincere belief, both in the existence of this figure and in the efficacy of his cures. This emphasis on the question of belief, the internal state of mind of the accused or his "intention," is the clearest indication that the question of demonic intervention in this case was not taken seriously.[83]

Thus, while the issue between prosecution and defense remained the dichotomy natural-supernatural, "supernatural" did not infer any genuine contact with spirits or demons but only foolish convictions contrary to the faith. Vásques was accused by the *promotor* (prosecutor) of heresy and idolatry, not because he had genuinely entered a compact with Satan but because his cures had been performed in a superstitious manner. It was not important whether his knowledge of the qualities of herbs, or of the meaning of the moles on his arm, had in reality been imparted to him by the old man of his dreams; Vásques's sincere conviction that it was so was sufficient proof of his guilt of superstition. His insistence, for example, on performing his cures only on certain days, believing them to be propitious while others were not, was an act of *credulity* clearly constituting superstition.

Similarly, his interior state of mind determined his guilt in the matter of heresy. His examination of the spittle of the sick to learn of future events or to reveal hidden things confirmed that he was a sortílego or diviner. However, the practitioner of sortilegio could be excused the offense of heresy by reason of ignorance. Thus it was very important to learn if he was ignorant of matters of the faith and of those things that do or do not exceed the capacity of the Devil. For if the practitioner of sortilegio was true to the faith *in his mind*, he was not truly a heretic, since heresy depended on *interior consent*. Therefore, although on account of the method by which Vásques had learned of the nature of the illnesses of his clients he should be held to be a *sortílego heretical*, he could not be considered truly to be a heretic because in repeated examinations he had been found to be firm in the faith.[84]

By concentrating on Vásques's beliefs and his state of mind, the promotor had apparently undermined his own case. His exoneration of the accused on the grounds of his firm faith also contradicted his own earlier charge that Vásques's knowledge of Christian doctrine was very poor. Indeed, he conceded that the accusation of divination that he himself had brought against Vásques had not been sufficiently proved and that therefore the resolution of this question should be left until such time as there might be more evidence. The promotor's purpose may have been to avoid a charge of heresy, which required the death penalty. He observed that although the punishment for the crime of sortilegio was death, by custom this punishment had always been arbitrary and could be reduced. More important, it seems that he was concerned to avoid disputes over whether the Inquisition should have jurisdiction over heretics. In the same sentence as his denial that the accused was a heretic, he attacked the proposition that all those found guilty of sortilegio and maleficio were heretics and as such belonged to the jurisdiction of the Holy Office. To justify ordinary ecclesiastical jurisdiction, he was compelled to dwell on nuances and subtleties that rendered his case inconsistent. Thus while he argued that his client might be a sortílego without being a heretic, at the same time he alleged that there was insufficient proof even of sortilegio.

To demonstrate the absence of superstition from his client's practices, the procurador, Melchor de Carvajal, sought to provide an explanation in purely natural terms. Vásques did not know the origin of his knowledge, which he had possessed since he was a child and which he had attributed to the will of God. His moles had not been formed in a vision but had been with him since the day of his birth. If he had reserved certain days for his cures, it was not for any superstitious reason but because the occupations of his patients only permitted them to attend on those days. He knew well that all days were equal for the purposes of his cures. As for recognizing the illnesses of patients from their saliva, it was well known that doctors could do the same. Vásques's ability with herbs was not to be taken as evidence of superstition or of dealings with the Devil, since knowledge of the properties of herbs had been given by the Lord to some individuals in his Divine Providence. In their pagan state, without doctors, the Indians had possessed this knowledge and used it to cure illnesses. Other heathen peoples, such as the Ethiopians, had known of the properties of plants and had used them for medicinal purposes. Since the medicinal virtues lay in the herbs themselves and the accused had learned of them from his grandfather through the grace of God, it could not be demonstrated that he had committed any offense against the faith.[85]

Vásques's defense rested on the contention that the herbs possessed their virtues according to the laws of nature and that knowledge of them could be acquired by natural means. The promotor proposed to resolve the issue by summoning a *protomédico* (officer appointed to supervise the practice of medicine) and a professor of medicine to offer their professional opinions. They were asked to consider if the herbs mentioned in the confessions could have the medicinal effects claimed by the accused and if he could reasonably have acquired knowledge of these effects. They concluded that the herbs did indeed possess natural virtues for curing serious ailments, that doctors had successfully used them, and that knowledge of their virtues could be obtained by natural means through continual observance of their effects. Although current medical knowledge of some of the herbs was incomplete, it was quite possible that through the tradition of his ancestors an individual might have acquired a detailed understanding of their virtues. However, the experts felt unable to give any opinion as to how Vásques himself had made use of the herbs, since it was a matter of religion and therefore under the jurisdiction of the *provisor* (vicar-general). Their evidence was deliberately noncommittal and ambiguous, since they wisely did not wish to appear to usurp the authority of the Church. Although their testimony appeared to vindicate the defendant, the promotor was not deterred. He insisted that even if it was true that the effects of herbs could be known by natural causes, there was no proof that this particular defendant had acquired his knowledge in this manner. The expert testimony was incapable of resolving the question. Indeed, it is clear that the question was fundamentally irresolvable, since Spaniards were aware that they were ignorant of many of the properties of herbs. This detailed examination of the question of the natural virtues of herbs, the most complete of its kind in the records, had brought the dispute to no effective conclusion.[86]

The final sentence passed against Vásques failed to resolve the question of the origin of his powers. Although it found him guilty of using "illicit and superstitious means" in his cures, it neglected to reach a verdict either about the diabolical pact or the significance of the vision of the old man. The failure to resolve the central theoretical questions of the case suggests that this was not the priority of the investigation. The appeal to demonological theory was only useful in providing an intellectual framework within which to set and, to a certain extent, explain the accused's actions. It was not of great value in determining the action to be taken against the prisoner. The priority was, after all, not to engage in theological disputes about the nature of diabolical intervention but to prevent individual subjects from relapsing into their deviant behavior.[87]

If the question of the natural or supernatural origin of herbal knowledge was not explicitly addressed, it may have been because of the latent contradictions it evoked, evident in the sentence and punishment imposed. On the one hand, the fact that Vásques was ordered never to perform such cures again, or to pass on his knowledge of herbs to any other person, suggests a conviction that this knowledge was reprehensible *in itself* and not simply by association with superstitious practices. On the other hand, the leniency of the penalty in relation to the apparent seriousness of the accusation implicitly recognized the plausibility of natural causes as the explanation of Vásques's cures. His punishment was restricted to two years service in the convent of the Bethlehemites, where he would be instructed in Christian doctrine.[88] The full weight of the law would only be brought against him if he relapsed into such an offense in the future. Such forbearance was not wholly consistent with a sentence that had spoken of "illicit and superstitious acts." By the logic of the prosecution's own argument, if demonic intervention was excluded as the real source of Vásquess' acts and the superstition lay only in the frame of mind in which he had performed them, what other explanation remained but that of natural causes? In effect, the outcome of Vásques's case was a tacit recognition of the role of natural causes in the use of herbal remedies and thus also an implicit acceptance of the arguments advanced in previous years in defense of other curanderos who stood accused of hechicerías.

At the outset of his analysis, the promotor had posited two possible explanations, excluding mental illness, for the apparent successful outcome of Vásques's cures: natural causes or the illusion of demons. Yet his own account concentrated on an argument, that of reprehensible superstitious beliefs, that, while providing a plausible pretext for punishment, could not account for the outcome of exterior acts. The promotor was ensnared in the contradictions of his own philosophy. The rejection of the intervention of demons, by minds that were skeptical of the claims of hechiceros, strengthened the case for natural causes. Yet, at the same time, acceptance of natural causes attributed a dangerous efficacy to the actions of curanderos. It seems that having posited two alternative theories, the authorities were not happy with either, unconsciously acknowledging, through their unease, that the terrain of the empirical evidence did not quite fit the map of their intellectual constructs.[89]

Vásques's relationship with the old man of his dreams testifies to the resilience of the eternal bond between shaman and tutelary deity, a bond that had survived the increasing atomization of the native world. Vásques differed from his predecessors in one important respect: his isolation from any intellectual framework or collective indigenous context for his abilities. Whereas practitioners such as Icha, Carva, Carvachin, and even Augustina performed their roles within the context of their traditional communities, from which they drew their inspiration, Vásques worked alone in the alien environment of the capital, cut off from the network of references that gave meaning to his office. It was true that he had been awakened to the possibilities of his calling by the example of his grandfather, but he had not begun to practice until he was alone in Lima. Once he began to receive intimations of his vocation, he was plunged into a crisis of doubts and uncertainties and a sense of existential unease that only the validation of an authoritative voice could assuage. In the normal course of events, the budding shaman would receive his spiritual initiation only in the context of the intellectual and physical preparation provided by the sustaining beliefs of his community. Vásques stood outside such a secure environment. He enjoyed the support of no master in his adult life to communicate to him, and sustain in him, a conceptual understanding of his powers. Therefore, it seems he was ineluctably drawn to an alternative source of numinous authority. To validate his unnerving experiences, he sought legitimacy from representatives of the strongest supernatural force he knew, Catholic priests. In the climate of tolerance demonstrated by the Church toward the practice of healing without superstition, it is not implausible that a priest might have given his approval to Vásques's cures. Thus his appeal to Christian authority for his cures should not be interpreted simply as a convenient defense. It was an original attempt to reconcile the two religious traditions, the collision of which had plunged Icha and her fellows into such confusion and anomie. Because of his total break with his native community, Vásques had succeeded in articulating a new hierarchy that set the two traditions in a logical relationship to each other, not as antagonistic and contradictory systems but as complementary and mutually sustaining parts of a greater supernatural whole. Vásques's answer, in seeking the blessing of the representative of the Christian tradition for indulgence in the rites of the native tradition, was to enact the subordination of the latter to the former. But the subordinate position of native religion did not signify its defeat. The relationship might be (and was) reversed under different circumstances. What was important was the reconstruction of the logic of the native world, the finding of its place in the new universe "turned upside down." Vásques's solution enabled him to maintain his dialogue with the native supernatural world, a dialogue he continued to interpret according to indigenous criteria. The Christian priest, although higher in the hierarchy, was manipulated by Vásques to reaffirm the validity of his own numinous world. This "supernatural" reality was lost on the ecclesiastical authorities, blinded as they were by their Manichaean world and its phantasms of demons and natural causes.

Four: THE IDOLATRY TRIANGLE

A priest avenges himself with the
doctrina on a litigious Indian.

I

THE IDOLATRY TRIAL WAS THE MANIFESTATION OF A POWER
struggle within the native community, in which the religious specialist was but one protagonist. This power struggle was a tripartite one between the Christian priest, the
native religious specialist, and the community's leading
native authority, the kuraka. Hence the idolatry trial
should be understood less as the automatic response of a
zealous parish priest in the face of stubborn pagan practices than as a chosen strategy employed to gain the advantage in the game of local power relations. The priest,
the native religious specialist, and the kuraka constituted
rival sources of politicoreligious authority within the

community that always coexisted uneasily. In this chapter I demonstrate how the idolatry trials were manipulated to serve the political ends of different factions within the community to alter this precarious balance of power.

If the most frequent victim of the idolatry trial was the native religious specialist, the most common instigator was the priest. Antonio Acosta has demonstrated the close correlation between surges of persecution of idolatry and the relationship between the priest and the Indians of his doctrina.[1] At the best of times, the priest represented an alien authority, both temporal and spiritual, whose unrestricted power inevitably provoked enmity among those who were subject to him. It was, above all, the economic demands that the priest imposed on his parishioners that converted repressed resentment into action. Unwilling to remain passive in the face of economic exploitation, natives were prepared to denounce their priests to the ecclesiastical authorities. To forestall potentially damaging investigations, the priest could bring a counteraccusation of idolatry and divert unfavorable attention away from his own activities.[2] Thus an idolatry accusation was frequently an act of revenge by the priest against his own parishioners. Felipe Guaman Poma de Ayala, the scion of the Andean native elite whose participation in the idolatry trials of the 1560s gives his observations an authoritative ring, alluded to the retaliatory nature of such accusations: "The padre avenges himself with the doctrina upon the miserable Indian because he complained and sought justice; he says: Recite the doctrina, litigious Indian, recite it immediately. . . . [I]f the chief caciques and Indians plead for justice, then *the padre brings testimony against them, accusing them of being hechiceros.*"[3]

The notorious priest Francisco de Avila, who gave the trumpet call for the first campaigns of extirpation in

Huarochirí in 1609, evidently used the charge, at least in part, as an act of revenge against the Indians for their denunciation of his economic exactions.[4] Avila was not the only Visitor to have been involved in legal disputes with Indians; shortly before his own role in the Extirpation, the Jesuit Rodrigo Hernández Príncipe was embroiled in a quarrel with the Indians of his doctrina over the use of their labor in his *obraje* (textile workshop). In fact, before their nomination as extirpators, almost all the Visitors of the period 1609–22 had been subjected to judicial proceedings by the communities for which they were responsible.[5]

Some priests used the charge of idolatry to improve their career prospects by drawing the attention of their ecclesiastical superiors to their existence. Many who participated in idolatry campaigns moved from administering obscure doctrinas to the position of ecclesiastical judge and Visitor-General of entire provinces. This could serve as a launching pad for promotion through the Church hierarchy. On the strength of his "discoveries" of idolatry in the doctrina of San Damián de Checa in the province of Huarochirí, Avila became, successively, the first Visitor-General of Idolatry, canon of the cathedral of La Plata, and canon of the Lima cathedral. Others of his colleagues, including Avendaño and Tello, followed similar paths.[6]

Not all priests rose to such heights, however. If some played the idolatry card to gain personal advancement outside their doctrinas, many more aimed, by winning the commission of Visitor-General and its sweeping concomitant powers, to tip irreversibly in their favor the uneasy and finely balanced coexistence between themselves and their flock. Thus it is not sufficient to suggest that idolatry trials were merely a response to Indian litigation against the priest. Both forms of litigation—the *capítulos* (ecclesiastical lawsuit) instigated by the Indians against the priest and the idolatry charge brought by the priest against his parishioners—were expressions of the same phenomenon: the outburst into the public sphere of profound, repressed tensions, of antagonisms over the exercise of power between competing sources of authority. Litigation served as an outlet for these tensions between the different forces seeking to assert control over village life.

The principal motive of the priest was the assertion of his unrivaled power. The charge of idolatry was employed as a means of punishing those Indians who dared to flout his authority. Guaman Poma recognized the hubris of the priest as the principal factor in idolatry trials when he put these words into the priest's mouth: "Understand that the padre is better than the corregidor, better than the kuraka, better than the *encomendero* and better than the viceroy himself. . . . [D]id you say you would testify against me? Who is the bishop, who is the king? They will not harm the representative of God. I will have them burn all of you, *on the grounds you are living in sin or are hechiceros*. . . . I will make you confess by the whip, litigious Indian."[7]

The idolatry accusation was one of the most potent weapons the priest had at his disposal for imposing firm social control. This remained true not only of the early campaigns of 1609 to 1622 but throughout the seventeenth century as well. Acosta has argued that by the mid-seventeenth century, the denunciation of priests by their parishioners had become commonplace and that therefore it was no longer necessary for priests to respond by making a reflex retaliatory accusation of idolatry, which, in any case, had lost the element of surprise. But he is unable to provide any alternative explanation for the renewed campaigns of idolatry, concluding that the origins of the campaigns of the 1650s should not be sought in the world of the doctrinas.[8] Such a conclusion does not seem warranted. It may well be that by midcentury, a priest no longer had so much to fear in a denunciation that in normal circumstances would not lead to any disciplinary action. But what had not changed was the nature of the relationship between the priest and his flock. An idolatry accusation could still function as the ultimate sanction against the subversion of the priest's authority by the Indians. It still served the purpose of drawing attention to the priest. In any case, if the idolatry accusation was useful for cynical political purposes, individual priests who exploited it were also convinced of its objective truth. Native religious rites were not an *invention* of the priest; they were a constant reminder of his own failure. Thus the principal determinant of accusations of idolatry remained the same in the mid-seventeenth century as during the early decades of the century.

It is important to recognize that the priest was not faced by the unrelenting hostility of a homogeneous society closed to him. His native community was in no way united, and he did enjoy the cooperation of his allies among the indigenous people. The Church officials who assisted the priest in his ministrations were drawn from the native population to reinforce his authority among the Indians. These included a sacristán, who was responsible for the maintenance of the church, *cantores* (choristers) to lead the choir, and, the most important for the assertion of the priest's authority, a fiscal or *alguacil* (constable) to ensure attendance at mass. To maintain the credibility of his officials, the priest was obliged to choose candidates who would be able to earn and retain the respect of the parishioners; thus the fiscal would normally be a man over fifty who by his experience and reputation would assert sufficient influence over fellow villagers.[9]

But these allies were by no means entirely reliable, and their control over the village was not assured. The very fact that their authority derived from an external colonial source inevitably placed them in an ambiguous position. The role of the fiscal in obliging the Indians to attend mass inevitably undermined his standing among the indigenous community, on which the authority of the priest ultimately depended. At the same time, the priest could never be totally sure of the loyalty of his officials. It was not unusual for the fiscal or sacristán to refuse to cooperate with the priest if the latter's demands risked alienation of the entire community; some even led revolts against their nominal masters.[10] Furthermore, there are frequent references to the participation of precisely these Church officials, supposedly loyal to the priest's cause, in native religious ceremonies.[11] This was not only true of Peru. *Maestros cantores* were implicated in the idolatries uncovered in Yucatán by the Franciscan provincial Fray Diego de Landa in 1562.[12] It may have been precisely because of the ambiguity of their role and the tainted source of their authority that the priest's officials found themselves obliged to reestablish their credentials within their own community by occupying correspondingly official posts within the hierarchy of native practices. The same appears to have been true of kurakas, as I will demonstrate below.

At best, then, these officials were untrustworthy and potentially ambivalent allies. The influence of the priest had perforce to operate through ambiguous channels, but it was nevertheless a powerful one. The allies of the successful priest extended beyond his immediate officials into the community itself. So great were the resulting cleavages among native inhabitants that one can speak of the existence of factions within the community. It was the conflict between these factions that was to determine the frequency and extent of idolatry accusations. Clearly, the aim of the priest was to ensure that his faction drew, if not all the Indians, then at least most and certainly the most powerful into its orbit. Those opposed to the influence of the priest might feel sufficiently confident to flout his authority by encouraging attendance at public ceremonies of native religion. An idolatry trial could function as a preemptive strike against the disobedient faction.

Many native communities were characterized by the existence of two sharply defined mutually antagonistic factions: those grounding their authority in the maintenance of the traditional practices of their ancestors and those "allies" of the priest who secured their power base by conforming to the model of behavior required by the dominant colonial elite. These two factions might coexist in hostility for many years until the tension exploded in the form of violence or legal action. For example, the authority of the priest Marcos de Nuñovero and of his faction within the village of San Francisco de Guantan had experienced a precipitous decline in favor of the nativist faction. The initiation of an idolatry trial in 1680, intended to reverse the disequilibrium in the priest's favor, provoked a crisis. One of the leaders of the nativist faction, Francisco Pasqual Cantor, came with intent to kill the priest, who, according to his own admission, was only saved from certain death by the intervention of "the Christians" of his own faction. The eruption of violence and legal recriminations was the latest development in a long history of hostility. The chief witness for the priest's faction, Pedro Lázaro, was a long-standing enemy of the nativist faction, which had used violence against him and other members of his family on several occasions in the past. He and his kinfolk were reviled as "the priest's liars" (*los embusteros del Padre*) and, for refusing to go to worship the huaca, they were accused of sacrificing "the honor of the village."[13]

The rift within the community was so great, and presumably so evenly balanced, that it was reflected in the composition of the village *cabildo* (municipal council). The guardians of the community's religious traditions had used their representative in the cabildo, the alcalde Pedro Blas Sillero, to seize and punish their rival, Antonio de la Cruz, Lázaro's father, also an alcalde and member of the cabildo. The nativist faction's hold over the principal political institution of the village enabled them to withstand the disfavor of one whose influence, all things being equal, would have been enough to undermine them: the kuraka. The late ethnic lord, Simon Carlos Canchocapcha, had tried to put an end to the worship of the village huaca by removing it from its designated place. But its reputed powers of vengeance enabled the holy stone to strike back at even the most powerful. According to the kuraka Rafael Valerio, his father had fallen sick and died after having it removed. Consultation with a specialist had confirmed that the death stemmed from his audacity in moving "the stone which was god." Such powers could only enhance the reputation of the huaca. Even the hostility of the kuraka, then, had been insufficient to eliminate the power of the nativist faction; indeed, quite the reverse, the kuraka had been defeated by the powers of the huaca. The awed respect in which the huaca continued to be held originated from the efforts of the nativist faction to spread the myth of the stone's powers. Its reputation undiminished among the villagers, it had been restored to its rightful place in defiance of the current priest. Even with the kuraka in its favor, the Christian faction had not prevailed.

Even after Nuñovero had learned of the reinstatement of the huaca and had launched his campaign against it, the nativist faction continued to hold the village in the grip of fear. Nobody, including the powerful witness de la Cruz, would inform the priest of the location of their huaca. Relying on his intuition, Nuñovero had been "led by the Lord" to the stone. Only when he requested ropes to pull it down did de la Cruz acquiesce in rendering assistance. There followed the psychological triumph. The priest delivered a sermon in the church, scolding the Indians and threatening them with the punishment of God and of man with such vigor that the following morning all of them, except the leaders of the nativist faction, Marcos and Juana Asención and Francisco Pasqual Cantor, begged pardon in the public square. When the priest had gone, these three threatened the others for what they had done and met to prepare capítulos to bring against the priest in Lima. On subsequent occasions they tried again to kill both the priest and this witness. The *huaca* had been humiliated, but the nativist faction remained defiant. This defiance, expressed through the action of preparing capítulos, must have been the last straw for Nuñovero, who, unable to proceed alone any longer, invoked the aid of his superiors through an idolatry trial.

The cabildo was such an important forum for the expression of factional conflict that the impetus for an idolatry trial might derive from this source and not from the priest at all. When the notorious curandero Pedro Vilcaguaman was brought to trial for hechicerías in 1700, it was on account of the enmity, not so much of the priest, but of powerful figures in the political life of his community. These figures might find an idolatry accusation presented to the village priest a very effective attack on a dangerous rival for power in the village. The two principal witnesses against him were men of considerable power who had determined to bring his activities to public attention. The first was the ladino Juan Ilario Chumbivilca who had confiscated from Vilcaguaman the supposed instruments of his hechicerías. If he had failed to inform the priest of his findings, it was because he had suddenly fallen seriously ill. Attributing his sickness to the malice of Vilcaguaman, he had agreed to pay the curandero to heal him. After his recovery, he had remained silent about these events. It was Vilcaguaman's quarrel with a more powerful figure, the alcalde Marcelo Macuychauca, that proved his undoing. Whereas Chumbivilca had failed to inform the priest of his suspicions, Macuychauca had accused the curandero of hechicerías. Released with nothing more than a reprimand and a warning not to reoffend, Vilcaguaman had sworn to revenge himself on the alcalde. Falling ill without good cause and alarmed at the example of Chumbivilca, Macuychauca had believed himself bewitched and hence had come forward to denounce his enemy.[14] Macuychauca was able to defy the nativists because of his status as alcalde. Only someone with political power could, for example, order the search of Vilcaguaman's house, which uncovered the evidence of his hechicerías. It was the persistence of this one powerful individual that determined the case would come to prosecution.

The trial of another notorious curandero, Gerónimo Pumayauri, also originated in an accusation brought against him by a person in a position of power, the alcalde Juan Batista de Mendoza. Once again the political weight of the accuser was the determining factor in securing the prosecution. Determined to take revenge for the death of his wife from an illness for which he believed the curandero was responsible, Mendoza used his power to conduct a search of Pumayauri's house and found evidence of sorcery. The alcalde's family had a long history of enmity with the curandero, to whom they were related by marriage. If Pumayauri had predicted the deaths of several members of the family, including Mendoza's wife, it was because he had bewitched them in the hope that his own family would inherit their livestock. It cannot be insignificant that the principal mover in the case, as in that of Vilcaguaman, was a former alcalde and, as such, well placed to take his revenge through litigation.[15]

The resolve of powerful individuals determined whether practitioners of native rites would be prosecuted in idolatry trials. Only Macuychauca's determination to denounce Vilcaguaman before the ecclesiastical judge of the province ensured that legal action would be taken against

him. The intervention of Chumbivilca alone would have
been insufficient because the powerful forces supporting
native religious practices would have isolated him. Even
before his illness incapacitated him, an early attempt to
denounce the curandero had been suppressed by higher
authorities within the village cabildo. Unable to report to
the priest, who was out of the doctrina, he had consulted
the alcalde and alguacil mayor (one Don Lucas, clearly
not Macuychauca), who had advised him "to keep his
mouth shut" in order not to prejudice "the honor of the
village." Even in the absence of his illness, his silence
might have been secured by the intervention of this alcalde. Similarly, in San Francisco de Guantan, the nativist
alcalde Pedro Blas dissuaded the only eyewitness of offerings to huacas from revealing his knowledge to the
priest. Without the determination of the priest, Pedro
Lázaro's testimony might easily have been suppressed.
Such suppression of information must have been an effective means of concealing the traditional religious practices of the community. The subtle workings of these
processes ensured that denunciations for idolatry remained the exception rather than the norm. Most native
practices never entered the public domain.[16]

An idolatry trial was by no means, then, the automatic
outcome of the "discovery" of native religious practices.
Nativist factions protected clandestine pagan practices
for many years against excessive outside scrutiny. It was
the configuration of relations at any particular moment
between the competing factions of village life that provoked idolatry accusations. In San Francisco de Guantan,
the nativist faction held the village in such a grip of fear
that their religious practices would never have been "discovered" without the priest's decision to raise the stakes
and proceed to the juridical sphere, to resolve a power
dispute that he could no longer settle by other means.
Similarly, the timing of the prosecutions of Pumayauri

and Vilcaguaman was determined by the resolution of enemies to use legal means to destroy their power. It was only when the uneasy balance of forces reached a crisis that these eternal intercommunity resentments erupted into an idolatry trial. Any community was a potential victim of idolatry accusations. But under normal circumstances, the nativist faction, through its power in high places, was able to maintain a conspiratorial blanket of silence. This explains the relative infrequency of idolatry trials in relation to the frequency of native religious practices.

II

When the strength of the nativist faction was great, the priest needed a powerful political figure to act as a counterweight. The only native figure who could perform this role was the kuraka. There were *kurakas* who cooperated with the Christian priest in the uncovering of huacas and native specialists. The cacique Cristóbal Choquecaca revealed to Francisco de Avila the existence of the pagan festival of Pariacaca, and the kuraka Don Juan helped Hernández Príncipe in his investigations in the 1620s.[17] But even when the priest was assured of the cooperation of the native lord, it was not always sufficient. In San Francisco de Guantan, the combined authority of the priest and the kuraka proved insufficient to defeat the defenders of the huacas.

The position of the priest became even more vulnerable when, as was frequently the case, the kuraka colluded with the nativist faction. This was particularly dangerous since even the most charismatic priest had little chance of luring the mass of Indians away from allegiance to the deities patronized by their natural lord. The role of the kurakas in determining the religious allegiance of the Indians was recognized by Arriaga in his treatise on idolatry. He wrote that if the kurakas would only act in the interests of Christianity, this would be sufficient to eradicate idolatry: "They make of the Indians what they want; if they wish them to be idolaters, they will be idolaters, and if Christians, then Christians, for they possess no other will than that of their caciques and they are their model."[18] Since their responsibility was so great, they were to be severely punished for the protection of idolaters. In accordance with Archbishop Lobo Guerrero's *carta de edicto* of 1617, those kurakas who were masters of idolatry should be whipped, shorn, driven from office, and transferred to the House of Santa Cruz; if they were accomplices only, they should be deprived of the cacicazgo and reduced to the status of an ordinary Indian *mitayo* (a native assigned to the mita, or forced labor in Spanish mines, farms, or workshops). Even if they claimed to be unaware of the idolatrous activities of their community, they were still to be removed from their posts as such ignorance was considered morally impossible.[19]

However, it would be an oversimplification to see the role of the kuraka in terms of two mutually exclusive possibilities, as either an ally of the priest or a protector of clandestine native religious practices. In most instances there was no clear distinction between kurakas in the Christian and nativist camps. Many kurakas were able to work out a modus vivendi with their local Catholic priests, who overlooked native practices among the Indians for the sake of a quiet life.[20] Most kurakas played a double game. If they outwardly acquiesced in the propagation of Christianity in their community, at the same time they continued to patronize native religious ceremonies and, above all, to obstruct potential investigations into this aspect of the religious life of their community. It is important to understand why the kurakas chose to occupy this uneasy and extremely hazardous no-man's-land.

Luis Millones has emphasized the important link between the political power of the kurakas and the religious

beliefs of the community. The kuraka found himself in
the awkward position of having to maintain his power on
the basis of two alternative sources of authority: one de-
riving from the external, colonizing, dominant sphere
and the other from the internal, traditional, dominated
sphere. Although the legislation of the colonial regime
had established the native lord as the major local functionary, he could only legitimize his authority in the eyes
of his subject *ayllus* (kin groups) through patronage of the
traditional religious ceremonies, which represented a
continuity of political structures in place before the conquest. In other words, the external origin of the colonial
kuraka's power was not sufficient; despite it, or perhaps
because of it, the kuraka's authority, contaminated by its
association with outside influences, had to be legitimized
in the context of traditional references. Precisely because
the kuraka's commitment to these traditions might be
jeopardized by his enrollment in the ranks of colonial
functionaries, it was all the more necessary he should
participate in the revitalized religious traditions of his society. Thus the manipulation of the sacred was an important tool in the maintenance of traditional authorities.
Kurakas could make either covert or overt use of their relations with traditional cults, but they could not dispense
with them. They owed their authority to their capacity to
manipulate mechanisms of power that were recognized
and accepted by the Andean population. At the best of
times, then, the kuraka was obliged to maintain a double
role.[21]

This requirement to protect the native religious life of
the community obliged the kuraka to shield the religious
specialist from the priest's scrutiny. It is hardly surprising, then, that the priest should come to see as his greatest enemy, not the religious specialist himself, but his patron, the kuraka. Let us hear once more the priest's words
through the perceptive ears of Guaman Poma: "Under-

stand that the padre is better than the corregidor, better than the kuraka. . . . Understand me well! I am going to die here! I will leave only after having killed the kuraka."[22] The power struggle could be one to the death for the priest. And if it did indeed mean his own death, he would take with him his greatest foe. "Killing the kuraka," if it is interpreted metaphorically rather than literally, was the greatest challenge facing the priest; for the religious life of the community was determined by its chief. If he was to prevail, the priest had to make his word more respected or feared than the kuraka's. The kuraka became the priest's chief antagonist.

The high incidence of kurakas among the accused in idolatry trials can be attributed directly to this antagonism. Judicial proceedings could eliminate the priest's rival for power. The charge of idolatry was a very effective disqualification against a kuraka who was not only protecting native rites but also undermining the priest's authority in other areas. After all, it was hard to bring any effective sanction against a kuraka who discouraged Indians from going to mass or who neglected his duties in village fiestas; but there were clear legal remedies to destroy an "idolatrous" kuraka. Thus the charge of idolatry could be manipulated by an enterprising priest to score a definitive victory over his greatest rival.

In many instances the evidence advanced against supposedly idolatrous kurakas by their local priests contained few references to genuinely pagan practices, consisting instead of charges of subversion of the priest's authority. The principal accusation against the kuraka Diego Yaruparia, tried for idolatry in 1672, was not participation in native religious rites. Instead, he had earned the enmity of his priest by failing to fulfill his religious obligations. He had neglected his duties as *alférez* (steward) of the *cofradía* (religious confraternity) of the apostle Santiago, deliberately absenting himself from the village to prevent the celebration of the feast. Other charges, amounting to little more than gossip, were included to lend weight to the accusation. For example, he had allowed his wife to die without confession or sacraments, he had frequently indulged in drunkenness and led the Indians into the same bad custom, and he had subjected his subordinates to bad treatment by fining them unjustly. The only genuine charge of idolatry lay in the accusation that he had made sacrifices to native deities to bring a favorable outcome in a lawsuit and that he had invoked Lucifer while whipping an Indian woman.[23]

The origin of the accusation lay in the desire of the priest Diego Francisco del Castillo to rid himself of a powerful enemy. It was not the first time charges of idolatry had been brought against Yaruparia; he had already been tried for the offense on no less than three separate occasions by three different Visitors-General. Del Castillo had denounced him before the Visitor Ignacio Castel, after which, for reasons unknown, no action had been taken against him. The subsequent accusation of 1672 was a renewed attempt on the part of the frustrated priest to get the kuraka convicted. Presumably to disguise the repetition of the same charge, the later accusation was brought by a third party, one Rodrigo de Billalobos, the priest's ally, rather than by del Castillo himself.[24]

Many of the kurakas tried for idolatry had been subjected to repeated accusations of the same offense. Martín de Sosa alleged that the charge of idolatry against him originated in the ill will of his enemy, Pedro Gudino, the temporary priest of the *repartimiento* (administrative district) of Pacaraos. He protested at the revival of an accusation for which he had already been imprisoned on a previous occasion but from which he had been absolved when the evidence against him had been proved false. He insisted that Gudino had personal motives for persecuting him: "The priest bore hatred toward him and his son since they had complained officially to the government and church authorities about the mistreatment the priest had given the Indians and, as he had not been able to satisfy his anger by other means . . . [he had decided] to denounce them as brujos."[25]

If this was in fact Gudino's intention, his strategy misfired. The provisor, Lucas de Seguras, dismissed the case on the grounds that the accused had already been absolved of an identical charge twelve years before. Since the current accusation was nothing more than a repetition of the previous defamation, constructed on the testimony of the same untrustworthy witnesses without advancing any fresh evidence, the origin of the renewed attack could only lie in ignorance or malice. It seems that repeated accusations of idolatry could be counterproductive.[26]

The attempt to disturb the balance of power within the community by attacking the kuraka might backfire at the local level and, far from securing a victory for the priest, could result in the loss of any remaining authority to which he still laid claim. The communal closing of ranks around the kuraka that an idolatry accusation could provoke might ultimately pose a greater threat to the priest's position than the kuraka's original disobedience or subversion. When del Castillo imprisoned Yaruparia, the villagers rose up against him and, threatening the ministers of the Church with weapons, physically removed their native lord from his confinement. The secular powers of the village who should have helped the priest conspired against him. Even the Indian fiscal told him he would support the cacique before the priest. Such was his fear for his own safety that he asked permission to be allowed to leave the village lest they burn him alive in his house. The case was remitted to Lima for consideration but, like so many others, disappeared without resolution.[27]

The authority of the kuraka could well prove stronger

than that of the priest and ensure that the latter's manipulation of the idolatry charge should not pry open cleavages among those disaffected with his rule. On occasions, obedience might be secured through terror. The witness María Magdalena testified that her cacique, Antonio Ilario de Sosa, had had her whipped as a punishment for denouncing him and his family in an idolatry trial and had attempted to kill her when she was on her way to testify. He had also threatened all the Indians of the village of San Miguel de Vichaycocha that he would kill them if they declared against his father, insisting that "the Indians should have more respect for him than for the priest or the corregidor." It is interesting to observe that the mutual antagonism was recognized by the kurakas.[28]

Really skillful kurakas might divert attention away from their own activities and exploit tensions and rivalries among the prosecutors. Leandro Pomachagua succeeded in turning an idolatry investigation initially directed against himself into a legal dispute between the priest, Luis de Villavicencio, and the Visitor-General, Joseph Laureano de Mena. Although the accusation of idolatry seems to have originated in part from the cacique's patronage of clandestine pagan ceremonies, it is clear that his activities had long been known to the priest. The precise timing of the accusation was more closely related to the intolerable affronts offered by the kuraka to the priest's authority elsewhere, in particular, his persistent obstruction of Indian attendance at mass and at the doctrina, which was little short of an open act of defiance. Pomachagua was able to avert the vengeance of his priest by exploiting the enmity that had grown up between the latter and the priest of a neighboring village, Gabriel de la Cueva. By denouncing the idolatries committed by the cacique in this village, Villavicencio had offended his colleague's pride. To resist too close an inspection of his doctrina, de la Cueva was prepared to cooperate with Pomachagua. They courted the Visitor-General, bestowing gifts on him and poisoning his mind against Villavicencio until the priest was convinced that there was a conspiracy between the three to liberate the cacique from the charges.[29]

What had begun as a case of idolatry brought by the priest against the cacique had been transformed into a dispute between the priest and the Visitor. By the time the case came before the archdiocesan court, the chief accusation was concerned with the Visitor-General's complicity in idolatry. The attention of the promotor fiscal was given entirely to the actions of Laureano de Mena. He was judged to have acted in a manner unworthy of the authority of a judge, since not only had he formed a friendship with an idolater but he had also released the man from prison and dined with him. As a result of his negligence, he was suspended from his duties and replaced by a new Visitor appointed to investigate the actions of de la Cueva.[30] In the meantime, Pomachagua was absolved and freed from the charges by Archbishop Villagómez in December 1667, two years before the final decision against the Visitor-General was issued.[31] It seems that the cacique continued in his post unmolested. Villavicencio's zeal against idolatry had embroiled him in lengthy legal actions that the cacique had been able to exploit to his advantage. The enmity between the two priests and between priest and Visitor had eclipsed the question of the cacique's idolatries. Clearly kurakas were able to manipulate the idolatry trials against them; they were not passive victims but active participants. The eruption of local tensions into the legal sphere provided them with a weapon they might turn to their own advantage.

III

It was not only caciques who could turn idolatry trials to their own advantage; other members of the native community were able to do so. It is important to recognize that the priest was not the only instigator of idolatry trials. The initial impetus for an accusation frequently came from a member of the native community, even before it came to the attention of the priest. On many occasions kurakas became the victims of charges of idolatry brought by their own subjects, sometimes with the complicity of the priest but also on other occasions without his intervention.

Native communities saw an idolatry accusation as one of the most effective methods of "disqualifying" an unpopular kuraka from office. They were prepared to use Spanish colonial judicial procedures to resolve their internal political rivalries. Such willingness to resort to the legal norms of the dominant colonial elite when it suited their purpose is not entirely surprising. Stern has illustrated how Spanish judicial authority developed into "a major internal force used by Indians against their own authorities." The excessive and intolerable exactions of local priests were not the only colonial impositions resisted by means of the exploiters' own judicial system. Stern has shown that the indigenous communities of Huamanga were able to secure significant victories in the downward revision of mita quotas by exploiting their rights before Spanish justice. Because the colonial state defined the legitimate and illegitimate rules of exploitation, the natives possessed certain legal rights that gave them the opportunity to restrict the demands made of them. However, natives did not limit their judicial politics to actions merely against representatives of the colonial order. As Stern has stressed, "Andean litigants used their juridical rights and skills against one another" to such an extent that native society became divided and dependent on colonial authorities to settle internal disputes. The accusation of idolatry became one more weapon in the armory of rival groups for the cacicazgo.[32]

Such a strategy involved very high risks. There was an ever-present danger in provoking too close an examination of the clandestine religious activities of the community. But in at least some instances, the potential benefits of removing a hated cacique must have outbalanced the hazards. This is particularly evident in cases in which the cacique seems to have transgressed the acceptable bounds of cooperation with the colonial authorities, to the point of subjecting his community to harsh and intolerable burdens. The cacique always had to walk a tightrope between satisfying the demands of his Spanish superiors and defending the interests of his community. Those who showed themselves unable or unwilling to resist colonial exactions earned the opprobrium of their subjects. The most hated of the colonial exactions imposed on Indians was service in the mita. The obligation on caciques to serve as intermediaries in the provision of labor quotas could provoke furious resentment if they were seen to fail to protect their subjects from the full force of this colonial burden, or even worse, openly to collaborate in its imposition.

The cacique Alonso Callampoma, accused of idolatries by Indians of his village, was held in very great fear on account of his power to collect tribute and to send disobedient subjects to the mita. He had believed this threat sufficient to deter the Indians from denouncing his idolatries. But his consorting exclusively with Spaniards and his negligence in his duties to his own constituency had alienated a sufficiently large number of his subject Indians who were prepared to risk his vengeance. Failing in his attempt to prevent the idolatry investigation, Callampoma mustered many witnesses to testify to his good Christian standing and to accuse his detractors of spite, arising from his prompt correction of their nonattendance at mass. There is a pleasing irony in these accusations and counteraccusations. The charges of both parties, no doubt united in their dual patronage of Catholic and native gods, are couched in the language of Christian religious orthodoxy; the charge of idolatry is countered by the charge of failure to comply with Christian observances. There is an even greater irony in the villagers' use of colonial justice against a cacique who had alienated his subjects precisely by his overzealous collaboration with the dominant elite. His downfall was to be engineered according to the standards of religious orthodoxy of those whom he had been so eager to placate. Deprived of his post for life, Callampoma was ordered to serve for four years in the Franciscan convent in Lima. Thus the accusation of idolatry had become incorporated into the discourse of political disputes.[33]

Cooperation with colonial society was not the only issue of contention within native communities. One of the bitterest conflicts afflicting indigenous society was determining who was to occupy the cacicazgo. The succession was a tense, complex affair fought out between several rivals, often including the nephews and brothers as well as the sons of the incumbent chief. The identities of the major kurakas held crucial economic implications since the chiefs supervised distribution of tribute and mita burdens among the various ayllus. Small wonder that the colonial judicial system was often called on to gain a favorable judgment. But, as Stern points out, access to a legal system that presumed to resolve local disputes may actually have intensified them. A group too weak to accept a modus operandi based on local power balances could try to compensate by securing backing from a Spanish judge. Their rivals, even if legally at a disadvantage, could not then afford to forgo participation in the legal battle. The availability of a powerful external ally kept alive the damaging polarization resulting from a cacicazgo dispute. Litigation could, indeed, be a process without end.[34]

Increasing dependence on the arbitration of the colonial authorities necessitated the adoption of the norms of the dominant elite. The strongest tactic against a rival for the cacicazgo was to prove some form of disqualification for the post. Since idolatrous kurakas were deprived of their offices, a most effective attack on an opponent was to embroil him in an accusation of practicing native religious rites. Recourse to Spanish justice encouraged this concomitant search for evidence of "idolatry," not this time by external investigators or the local priest but by the community's native elite themselves.

Thus a large number of idolatry trials arose from the decision of elements of the native community to exploit judicial means to settle cacicazgo disputes. Such accusations became a covert form of eliminating rivals for the chieftainship, a continuance of the battle for domination of village politics by other means. The idolatry accusation against Auquinivin was put before the local priest by the cacique's own nephew, Alonso García, whose ambition was to replace his uncle as native lord. Although the investigation was originally instituted to consider the accused's supposed hechicerías, the case soon became dominated by the question of the legality of Auquinivin's status as governor. García argued that the original governor of the doctrina had been his own father, Alonso González, under whom Auquinivin had been an ordinary subject tributary. It was Auquininvin's pride that had led him to usurp the cacicazgo to avoid paying tribute. All the witnesses brought before the Visitor, Juan Gutiérrez de Aguilar, agreed that the legitimate governor had been Don Alonso González and that therefore the true heir was his son, Alonso García, and not Auquinivin. As in the case of Pomachagua, the impartiality of the Visitor-General was called into question. The procurador de los naturales accused Gutiérrez de Aguilar of conspiring with Gonzalo Cano, the village priest and notorious enemy of Auquinivin, to deprive the kuraka of his

post. The testimony of the witnesses procured by García
was couched in identical terms, which would suggest concerted coordination and thus lend credence to the notion
of a conspiracy. As a result of these suspicions, the Visitor
was replaced in September 1648 by Bernardo de Noboa,
the priest of Sucha.[35]

The rigorous investigations of Noboa revealed that the
evidence had been concocted and that politics was the
basis of the accusation. All the witnesses withdrew their
accusations. They denied testifying that Auquinivin was
not the legitimate kuraka or that they had seen him perform idolatrous ceremonies in his house or invoke the
huaca. Felipe Guaman, for example, retracted his statement that Auquinivin had called the Indians to his house
with chicha and cuyes and had communicated with
hechiceros. If he had earlier sworn the contrary, it was because the notary had made him sign without reading his
statement to him. He personally had not observed any
idolatrous actions by the kuraka; he had merely heard
such stories secondhand from Alonso García, who had
been waiting at the door for him when he entered to testify and had instructed him to repeat these accounts.
Cristóbal Llibiac Poma similarly confessed that he had
not witnessed the events he had reported but that Alonso
García had told him about them. Joseph García denied
having testified that Auquinivin was not the kuraka. If
his cacique had been absent when the Visitor arrived, it
had not been on account of his own guilt but rather out of
the need to collect tribute. Nor had he seen with his own
eyes any idolatrous acts. Likewise, Pablo Alfonso Mallqui
denied he had said that Auquinivin was not the kuraka;
what he had said was that he had been involved in a lawsuit to deprive Alonso García of the cacicazgo. García rejected his entire deposition when it was read to him. Instead he argued that Auquinivin's arrogance, especially
his failure to obey the priest, had lost him the respect of the

authorities of the village. Clearly the denunciation of idolatry and the enmity between the priest and Auquinivin had been manipulated to disqualify the unpopular kuraka. But the strategy backfired since the explicit confession of the fabrication of testimony led to the absolution and release of the accused. The result was a stalemate.

The issue between rival pretenders to the cacicazgo could be the very nature of the relationship with the dominant elite. As has been illustrated, the reaction to Spanish colonial exactions and the question of how far an accommodation was to be made with the conquerors could provoke profound cleavages within the community. These divisions were reflected in the contest for the principal native office. The idolatry accusation leveled against Tomás de Acosta, the *kuraka segunda persona* (deputy or secondary kuraka) of the village of Santiago de Maray, derived from the hostility that his good relations with the Spanish colonial powers had engendered within his own community. The charge against him was that he had kept a huaca in his house to which he and his family made offerings and that he had contracted an hechicero to perform sorcery against the village priest. But the prime mover in the case was Acosta's illegitimate younger brother, Antonio Pomalibiac, whose fundamental grievance against his relative was not the worship of ancestors but the latter's willing cooperation with the priest and corregidor. His intention was to deprive his brother of the cacicazgo so as to secure it for himself.[36]

The procurador de los naturales rejected the accusation against Acosta on precisely the grounds that it was the result of a conspiracy to unseat the kuraka. The two key allies of Pomalibiac were Rodrigo Guamanchagua, principal of the village, and Antonio Chupica, governor and principal cacique of the province. Many witnesses testified that all three men were Acosta's sworn enemies. The first cause of resentment was the long-standing legal wrangle between the two brothers over the cacicazgo, which, according to the procurador's witnesses, belonged by right to Acosta as the legitimate son. Guamanchagua had also been in litigation with Acosta over the cacicazgo. But the fight for the principal office formed only one part of a wider struggle for the reins of power in the village. Chupica still smarted under the humiliation he had endured at the hands of Acosta's father, who had ordered that the right to collect the tribute of the village should remain exclusively the responsibility of his own son. Envy of Acosta's powerful political position was not the only motive for growing resentment. The kuraka was especially reviled by the conspirators for his good relations with the corregidores and the priest. His punctuality in the payment of tribute earned him particular opprobrium. Chupica had further personal reasons for objecting to the alliance between Acosta and the Spanish authorities since the kuraka had insisted he should pay for some damage he had done to the church. When Chupica failed to comply, Acosta had seized his lands as security for the payment.

Acosta had generated the hostility of powerful members of his own community by identifying himself too closely with the interests of the Spanish authorities. What better manner to destroy his credit with the dominant elite than to accuse him of idolatry? It is difficult to determine whether the accusation bore any relation to fact, whether indeed the kuraka had been playing a double game, openly patronizing the village church while at the same time sponsoring clandestine native ceremonies. The transparency of the motives of Acosta's accusers diverted attention from the issue of idolatry. The final decision in the case recognized the arguments of the procurador, and Acosta was absolved and freed. As in the case of Auquinivin, the evident malice of the witnesses had nullified the accusation.[37]

Such an outcome was the rule in cases in which ill will was perceived to be the primary determinant of an accusation of idolatry. Even in cases in which there was considerable incriminating evidence of idolatrous acts, the suspect could escape unscathed if there was a clear indication of malicious intention behind the denunciation.

The trial in 1696 of Miguel Menacho and Juan de Guzmán, principal caciques of the repartimiento of Huamantanga, was instigated by Juan de Campos, a rival candidate for the cacicazgo. Once again, the initial accusation of idolatry became overshadowed by the political nature of the accusation. Menacho and Campos were already parties in a long-standing legal dispute to determine who was the legitimate native lord. That this dispute over the cacicazgo predated the idolatry trial suggests that the latter accusation was simply another means by which Campos could attack his rival. The procurador argued that the accusation should be discounted because it arose from this enmity. It was untrue that Menacho had contracted an hechicera, María Pilcosuyu, to perform maleficio against Campos, in order that the rival cacique would be unable to maintain his appeal for the governorship of the repartimiento. Rather, his client was the victim of the woman's spite. Suspecting her of harming his nephew through occult means, he had threatened her with correction; her revenge had been to join his enemies and present the denunciation so favorable to Campos's cause. When the case was transferred to Lima, the evidence of both caciques was dominated by the dispute over the cacicazgo. Menacho denied the charge of maleficio, pointing out that he had been in litigation with Campos for more than ten years over the cacicazgo. Campos insisted that he was the only legitimate principal cacique. The charge of idolatry became a secondary issue. Indeed, consultation of an hechicera was the only evidence ever presented by Campos to substantiate the charge. In the absence of clear proof, Menacho's defense that the denunciation was motivated by animosity was upheld and he was absolved.[38]

What makes this decision curious is the fact that there was further evidence that Menacho had consorted with hechiceros. In the same year charges were brought against other supposed hechiceros implicated in acts of maleficio against Campos, apparently instigated by Menacho himself. María Quillay accused Juan de Guzmán, segunda persona of the repartimiento of Huamantanga, of having contracted her, on behalf of Menacho, to perform maleficio against Campos. Her account describes Campos as being the governor at the time. Both Menacho and Guzmán had denounced Campos to the authorities as an hechicero. In the ensuing investigation, Guzmán had retracted his declaration, admitting it was false and motivated by hatred and revenge. Since the commission to investigate had been issued by Villagómez (whose tenure of office ended in 1671), these events must have taken place at least a quarter of a century before the 1696 trial, which was itself only the latest manifestation of a deep-seated and long-running enmity between the principal contenders. What is curious is that this woman's evidence does not seem to have damaged Menacho. After all, if Campos occupied the position of governor at that earlier time, it should have lent credence to his claim that he was the true cacique. Furthermore, the declarations of multiple witnesses that Menacho had contracted various hechiceras constituted strong evidence of his guilt. Nevertheless, he succeeded in securing his release without punishment. There can only be one explanation. Although it is not explicitly expressed, the long history of litigation between the two protagonists must have left the authorities very skeptical as to the truth of any accusation brought against either of them. Once again the mutual hostility of accused and accuser had resulted in stale-mate.[39]

It may be concluded from these cases that idolatry ac-cusations against kurakas became a tool to be manipu-lated in disputes for the cacicazgo, which were themselves part of a wider struggle for the assertion of power within the community, and that the evident political motivation behind such denunciations resulted in cases being dis-missed and the accused being absolved. There are other cases in which the fight for the cacicazgo may be demon-strated as the principal motive behind the accusation but in which the final sentence or decision is missing. Though no unequivocal conclusions may be drawn, it would not seem unreasonable to suppose that the failure of these cases to proceed to final sentence also derived from a sim-ilar distrust of the motives behind the accusation.

The protracted trial, from 1665 to 1669, of Francisco de Vergara, cacique of the village of Santo Domingo de Ocros, was instigated by his rivals for the cacicazgo. The chief witness against him, Francisca Flores, had a case pending concerning the cacicazgo, claiming superior right to the governorship over Vergara, who was an out-sider. Vergara retaliated by accusing Flores of having planted the witchcraft bundle that constituted the in-criminating evidence against him. As in previous cases, the competing factions of the village were able to take advantage of the partiality of the Spaniard delegated to resolve the legal dispute. The ecclesiastical judge, Fer-nando de Arce, was implicated since the evidence against Vergara had been uncovered at the moment that the judge had entered his property by force, in the cacique's absence, in order to transfer ownership to Flores. Vergara brought a case before the audiencia against de Arce for having exceeded his commission. This only added to the litigation in which the two were already engaged over some of Vergara's property, which de Arce had sold without his permission in order to pay his own salary. Vergara earned the enmity not only of the judge but also of his own village priest, Gabriel Menéndez de Coca, who had unsuccessfully initiated a case against him to regain ownership of property that he claimed belonged to the village confraternities. The idolatry trial was simply one more act of litigation with which to ensnare the cacique. By extending the quarrel to the sphere of ecclesiastical justice, the priest was able to bring more powerful forces to bear on Vergara and enlist the aid of the Visitor-General in his struggle to neutralize a rival power center. The mutual enmity between the protagonists of the case—the priest and the ecclesiastical judge, Flores and Vergara—dominated the inquiry and eclipsed the accusation of idolatry. Such were the complexities that the case continued for at least four years without resolution. There is no decision or sentence included with the case, so it is impossible to know with certainty if it was dismissed on the grounds of motivation from enmity. But the very fact that the trial led nowhere may indicate that the case was abandoned because it was impossible to determine the truth of the matter.[40]

The idolatry trial of the cacique Juan Soclac in 1676 found no evidence of native religious practices but uncovered a festering quarrel over the cacicazgo. Soclac was accused of employing maleficio against the "true" native lord, Diego de la Cruz, to install himself in his place and prevent the return of the legitimate cacique to the village. Under examination, he denied being an idolater or hechicero but admitted that he was not the legitimate governor. He professed to be willing to hand over the cacicazgo and its property to de la Cruz but argued that the latter had never come to the village to assert his rights. No final decision was recorded, presumably because the case was dismissed for lack of evidence of idolatry. The question of legitimacy in the cacicazgo had overshadowed the charge of idolatry. Aside from the unsubstantiated charge of maleficio, Soclac's only sins against the faith had been failing to maintain the church in good repair and preventing the gathering of the Indians in the village for instruction. The only hint of hechicería was the testimony of certain witnesses that they had seen Soclac move around his estate in the form of animals, such as a snake and a white horse. Since these witnesses were implicated in the theft of goods from Soclac, their testimony was dismissed as unreliable. The principal achievement of the accusation was to uncover Soclac's illegitimate claim to the cacicazgo, and hence it may be supposed that the motive for the denunciation was the attempt to effect a change in the leadership of the village that could not otherwise be achieved.[41]

The accusation of idolatry brought against the interim cacique Juan Picho was understood to be a strategy to deprive him of the cacicazgo and failed to proceed to judgment and sentence. The prosecution took the form of two separate cases, of which only the second, in 1691, was a direct attack on the cacique himself; the first, of 1690, was restricted to three hechiceros, the agents of his supposed maleficio. However, the intended victim of the first prosecution was clearly Picho, whose prosecution quickly overshadowed that of the mere executors of his bidding. The hechicero Pedro Guaman testified that he had been summoned to Picho's house to participate in an act of maleficio against Francisco Llucllicachin and Diego Hernando de Mendoza, whom the cacique suspected of conspiring to deprive him of the cacicazgo. Failing to inspire his native lord with confidence, he had been dismissed. But he knew the hechicero Diego Yacan had acted to destroy Picho's enemies by casting a bundle of coca into the river. This testimony was sufficient for the Visitor-General, Antonio Martínez Guerra, to imprison Picho pending further investigation.[42]

Once again attention fell not on the alleged idolatrous activities of the accused but on the motives of his accusers, including his enemies within the village and even the Visitor-General himself. The first to raise the cry of brujo against Picho had been his rival for the cacicazgo, Llucllicachin. But the idolatry trial was not the first act of litigation in which the cacique was embroiled. The accusation of idolatry must be understood in the context of preexisting internal conflicts. Disputes over tribute collection (which, as we have seen, could cause great resentment against a cacique within his community) had brought him into litigation in the audiencia with Augustin Aylas. Aylas denied owing the cacique dues from the collecting of tribute; if Picho had accused him, it was in retaliation for his role in bringing capítulos in Lima against the cacique. Clearly Picho was already ensnared in a vicious circle of accusation and counteraccusation. Feuds and tensions within the community had already broken out into the colonial judicial sphere. The resort to an idolatry accusation was simply another step in the conflict.

The presiding Visitor-General had motives to resent Picho that threatened to invalidate the entire prosecution. By acting in defense of Indians whose rights had been usurped by two of the Visitor-General's relations, Antonio Martínez and Juan Martínez, the cacique had earned the anger of his prosecutor. According to the procurador, Melchor de Carvajal, Martínez Guerra had colluded with Llullicachi and Hernando de Mendoza in a conspiracy to deprive the cacique of his properties and rights. It was to prevent any further obstruction of Picho's case that the procurador requested the replacement of the Visitor-General by a disinterested party. The evidence of ill will was sufficient to cause the archbishop to accede to this request and to name a new judge, Juan de Blancas Coloma, to the case. The outcome of the case, which continued into 1692, is unrecorded. But the large role of evident enemies of the cacique in the denunciation must have been influential in the failure to proceed to judgment and sentence.

The role of factions disputing the cacicazgo in generating idolatry trials is nowhere better illustrated than in the trial of 1689 to 1691 of the hechicera María de la Cruz. The alleged hechicerías had been employed to determine the occupancy of the cacicazgo of the repartimiento of Atunjauja. The office was contested in litigation by two members of the same family, Lorenzo Surichac and Cristóbal Surichac, in which the former was successful. The hechiceros on trial were accused by Carlos Apoalaya, cacique of Hananhuanca and head of the faction supporting Lorenzo Surichac, of using witchcraft against his family to take revenge after the selection of their candidate and to prevent him from succeeding to the cacicazgo. In particular, the death of his wife, Sebastiana Surichac, Lorenzo's aunt, was to be attributed to their intervention. These diabolical arts had been encouraged by the faction supporting Cristóbal, led by the interim cacique Cristóbal Agustin Calderón Canchaya.[43]

This case is curious in that it fails to follow the usual pattern. The object of the idolatry accusation was *not* one of the candidates aspiring to the cacicazgo, or one of the leaders of the rival factions. If the enmity had not resulted in a direct accusation against, for example, Calderón himself, it may have been on account of the role of the same Antonio Martínez Guerra who was the Visitor-General in the previous case. When both Sebastiana Surichac and her daughter died suddenly, Apoalaya strongly suspected witchcraft and Martínez Guerra was appointed to investigate. Apoalaya accused several Indian women of causing the death of his wife, but Martínez failed to proceed against either Calderón or his protégés. Convinced that the Visitor-General had been threatened, or worse, had colluded with his enemy, Apoalaya resolved to bring the case directly to the attention of the procurador, Joseph Mexia de Estela. The procurador's intervention, complaining at the lack of progress and the failure to punish the guilty, led to the replacement of Martínez Guerra by the same Juan de Blancas Coloma who had already replaced his colleague in the trial of Juan Picho.[44]

The defense of de la Cruz rested on the clear enmity of the witnesses and of Apoalaya himself. All the witnesses were either dependents of the cacique or mortal enemies of the accused. The witness María Regina, for example, a sworn enemy of de la Cruz for family reasons, had a reputation for superstitions and could have planted the evidence of witchcraft. Furthermore, the defense pointed out that these allegations were a repetition of those advanced three years before during the lifetime of Sebastiana Surichac. The cacique's wife had investigated charges of witchcraft made by the same María Regina and had found no evidence for them. Since no action had been taken at that time, it was unreasonable for the cacique now, after three years had passed, to bring charges against these women.

Apoalaya denied that his wife had ever inquired into the matter and said that she had only warned the accused against their actions; if the women had not been brought to justice at that time, it was because there had been no judge competent to hear the case, since the Visitor-General Martínez Guerra had done nothing about it. Since then, the women had committed further acts of maleficio that had led to several deaths in his family, including that of his wife. The women had been heard to boast of placing witchcraft bundles in Apoalaya's house and of having taken action to ensure that the judges in this case had their "mouths and hands sewn and tied." Apoalaya took care to express his denunciation in the language of the pact, arguing that if de la Cruz had reduced a toad to her obedience, this could only have been done through an explicit pact with the Devil.

It seems that the provisor in Lima was unconvinced. Although Blancas y Paloma insisted that the women were guilty of idolatry and diabolical arts, the principal issue was the hatred arising out of disputes over the cacicazgo. The absence of final judgment and sentence may indicate that the case was abandoned on account of the suspicious motives for the accusation.

The idolatry accusation brought against Cristóbal Yaguas of Huamantanga in 1664 was the work of his capital enemies, Juan and Ana María Carguacapcha, who sought to punish him for his support for the cacique, Rodrigo Rupaychagua. When the villagers had brought capítulos against their native lord, Yaguas had testified in his favor and derided Carguacapcha, one of the principal litigants and pretender to the cacicazgo, as a mere plebeian Indian mitayo who had no right to move charges against his own cacique. In revenge, Carguacapcha had induced his wife to testify that she had seen Yaguas worshiping huacas in the ancient village of her people. The charge was opportunistic and exploited the doubts surrounding Yaguas's religious allegiances ever since he had been punished by the Visitor-General Pedro de Quijano Bevellos as an idolater and hechicero. Despite the accused's apparent recidivism, his interrogators chose to examine witnesses closely on the alleged enmity of the Carguacapchas. The defense offered by the procurador Estela, rested principally on the evident malice of the chief witnesses. Estela argued that even if she had been an exemplary and worthy witness, which in any case was doubtful, especially as her account was uncorroborated by other parties, her testimony should be discounted.[45]

The suspicion of enmity was the crucial factor in the failure of these cases to proceed to sentence and punishment. In cases in which there was no such suspicion of malice, the accused would readily be punished. The cacique Lorenzo Guaraca was deprived of his cacicazgo in 1671 after the segunda persona of his village denounced him for participating in heathen ceremonies on the occasion of a roof covering and for consorting with known hechiceros. Guaraca was held to have forfeited his position as head of the village and was forbidden to exercise the cacicazgo or any other public office in future and reduced to the status of mita Indian. Unfortunately, his replacement as cacique is unknown, but if it was his segunda persona, the motive would be clear. However, there is no record of Guaraca having denounced the accusation as one arising from enmity. Where there was no reason to suspect enmity, a case proceeded to sentence.[46]

I have shown that the idolatry trial could be manipulated by factions within the community to strike a blow for their own side in a dispute over the cacicazgo. Of course, it is not remarkable that enemies would take the opportunity to denounce one another before judicial authorities. It is only to be expected. What is remarkable is that the idolatry trials came to occupy such an important role within the native community as a means of resolving internal disputes, to the extent that the trials themselves were invalidated in the eyes of their own creators. By manipulating the trials for their own factional advantage, native communities rendered them useless as a weapon of punishment for indigenous religious practices. An institution of the dominant colonial elite became increasingly invalidated by the willingness and ability of native communities to exploit it for their own purposes. It is true that in many instances the attempt to unseat a cacique by means of an idolatry investigation failed. But two caveats must be recognized. First, idolatry trials seem to have been effective, at least on some occasions, in changing the occupancy of the cacicazgo. Even this represents an impressive achievement for the native communities. Second, if the idolatry accusation ultimately proved futile or counterproductive, as the authorities came to understand native abuse of the trials and refused to accept accusations at face value, in the process, the trials were rendered ineffective in their primary purpose: the control and punishment of deviant religious behavior. Thus, despite limited success in manipulating idolatry trials for their own ends, native communities had at least neutralized the trials as an effective method of repression. Most cases ended either without a final decision or sentence or with the absolution of the accused. Such an outcome hardly represented a serious method of enforcing religious orthodoxy.

The final irony of these trials is that the provision by colonial society of judicial means to resolve disputes over the cacicazgo generated increased "idolatrous" activities. The pivotal role of the cacique in village life meant that the identity of the occupant of the office was the central politicoreligious question of native society. The uncertainties of the workings of the Spanish legal system encouraged native communities to seek the intercession of their ancestral deities in favor of a particular candidate for the cacicazgo. Because the Indians could have no direct influence over the result of Spanish deliberations, they were obliged to resort to supernatural, occult influences. In an early idolatry trial of 1617, one witness testified that his kuraka, Juan Caxaatoc of San Miguel de Ullucmayo, had made offerings to his huacas and mallquis to win a lawsuit over the cacicazgo against his rival and to propitiate the ancestors in order that the result would be in his favor. The witness added that to ensure victory and a sound knowledge of how to govern, the cacique had ordered the Indians to go with him to where their ancestors were buried and sacrifice a llama to them, as their forefathers had done. This was their custom whenever they had differences over the cacicazgo or over how to govern.[47] Similarly, half a century later, Diego Yaruparia had made sacrifices to his gods on the way to Lima so that he would be successful in the lawsuit in which he was involved in the capital.[48] The consultation of native deities in moments of political crisis had been established long before the arrival of the Spaniards. In the colonial period, it not only survived alongside recourse to Spanish justice as a complementary means of ensuring a favorable result; it was also generated as a by-product of Spanish legal processes. Moreover, these communications with native deities themselves became the substance of the accusation by which their enemies sought to deprive them of the cacicazgo. It is a supreme irony to reflect that the idolatry trials were subverted by Indian manipulation of communications with native deities, which themselves had been provoked by the very organization that sought to suppress them. The snake had ended up eating its own tail.

Five: "Stones That Are Gods": The Response to Extirpation

A priest vents his anger on an Indian.

So tell me, how is it you have put your hopes in a stone as if it were the true God, do you not see that this stone cannot understand what you ask of it? . . . [I]f it could speak it would tell you, Indian, you are mad and blind. . . . [D]o you not see that I am a stone, that the birds and foxes dirty themselves upon me, if I am a stone as you can see, how can I be God?

—Hernando de Avendaño, *Sermons* (1649)

The witness said he had heard from the old people that their ancestors had worshiped the stone Cari as their god. . . . [S]ome Indians threatened their children that if they touched the stone they would die. . . . [T]he son of Francisco Pascual Cantor had gone lame and then died because he had dirtied himself upon the stone.

—Testimony of the witness Antonio de la Cruz, *Idolatrías* (1680)

This witness taught the villagers that they should not worship the Lord Our God or the saints because that was for the Spaniards, they were their huacas and camaquenes, they were painted and gilded bits of wood that did not speak, that could not grant the Indians what they asked of them. . . . [A]lthough the Lord bishop burned some mallquis and idols, they must worship them and make sacrifices to them because their souls live on, they are immortal and descend to receive the sacrifices their children make to them.

—Testimony of the defendant Hernando Hacaspoma, *Idolatrías* (1658)

I

THE EXTIRPATION WAS NOT LIMITED TO PHYSICAL destruction but extended to psychological destruction as well. The extirpators sought nothing less than the desacralization or "disenchantment" of the native religious world. They were determined to deprive Andean sacred entities of their immanent numinous significance. Their principal weapons in this struggle were the separation of natural and supernatural forces (which played an important role in the prosecution of curanderos) and a materialistic interpretation of the significance of Andean sacred entities. They denied that the huacas were repositories of the sacred; they were endowed with no supernatural life, nor could they exercise real powers in this world or the next. The sermons of Avendaño sought to persuade the Indians, by the use of reason, that huacas could not be god. The proposition was so self-evident to the learned Christian mind that contradiction provoked ridicule. How could an object on which the birds and foxes relieved themselves be the Creator and True God? Should not the hechiceros be ashamed to have worshiped a stone covered in the excrement of such creatures? They were, after all, mere inanimate objects. By classifying huacas as either mobile or immobile, Arriaga employed the native term as a category of an "object," not as a form of divinity. The Indians did not even believe in false gods but simply attributed animate qualities to inanimate objects. Huacas were fetishes rather than divinities. Thus by a process of attrition native deities were transformed into a collection of objects, a process Bernand and Gruzinski have called the "reification" of native deities.[1]

To avoid disappearing into the realm of inanimate objects, native deities would have to fight back and prove their supernatural powers. Christian denigration of their huacas obliged practitioners of native religious rites to demonstrate the continuing relevance and potential of their otherworldly masters. The huaca Cari of the village of San Francisco de Guantan retained the power to inflict harm on all those who trod on it or mistreated it. Its reputed powers of vengeance enabled it to strike back at even the most powerful. The cacique who had ordered the stone's removal from its traditional site had, shortly afterward, fallen sick and died; the village understood his death as a punishment for his audacity in moving "the stone that was god."[2] The persistence of such beliefs represented the determination of the practitioners of native religion to resist the Spanish belittlement of their deities and a significant challenge to the power of the local priest. To destroy the myth of the huaca's powers, the priest not only ordered the Indians to pull it down and put in its place the cross the idolaters had removed; he also insisted they publicly urinate on it. His intention was to demonstrate the inability of the stone to punish those who abused it, to consign it firmly to the realm of the inanimate, to prove it could be subdued with impunity.[3]

The refusal of this huaca to lay down and die and the persistent tales of its revenge on those who mistreated it are examples of the resistance offered by native beliefs and practices to the attacks of Christianity. The deposition of the witness Hernando Hacaspoma reveals that native practitioners reacted to Christian vilification by a retaliatory reification of Spanish "deities": the saints could not be "real" huacas but were mere "objects" because they did not speak. The true location of the sacred, the repository of the numen, lay in the huaca and mallqui. This eternal truth could not be shattered even by the physical destruction of the object of worship. The spiritual life of the huaca, represented by the force of its camaquen, did not depend on the continued survival of its material manifestation. Its "soul" lived on.

Such ideological adaptations represent such a significant response to the Extirpation that one may speak of an ideological resistance. It was accompanied by more direct obstruction of the effective functioning of the extirpation visitations. Thus, through a combination of subtle noncooperation, deception, and the manipulation of legal rules, Indians sought to slow down or halt the visitation. If a visitation could not be obstructed, then they worked to ensure the minimal disruption of traditional native practices. But since the persecution was frequently successful in locating and destroying huacas and mallquis, the ideological adaptations became the most significant form of response, by shifting the conflict into the realm of the abstract where the Extirpation could not triumph.

Although outright physical rebellion was not an option available to native communities, their response was unequivocally combative. Defiance could take many forms. They could refuse to cooperate in any way, by remaining silent before the Visitor's questions and closing ranks to prevent any revelations of religious practices. Such a strategy involved substantial risk and could, in any case, be effectively countered by an intelligent Visitor who knew how to uncover sources of information (through the use of the vulnerable, such as old people or children, or the exploitation of enmities). Another form of defiance, more symbolic than efficacious, might be the maintenance of native practices even during a visitation. The physical presence of the Visitor could not prevent the religious specialists of San Pedro de Hacas from continuing to make offerings to their huacas during his investigations.[4]

More effective was a strategy of clandestine obstruction through deceit. For example, the cacique of Otuco, learning of the imminent arrival of the Visitor Felipe de Medina, ordered the corpses that had been moved to the *machayes* (indigenous aboveground resting chambers, in the form of caves or niches carved out of rock, for mortal remains, mummies and funeral offerings) to be returned to the church; at the conclusion of the visitation, they were transferred once again to their traditional resting ground. Thus natives made temporary concessions to the demands of the Extirpation to allow long-term survival of their practices.[5]

The first priority of the strategy of deception was the protection of native deities from physical destruction. An obvious tactic was to conceal huacas or mallquis in locations inaccessible to the Visitor. Hacaspoma admitted the concealment of mallquis at the time of Avendaño's visitation. Alternatively, minor huacas might be surrendered while more important ones remained concealed. Common stones with no sacred significance might be handed over in the guise of communal deities.[6]

If these tactics failed and the true huacas were uncovered, the community could resort to bribery. If the Visitor's assistants could be induced to turn a blind eye, the deities might remain unmolested. The Indians of San Francisco de Mangas offered the fiscal sent by Noboa ten pesos if he would inform the Visitor that they themselves had revealed their huacas of their own free will, an offer he declined to accept. Other fiscales were less fastidious and agreed to overlook huacas. The Indians of San Pedro de Hacas admitted that during a previous inspection they had successfully conspired to suborn the mulatto assistant of Visitor-General Avendaño. Since he had failed to verify the destruction of their mallquis in person, they had been able to preserve their machayes intact. The kuraka Alonso Ricari, who was also the principal religious specialist of his community, confessed that he had bribed the Visitor's assistant to secure his complicity in the substitution of other mallquis for those of his village's ancestors so that they should not be consigned to the flames.[7]

Not only the deities themselves but also their officiants had to be protected from persecution. The best strategy was to conceal the existence of the guardians of the huacas. Often the kuraka was in the best position to do this. Tomás de Acosta had maintained in clandestinity the keeper of his huaca, Angelina Quillay Llacsa, deliberately excluding her from the mita and other obligations. Alonso Ricari had engaged his niece and four young female assistants in the service of their huaca, Huacaquillay, for more than thirty-five years. The woman had remained uncontaminated by baptism, taking the name of the huaca for her own. She had never attended mass and had preserved her virginity. Her existence had been kept secret by not registering her in the parish book of baptisms, recording instead a child who had been born dead.[8]

Although the records attest that by these methods many native communities were able to conceal huacas, mallquis, and their caretakers during successive visitations, many others found that the persistence of the extirpatory team robbed them of their ancestral spiritual guardians and threatened to destroy the traditional religious life of their community. In such circumstances, alternative means had to be sought to confound the Visitor. In every diocese there existed an ecclesiastical tribunal, whose sentence could be appealed to the archdiocesan tribunal in Lima. Every province was also endowed with a *protector de los naturales* who presented the cases on behalf of the Indians. Since bringing charges against their superiors was the only legal weapon available to the Indians under the colonial regime, they used it frequently. In their denunciations and declarations, they exhibited an identification with the Christian Church and its norms that they were certainly far from espousing but that the need to rid themselves of their priest obliged them to adopt.[9]

It is not surprising, then, that recourse to legal action became a powerful instrument with which to confront the executors of the Extirpation. By the time of the visitations of the 1650s and 1660s, litigation between Indians and their Visitors had become relatively commonplace. The Indians were generally not successful in securing permanent removal of a Visitor, but it was in their interest at least to slow down the processes of law and put as many obstacles as possible in his path. If he could not be driven out altogether, at least the costs and inconvenience of his activities could be increased.

As far as can be determined from the surviving documents, Bernardo de Noboa and Juan Sarmiento de Vivero were the most persistent persecutors of native religion. It is small wonder that both became victims of virulent accusations by communities they had investigated for idolatries. Noboa was subjected to litigation by representatives of four villages of the province of Cajatambo where he had conducted extensive idolatry investigations between 1656 and 1658. The case against him came before the provisor in Lima between February 1658 and January 1660. The procurador de los naturales, Tomás Hurtado, had already attempted, unsuccessfully, to secure a nullification of Noboa's proceedings on the grounds of irregularities. The procurador insisted that by threatening, torturing, and imprisoning his suspects and confiscating their property, Noboa had succeeded in extracting evidence of idolatries in villages where no such practices had ever been suspected or reported. Since priests of high caliber had been working there, it was inconceivable that such activities would have remained undisclosed. The procurador evidently believed that Noboa had invented the idolatries. Adding a further slur on the Visitor's character, Hurtado suggested that he had confiscated the Indians' property under the pretext that it was destined to the worship of idols. Such arguments failed to convince the promotor fiscal. He argued that there were no grounds for nullifying the Visitor's proceedings, since the evidence against the accused was based on their own confessions and the procurador had presented no evidence to indicate that they had not committed the offenses. The suggestion that the Visitor wanted to find the Indians guilty was an insult to the integrity of a priest, and the accusations of the use of torture and the misappropriation of goods were false calumnies.[10]

In the ensuing investigation into Noboa's activities, representatives of several villages of the doctrina of San Pedro de Hacas accused the Visitor of having used torture and imprisonment to make the Indians confess to idolatries. Witnesses testified that Noboa had imprisoned Hernando Chaupis Condor and Hernando Hacaspoma, beating them when they failed to answer his questions and threatening to take them to Lima if they did not reveal their huacas. The subsequent deaths of these two suspects, and that of Pedro Paucar, who had been hung upside down until blood came out of his mouth, were attributed to the Visitor's excesses.

However, the priest Francisco de la Llana painted a different picture. He asserted that the accusation of financial interest on the part of Noboa was entirely without foundation. Furthermore, he said that Noboa had done all that was necessary to secure a proper defense for the Indians and that when they had confessed to their crimes fully and voluntarily they had been treated with kindness. It was certainly not true that Noboa, wishing to find the Indians guilty, had tortured them so that they would confess things they had not done. There had been no mistreatment of the accused. Paucar had died of natural causes, and Hacaspoma had died many months after the visitation. The motive behind these false accusations was clearly that the Indians wished to prevent their ministers of idolatry from being taken to El Cercado. He had heard it said that the finances of the village had been depleted to bring the action against Noboa to frighten and discourage other potential Visitors. This was consistent with the notorious reputation of these Indians as idolaters, especially those of the villages that had brought the charges. To avoid punishment for their sins, the Indians were determined to cause their persecutors the greatest possible inconvenience.[11]

There were limits to what the Indians could achieve by litigation as the authorities defended the integrity of their officials. Noboa seems to have suffered no consequences from the litigation against him. Indeed, he continued to function as a Visitor throughout the 1660s, as is indicated by his *Información de servicios* of 1664, in which he gave details of the idolatries he had uncovered in twenty-eight villages he had visited.[12] He later emerged unscathed from an investigation into his conduct in 1668, which concluded that he had behaved in an exemplary fashion.[13]

The Visitor-General, Juan Sarmiento de Vivero, was prosecuted by the principal cacique and segunda persona of Juan de Lampián in 1665 for excessive financial exactions and mistreatment of individuals and property. The caciques objected that the Visitor had remained for an entire year in their community, causing great expense and inconvenience to the Indians of many villages who were already overburdened with the mita. The sustenance of his large delegation (which had included a notary, two fiscales, two interpreters, one alguacil mayor, a defense representative, and two servants) had fallen on the village, Sarmiento himself contributing nothing at all.[14] Payment had been required for the administration of the sacrament of marriage, which was against the norms laid down by the synods. The cacique's son, Alonso Pariasca, had been obliged to pay eight pesos; when he resisted, the Visitor's men had beaten him without regard for his social position. The church and the confraternities had also been forced to make payments. Other Indians had been fined from twelve to twenty-five pesos on the unsubstantiated grounds that they were living with their lovers and had been subjected to the indignity of whipping and imprisonment without food. Even the segunda persona had been imprisoned and five of his houses had been destroyed. Last, Sarmiento had caused great inconvenience by keeping the Indians from their work in the fields and terrorizing them, such that they had fled from the village and would not return.[15]

The fiscal responded with the same skepticism with which he had met the charges against Noboa, arguing that it was impossible that a Visitor named twice by the archbishop would have proceeded in such a manner. But since many Indians from different villages concurred in their stories of maltreatment and financial exactions, the accusations had to be investigated, if only to prove that they were false. Sarmiento was instructed to send an account of his activities, including details of the number of people he had taken with him, how many days he had spent in each place, and what support he had required from the Indians. Evidently this was not forthcoming, since a petition of January 1666 by the promotor fiscal, Joseph Lara Galán, complained that Sarmiento had still not handed over the account despite being told to do so several times. The provisor ordered Sarmiento to comply within three days under pain of excommunication. There is no record of his response or of the result of the proceedings brought against him by these Indians. But as he continued in his office, it must be assumed that the decision was in his favor.[16]

These investigations were not isolated examples. It was

not uncommon for secret inquiries to be made into the conduct of Visitors, though as far as can be determined, the universal conclusion was that they had behaved in an exemplary manner.[17] The judicial system could not provide foolproof protection for native communities.

However, the manipulation of the judicial system against the Visitors undermined the efficient operation of the idolatry trials to such an extent that Villagómez felt obliged to complain to the king about it. In a letter of 1663, he wrote that the Indians had "maliciously" and "insolently" engaged in litigation against three current Visitors.[18] But the threat of counterlitigation does not seem to have deterred individual Visitors. Sarmiento, for example, went on to conduct more idolatry investigations after being absolved in the case against him. But the spiraling chain of litigation and counterlitigation that the visitations provoked can only have made the campaigns seem cumbersome and inefficacious in the eyes of their instigators. The transferral of idolatry trials to Lima increasingly may have been seen as a more effective alternative, since the Indians would not be able to derail the prosecutions by countercharges. Thus the Indian practice of bringing charges against the Visitors contributed to the decline of the campaigns of extirpation.

Those Visitors who could not be deterred by legal means might succumb to occult influences. The use of witchcraft to deflect investigations was not at all uncommon. The Extirpation provided a new source of anxiety and insecurity in the life of the native community that only encouraged the consultation of indigenous deities. The cacique of the village of San Gerónimo de Pampas, Gerónimo Auquinivin, testified that some Indians from his village had sacrificed cuyes at a spot on the road where the arriving Visitor would pass before entering the village.[19] Such propitiatory offerings, made to exert occult influences on the behavior of the Visitor, were evolved as a response to the threat of the Extirpation. Thus, far from eliminating the relevance of sources of indigenous supernatural power, the prosecutions for idolatry had generated increased recourse to native practices as a counteragent. Indeed, these native practices would receive renewed validation by ensuring success in the struggle against Visitors or the local priest. By consulting the huacas and mallquis, Hernando Hacaspoma was able to predict the success of his village in its legal proceedings against successive priests. He divined, for example, that they would be rid of Licenciado Cartajena within a year, which proved correct. Hacaspoma seems to have engineered the removal of at least four priests, Licenciados Cartajena, Morales, Vintin, and de Escuer. Thus the use of legal action became a method whereby the religious specialist could reaffirm the validity of both his ancestral guardians and himself.[20]

II

Resistance was not confined to the material and physical; it could also take the more sophisticated form of ideological adaptations. The inability of communities to save their huacas from physical destruction engendered philosophical innovations to preserve the "posthumous" significance of their deities. Material annihilation did not automatically entail an end to "spiritual life." Either huacas might continue to be worshiped despite having been burned or smashed to pieces or they might be replaced by substitutes. Noboa's investigations in Santa Catalina de Pimachi uncovered a host of huacas and mallquis that had been restored after previous visitations.[21] The Indians of San Pedro de Hacas replaced two stone huacas in human form, which had been burned by Avendaño, with two similar wooden forms, to which offerings continued to be made. Such replacements might be rationalized as "the children" of destroyed mallquis or huacas. The Indians of San Gerónimo de Copa revealed some mallquis that were said to be the offspring of those destroyed by Alonso Osorio. If the ashes or broken remnants of sacred objects survived, they might be placed in the identical spot where the huaca had formerly stood or the mallqui had reposed. The remains of a sacred white stone, broken up by Osorio, had been restored to their rightful place where they continued to be worshiped as before. The ashes of the mallqui Carcoyanac, burned by the Visitor, had been returned to the same sacred cave where the body had originally been laid to rest. The Indians of San Francisco de Mangas explained that not only had they managed to keep their principal mallqui Auca Atama hidden from Osorio but they had also collected the ashes of the mallqui's "children" after their ritual burning and buried them in the same spot.[22]

Some huacas and mallquis seem to have been regenerated and even to have gained in spiritual significance as a result of being consigned to the flames. Domingo Nuna Chaupis testifed that the religious specialist of his village, Catalina Guacayllano, replaced the huacas and conopas burned by Avendaño with ten more huacas and taught him to be their hechicero, invoking them as "Our burned Lord and Father" (Señor padre quemado). The very experience of destruction by fire was incorporated into their divine status. In marked contrast to the Taki Onqoy, when those gods vanquished by the Christians had not returned to play a key role in the millenarian battle of the religions, these native deities arose Phoenix-like to fight again. Although it is true that some destroyed huacas lost their spiritual significance and their worship was abandoned, in the vast majority of cases, persecution led to renewed vigor.[23]

This phenomenon was so common that the extirpators were forced to resort to extreme measures to prevent the physical revival of deities, such as the grinding down of the stone remains and their disposal in fast-flowing rivers.[24] Even this strategy could be overcome by native communities that insisted that the site where the huaca had formerly stood remained sacred, even in its physical absence, or that the camaquen or spirit of the mallquis lived on. Hacaspoma told the Indians of San Pedro de Hacas that they should continue to make sacrifices to the mallquis and huacas burned by the Visitor because their camaquen, or "souls," were immortal and were watching over the Indians and would be present to receive offerings. The mallquis Paquirachin and Cuñarachin, whose physical remains had been destroyed by Avendaño, were still worshiped and could still give replies in the spot where they once stood. The huacas Apu Urauc and Caruatarpo Urauc, which had been physically removed by Avendaño, continued to receive the sacrifice of a llama kid in the identical place because their camaquen, or "souls," were said to inhabit the spot. The huaca Macacayan, despite no longer persisting in physical form, was reputed to attend sacrifices in its honor in spirit form.[25]

A further adaptation to the Extirpation lay in changes to the method of recruiting religious specialists. A frequent comment of witnesses was the difficulty in persuading candidates to assume responsibility for the huacas of their ayllu or village. The crisis in recruitment occasioned a relaxation in the criteria for selection, whereby the process of initiation became considerably shortened and less rigorous. Andrés Guaman Pilpi testified that Hacaspoma had instructed him to serve the huacas of his ayllu for no better reason than that, with the death of the former huacapvillacs, he was the oldest surviving member of his ayllu. His initiation consisted of sacrifices of cuyes to the mallquis in the ancient village of his ayllu. This was sufficient for him to embark on the exercise of the offices of mallquipvillac, huacapvillac, and *aucachi* (confessor).[26] Some witnesses had been threatened so as to oblige them to assume the function of religious specialist against their will. Alonso Quipi Guaman of San Pedro de Hacas had acquiesced to Hacaspoma's demands that he should minister to the huacas of his ayllu only after threats that he and his fellow Indians would die, cursed by the mallquis. He was initiated by means of a simple sacrifice of cuyes, with no rigorous training or preparation.[27] Most remarkable is the lack of spontaneous selection through dreams or trance experiences. No longer was the function of specialist reserved for exceptional people. It was as if there was a new urgency to conserve and transmit the knowledge threatened by Catholicism.[28]

The Christian practice of church burial posed a strong challenge to native practices that evoked significant adaptations in response. Obvious strategies were the removal of bodies buried in the churchyard or the concealment of corpses in secret places to avoid burial. The greatest change in traditional practices was in relation to the fate of the bodies of Indians who had received Christian baptism. Noboa discovered the existence of segregated machayes, with separate resting grounds for baptized and unbaptized Indians. In this way the ancestors were not contaminated. It is possible that the practice of segregation had been adopted during the lifetime of the declarants in these cases. Hacaspoma testified, that, *as a boy*, he had seen the bodies of dead Christian Indians buried in a cave where they were mixed with bodies of heathen Indians. The corpses of both baptized and unbaptized had been revered equally. This was in marked contrast to the separation of burial grounds characteristic at the time of the trial. The common explanation for removing the corpses from the church was that they suffered greatly under the weight of the earth on top of them. If the dead were neglected, they would curse their descendants and deprive them of crops and food. This notion developed in response to the Christian disruption of traditional burial practices and restored dignity to the ancestors.[29]

Ideological resistance was also necessary to resist the wider phenomenon of evangelization. This might not take the form of adaptation and change but instead, the reassertion of traditional native principles in areas where Christianity had posed serious challenges, particularly in terms of the relations between humans, their ancestors, and the supernatural world.

Religious specialists reasserted traditional rites of name giving to combat the conquests of Christian baptism. Indians were encouraged to abandon their Christian names and take the names of their huacas. The young Indians were taken to speak with the huacas so that their native names might be conferred in a ritual context. Henceforth they would be known, not by the saint's name, but by the name given them by the huaca.[30] Such names represented not merely the memory of a huaca but were also a means of establishing a continuity of lineage and bonding with territory. As the investigations of Hernández Príncipe showed, the perpetuation of indigenous names allowed the establishment of genealogies.[31]

The native concepts of damage to harmonious social relations (called *hucha* in Quechua) and verbal acknowledgment of transgressions of social norms were reinforced at the expense of the analogous Christian concepts of "sin" and "confession." The well-being of the community was still understood to depend on Indians' acknowledgment of transgressions to their native specialists twice a year; if they neglected this obligation, the springs would dry up and there would be no food. The transgression or acts of neglect to be confessed were judged by indigenous, not Christian, criteria. Indigenous transgressions included failure to keep fasts, neglect of sacrifices to mallquis, consorting with lovers who had slept with other men (a sin called *cutipatigrapa*), attendance at church at the time of making offerings, and lying under oath to the huacas. Failure to attend the worship of huacas was punishable by public whipping. Christian definitions of sins were explicitly refuted. Sexual relations with close relatives and married women were outlawed but not those with single young girls. It was, however, unacceptable to maintain relations with two women at the same time. Neither evil thoughts nor lying under oath to the Christian god were worthy of acknowledgment. Although Indians could not be forbidden to attend Christian confession, they could be encouraged to invalidate it. They were told not to reveal their idolatries or the transgressions that they had acknowledged to indigenous ministers. For example, they should only confess nonattendance at mass or eating meat on Fridays, since these were not real transgressions and did not need to be acknowledged to their own specialists.[32]

The causal link between the neglect of the native deities and personal or communal catastrophe was reaffirmed by religious specialists. The abundance of crops and the supply of water were dependent on continued attention to the huacas and mallquis; failure in these duties would entail human illness and agricultural disaster. The relatives of one dead man were told that he had died because he had not worshiped the mallquis and that they too would die soon if they continued their neglect. They gave an offering to the specialist to sacrifice to the mallquis, and the ashes were taken to the church to put on the grave of the dead man. Many neglectful Indians hurried to make amends to their deities when threatened with a curse from the other world, which might weaken them by draining their camaquen, or life force.[33]

The competence of native deities and their earthly representatives reigned supreme in the sphere of illness. The Indians of San Pedro de Hacas continued to bathe and wash their sick where two streams joined in one river.

Both streams ran down from the mountain where, in a niche in a rock, they had lain to rest the body of Tuqui Atipac or "All-conquering," who had been a curandero consulted by all for his prognostications and cures. In this way, from beyond the grave, the old man was able to continue exercising his healing powers.[34]

By insisting on the "all-conquering" power of the ancestors to determine the course of illnesses, religious specialists were able to exercise real power within their communities. The fiscal Francisco Poma was seduced from execution of his duties to the village priest by his conviction that Hacaspoma had called on the huacas to afflict him with a severe illness. Obliged by the priest to ensure Indian attendance at doctrina, he encountered the resistance of the villagers, who refused to go to church while they were fasting for the mallquis. Despite threats that something terrible would befall him if he interfered, he took Hacaspoma and the others to the church by force. That night he fell seriously ill and was confined to bed in great pain for six months. At the end of this time, Hacaspoma's wife came and requested a llama to be sacrificed to the mallquis to secure his recovery, to which he consented. Hacaspoma went to dig up some of the witness's hairs, which he had buried near the huaca in the ancient village, and made sacrifices, after which the witness began to get better. When he went to thank Hacaspoma, the hechicero told him that he had cast the spell himself and warned him not to interfere with the Indians' fasts again. By causing and curing the illness, Hacaspoma had reasserted his control over the fiscal and compromised his loyalty to the priest.[35]

The relationship between the Indians and the Christian god represented the most serious challenge for the native religious specialists. Even the most militant propagandists against Christianity did not entirely reject the competence of Christian supernatural forces. Instead, they insisted on a clear separation between the Spanish and the Indian supernatural worlds. Hacaspoma taught the Indians that they should not worship the Christian god because he had not created them or their *chácaras* (agricultural plots); rather, they should worship their true creators, the huacas Libiac and Huari. Although the saints might be effective as huacas and camaquenes for the Spaniards, they could not serve the Indians' supernatural needs. They were, after all, only dumb objects of wood, incapable of communicating with the Indians, as their huacas could. Resisting the Spanish classification of their huacas as "objects," native specialists responded by a retaliatory reification of Spanish sacred entities. The huacas were for Indians; the Christian god and his saints were for Spaniards.[36]

This demarcation between the competence of the two religions provoked a demand that those participating in Christian worship should be disqualified from native ceremonies. The chapel master of San Juan de Machaca, Pedro García, was excluded from the traditional native religious practices of his village because he kept the company of priests. If he returned to his village during a period of fasting and confession, he was instructed not to enter or communicate with anybody because he was *raccha*, or "dirty," from his contact with the priest and the church. If he joined them, the mallquis would be enraged and the sacrifices to them would be ineffective. He confessed that he had abided by these norms for fear that otherwise the Indians would kill him.[37]

The Indian elite of the Christian Church could be marginalized from native practices, but it was not easy to isolate the mass of Indians from contact with the alien religion. Most specialists preached that the huacas had forbidden the Indians to worship the god of the Christians and that they should not go to church because it was "a dirty place." However, they were obliged to make concessions.

Hacaspoma told his followers that while performing their fasts and sacrifices, they should not enter a church to pray lest the sacrifices be nullified; but if the priest should come at that time and oblige them to go, then they should attend "in body only and not in spirit." They were forbidden to receive the sacraments of communion and penance "with all their hearts" *(de todo corazón)* but were instructed to do so "in mockery" as "it was a custom for Spaniards and not for Indians." The physical presence of the Indians in the church might be unavoidable, but they should deny the Christian god their true participation. No compromise was admitted during the five days of fasting, when they were not to go to church to pray or worship the Christian god even in outward appearance. Nor were Indians allowed to go to church immediately after worshiping the huacas.[38] Thus the conditions on which Indians were allowed to attend Christian worship were determined by native religious specialists, and then it was only to be on sufferance.

Even where consultation of Christian deities was allowed, it was on native terms. According to Isabel Poma Chagua, the older Indians told them that they could worship the mallquis and the Christian god together to avert the onset of illness and shortages. The Christian god was interpreted as an alternative source of supernatural power that could be drawn on in the same way as indigenous supernatural power.[39]

If Indian attendance at Christian worship could not be avoided, it could at least be contextualized within the native tradition. Instead of forbidding outright attendance at church, religious specialists sought to subordinate it to the worship of the huacas. This could be achieved by prevailing on the huaca to grant permission for participation in Christian religion. Before the celebration of the feasts of Corpus Christi and Saint John the Baptist in the village of San Juan de Machaca, the religious specialists took offerings to the mallquis and requested their permission for the coming feasts. On their return, they reported that although the mallquis had been angry and reluctant at first, they had ultimately consented. On the day of the fiesta, the first cups of chicha were poured in the square in honor of the mallquis. That night they poured more offerings to the mallquis, begging them not to be angry because the fiestas were in honor, not of the Spanish god, but of themselves. They danced all night without sleeping, for those who slept were accused of not loving the mallquis.[40]

Hacaspoma testified that all the mayordomos (stewards) of the cofradías and the alférez of San Pedro de Hacas were instructed that before celebrating the feasts of the patron Saint Peter or Corpus Christi, they should supply offerings of llamas and cuyes for the mallquis and beg their permission, as "they had to show greater respect to their huacas than to the saints." On the day of celebrations, when the entire village had gathered in the main square to eat and drink, the first act was to pour some chicha on the ground and dedicate it to the mallquis and huacas and their ancestors buried in the church, as the fiesta was conducted in their honor. Then they would spread coca in the square and perform the *vecochina*, which was a ceremony in which all the ayllus passed through the village singing, dancing, and beating drums and relating the past deeds of their mallquis. One witness, Miguel Sánchez, testified that the image of Saint Peter was taken to the house where the mallquis were kept so that it might witness the offerings made to the native deities and be present at the dedication of the fiesta to them. Not only on this occasion but before any Christian feast the Indians were obliged to seek the permission of the huacas before celebrating. Thus not only were the Christian saints subordinated to the Andean pantheon but the fiesta itself was converted into an act honoring the native huacas. The native religious system had absorbed the alien supernatural deities into its own structure, and an accommodation had been made between the two religious systems on native terms.[41]

III

The new accommodation between the two religious systems may best be appreciated by examining how the religious specialists of one community adapted to the Extirpation and the challenges of Christianity. The confessions of the religious specialists of the village of Santiago de Maray in 1677 reveal the growth of a renewed native religious synthesis.[42] This synthesis continued to serve the traditional needs of the indigenous community, by ensuring the smooth functioning of the agricultural cycle and freedom from sickness and pestilence. At the same time, the community had responded to previous idolatry investigations with a great adaptive capacity.[43] Despite, or because of, such modifications and additions to the native tradition, the religious life of the community did not dissolve into unconnected, constituent parts but remained a seamless whole. The fate of the individual, the community, the ancestors, and the tutelary deities was still perceived as interconnected and inseparable. Thus the meaningfulness of the native religious world was preserved and a holistic interpretation of reality not only conserved but reaffirmed.

The native religious tradition continued to safeguard human material survival. In Santiago de Maray, this was secured by the participation of the whole community in native religious rites, dedicated to the huanca Huacrallani, which was the *marcaioc*, or guardian of the village. The religious specialist, Juan Gutiérrez, confessed that the entire village made twice-yearly offerings of chicha, coca, and llama fat to the huanca, once when the Pleiades appeared, to protect the crops from frost, and a second time in November, when they plowed the maize fields. Sacrifices were also proffered twice a year to the mountains Uguanpucaru and Llaullactullu (the village *paqarina*, or primordial ancestor), which were the guardians of the principal source of water for the village, the spring Curicalla. These sacrifices were made in October when they plowed the fields and in April when they cleaned the water source. The entire village continued to worship the sun as their creator under the name of Inti, to whom sacrifices were offered four times a year, indicating that the summit of the pantheon was still occupied by this supreme indigenous deity.[44]

The role of the religious specialist as privileged communicator with the native deities was reaffirmed. One of Gutiérrez's principal functions was to supplicate the huanca Huacrallani (reputed to be a petrified high priest of the sun) to intercede for the Indians with the sun and the mountain spirits. His intervention depended on the fulfillment by the Indians of their duty to confess their sins to the specialist. Gutiérrez maintained the shamanic traditions of his ancestors. Having inherited his office from his father at the age of fourteen, the method of his initiation had been, characteristically, selection by the strike of a lightning bolt. Thus it was in the name of Libiac that he offered sacrifices at the huanca, invoking its name to secure good health.

The religious specialists of Santiago de Maray preserved their multiplicity of functions. Gutiérrez's colleague, Gonzalo Paico, combined his role as minister to the huacas with that of curandero. He used to rub the body of the sick with corncobs smeared in llama fat, invoking the maize and pleading with it to cure the patient, afterward burning the cob, which had absorbed the illness into itself. Furthermore, he also acted as a mosa, or diviner of dreams. After sacrificing to the mountain spirits, he was visited in his dreams by the mallquis who, advised by the apus, would tell him if the item about which he had been consulted would appear or not. Other times he acted as a rapiac, foretelling events from the movements of limbs, which he claimed conveyed messages from the mallquis.[45]

Under the guidance of these specialists, the huacas and mallquis had emerged fortified and renewed from the experience of persecution by the Extirpation. In former times and according to their ancient custom, the Indians had preserved their mallquis in their own homes. The mass destruction and burnings undertaken by the Visitor-General Bartolomé Jurado had forced them to adapt their practices. They had taken the ashes of the mallquis burned by Jurado and buried them, together with the surviving mallquis, under the huanca Chuchupuquio. This huanca was the "child" of Huacrallani. The result was to create a new relationship between Chuchupuquio and the mallquis, whereby the huanca stood sentinel over the ancestors' mortal remains, thereby serving not to weaken but to fortify its sacred resonance. This ideological adaptation functioned as an act of retaliation for the burning by Jurado of the huanca's "brother," Rupaigirca. Alarmed at the irreducible strength of the numen, the presiding priest, Juan de Esquibel y Aguilar, now had these remains ground into ashes and thrown into a river three leagues from the village without the Indians' knowledge. But this act of spiritual vandalism did not guarantee an end to the powers of the numen, since the river itself was indestructible.

The most notable breach in the edifice of the native system lay in the growing self-doubts experienced by Juan Gutiérrez. Here he was apparently alone. His colleague Gonzalo Paico left no doubts about his strong belief in the significance of his own role; far from being a charlatan, he had exercised his office, not merely to survive, but because he truly believed he could placate the sun, his creator, in this way and that otherwise the deity would be offended. But Gutiérrez had not felt the same certainty. Originally he had been convinced that the Christian faith was untrue and that the saints were conopas only for Spaniards. However, after the death of five of his sons, some eighteen years before, he had begun to suspect "in his heart" that the Spanish god might be more efficacious, for which reason he had learned to pray. After only a few days, he had returned to his old ways. He confessed that now he was in doubt both about the powers of his huacas and about the mysteries of the faith.

If these feelings of self-doubt had been suppressed by Gutiérrez for many years, other religious specialists and their clients experienced stronger anxieties. A sense of profound unease accompanied the realization that traditional methods were failing to stem the outbreak of devastating epidemics. In response to a sudden epidemic that had struck the village of San Pedro de Pilas, the inhabitants made sacrifices to the mountain Huacahuasi. Despite these offerings, the epidemic had spread and many of the participants in these propitiatory acts had died, including the cacique who had ordered them. The witness Pedro Villanga admitted that he had made subsequent sacrifices to the same mountain in the company of an hechicero, Juan Tomás, who had "fed" llama fat, maize, sango, and chicha to four large stones, said to be his ancestors. He had also observed Tomás go to another mountain, Huamantinga, where he had splattered a huaca with cuy's blood and supplicated it thus: "Drink this blood, Huamantinga, so that the sickness will rest." He had then taken a stone from the mountains to his house to act as an altar for sacrifices to the huacas. The motive of both sacrifices had been to plead with the huacas for their intercession and the swift elimination of sickness from the village. Although initially the defendant had believed that the huacas had the power to end the epidemics, subsequently, when those who had taken part in the sacrifices died, he had been left greatly troubled. The failure of the huacas to reciprocate in their duties had left him uncertain about the effective powers of his deities.[46]

In pre-Hispanic times, the failure of native deities to put an end to sickness could only have been accepted with resignation, or with a determination to assuage their anger by renewed sacrifices. In the colonial period, however, the existence of an alternative source of supernatural power allowed the disappointed to seek their remedies elsewhere. When a native curandero failed to cure the daughter of Diego Pacha, he turned to Christian magic to aid him. At first he had trusted the curandero's word that a rock, which had formerly been worshiped by his ancestors, was punishing him for his neglect by eating his children. But when he went to the rock with a placatory offering of chicha, it had informed him through the mediation of the curandero that his child would die. Refusing to accept this prediction and deciding that the rock was a fraud, he went to his priest to denounce the man and, contributing twenty reales to alms, he requested a mass for the health of his child. His rejection of the native deity was so great that he even helped the priest to set fire to the rock and cover it with crosses. The failure of the huaca to fulfill its reciprocal obligations was no longer interpreted as a manifestation of its anger but as a sign of its weakness. The huaca's inefficacy induced a willingness to resort to more effective Christian magic.[47]

By the eighteenth century, this crisis of confidence had become more evident. Several witnesses testified to the growing indigenous despair at the powerlessness of the huacas. Martín Felipe had been taught by the village elders that worship of the huacas would be efficacious, but he and his fellow villagers had only believed it *on occasion*. This tantalizing statement fails to indicate under what circumstances the Indians would cease to believe. However, the testimony of other witnesses confirms that the spread of disease was the most powerful factor. Sebastian Ripas declared that although he had believed that his huacas had the power to grant good harvests of maize or potatoes, he had not always received the things he had requested and that "therefore he was asking for mercy." His disillusionment had set in after most of those who had gone to worship the huacas had died of plague. Similarly, the anxieties of María Juana were related to the pestilence that had struck down the older Indians of her community. In former times, a huaca in the shape of a llama had spoken to the Indians and granted each what he had asked for. But then "everything had turned out against them" and they had all died of plague. Without prompting, the witness interpreted this event as "the punishment of God" since not one llama, to whose preservation the huaca had been dedicated, had remained alive in the village. The disillusionment of these witnesses originated in the failure of the native deities to fulfill their part of the age-old reciprocal bargain struck with the community, in particular, protection against the plague.[48]

But this withdrawal of confidence reveals native disillusionment with the huacas rather than indifference or complete disbelief. It was not so much a rejection of the huacas as a bewildered incomprehension at their inability to counter the enormity of the epidemics. The rejection occurred because the Indians still expected the huacas to help them and were enraged at their failure to do so. Thus the Extirpation had not altered the expectations of the Indians in relation to their huacas. Their anger and despair remained a response completely comprehensible within the native religious logic.

Even by the eighteenth century, although the Andean religious world had entered a crisis of self-doubt, it had not been obliterated. If native communities had adopted strategies to resist interference with their practices and allowed accretions, adaptations, and transformations to take place in those practices themselves, the fundamental conceptual framework had not been replaced. Native religious practices during the first third of the eighteenth century still preserved certain consistencies with their pre-Columbian and early colonial past that testify to their resilience in the face of the Extirpation. Above all, there still existed *communal* rites, undertaken to ensure the *collective* survival of their participants; furthermore, the avowed purpose of these rites conformed closely to indigenous paradigms, since they were undertaken for the preservation of the good health and fertility of livestock. These ceremonies were not simply isolated throwbacks to a former time; they represented a symbolic reaffirmation of the shared beliefs and value systems inherited from the aboriginal past.[49]

Such ceremonies reflected the strong belief that only *collective* rites could ensure the survival of the community as a whole. The religious specialist Pedro de la Cruz devoted his office to the maintenance of *group* worship of two stone images, Apulibiac and Apulibiac Cancharco. Similarly, the ceremonies presided over by the specialists Juan de Rojas and Francisco Libiac Condor were attended by most of the village. The primeval bond between sacred rites and the fate of the livestock was manifest in the dual responsibility exercised by Rojas as both the chief religious specialist and the tender of the village herds. The inhabitants of San Agustín de Canin also celebrated collective rites of worship. The religious specialist María Tincya officiated at sacrifices at a place called Canin Tacray (House of the Ancients), which lay opposite the village's ancestral home, in the presence of "all the Indians of the village," who came to avail themselves of the advice of three stone images. The acts of worship ritualized the "marriage" of Tincya's young female assistants to the stone images. Finally, more than fifty Indians of the village of San Antonio de la Lancha had participated in the worship of a rock face on a hill named the Visitor's or Inquisitor's Hill, the extraordinary name of which presumably commemorated a previous (and clearly unsuccessful) visitation.[50]

The resilience of native religious practices still lay not simply in an ability to survive or "persist" but in the capacity to adapt to repression. These depositions reveal less a weakening than a strengthening of the role of the apus and huacas as a response to the insecurities of colonial life. Offerings were made by Pedro de la Cruz to Libiac Cancharco in return for attending to the community's needs. These included not only providing good harvests but also ensuring that the priest would forget to charge the dues on the confraternity or fail to return from Lima. Thus, ironically, the power of the priest, the native deities' greatest foe, could most effectively be counteracted by supplication of an alternative source of supernatural power, the apus whom the priest sought to destroy. The Catholic priest's combination in his own person of both religious and political authority was paralleled by Cruz's joint function as religious specialist and village *quipucamayoc* (the expert in the recording of information on the native system of knotted cords that had constituted both the accounting system and collective memory of the Inca Empire). He knew, for example, the total population of the village (more than four hundred), the material possessions of each inhabitant, and the amount each owed in contributions. As a result of this dual role, he held an extremely privileged position as the guardian of both material and supernatural knowledge. Such a position fortified his role as the rival of the Catholic priest.[51]

The Indians of Carampoma had responded to persecution of their religious specialists by maintaining a guardian of the huacas in clandestinity, isolated from the contamination of Christianity, who encouraged them in clandestine native rites. Annual rotation of the office among suitable candidates facilitated the individual's concealment. This marcaioc or alférez was responsible for the basic needs of the community. When there was a water shortage, he went up into the mountains to summon rains; when there were floods, he used native rites to bring the rains to an end. He sponsored public native ceremonies and processions with the support of the alcaldes, in such secrecy that neither the priest nor the corregidores ever knew. He was forbidden any type of subordination, political or religious, to the colonial authorities. He avoided tribute payment, since the rest of the community contributed in his place, and he never attended mass, since it was believed propitiation of the Christian god would destroy the crops. The Christian village feasts were subordinated to native ones. Thus the most important day for indigenous rites, when more than fifty or one hundred llamas were sacrificed to the dead, was the day after the feast of Santiago. On the saint's day, before going to their ancient village where they had formerly lived, all the Indians from Carampoma congregated in a high place where there was a cross. In defiance of the symbol of Christian victory, they danced and celebrated their native rites there before going to a large lake near the old village where they worshiped all night. The Christian celebration was deftly confined to a subsidiary position in the native hierarchy.[52]

The native religious system frequently proved adept at accommodating Christian elements within its structure. The Indian brothers of the cofradía of Nuestra Señora de la Natividad had made offerings on their own estate to the huacas of Juan de Rojas to promote the fertility of their livestock. Even the membership of Christian confraternities could be integrated within the native religious system.[53]

The principal native response to Christianity was to

domesticate the alien religious tradition, to incorporate its deities into an indigenous framework, and thus to tame it. In this way, neither religion absorbed the other; but then, nor were they simply juxtaposed; they were articulated into a symbiotic relationship, whereby one system was subordinated to the other. Among the marginalized communities that fell victim to the Extirpation, the Christian synthesis had been subordinated to the native synthesis, yet both functioned as alternative sources of supernatural support.

Persecution left its imprint on Andean religion. Possibly the most important effect was to force adaptations in the role of the native religious specialist. The pre-Columbian religious specialist was characterized by a multiplicity of functions, whether exercised separately or combined in a single officiant. He was the communicator with sacred beings, the interpreter of their desires, the transmitter of myths, the guardian of the huacas and mallquis, the officiant at sacrifices, the confessor, folk healer, sorcerer, and diviner. All of these functions continued in the postconquest period, though some became more or less important, new ones were added, and others were exercised in a different manner. For example, the persecution of native rites of worship and their consequent refuge in clandestinity conferred an increased significance on the specialist's role as organizer of ceremonies. At the same time, to maintain his authority, he demanded that his flock ask permission to participate in Christian ceremonies, thus apparently including Christian worship in his own religious jurisdiction. Another function that became qualitatively different in the wake of persecution was that of "dogmatist," or transmitter of the traditional beliefs and rites of the native world. This educative function became an aggressive defense against the attacks of Christianity. Closely related was a wholly new function of "antidoctrinero." This was the task of contraevangelizing and refuting Christian dogma and worship. Some of the Christian methods of propaganda were adopted to complement traditional methods. The antidoctrinero destroyed Christian symbols and ensured that the Indians participated as little as possible in Christian worship.[54] One characteristic of the colonial native religious specialist was the combination in one individual of a variety of functions (diviner, healer, sorcerer). It is impossible to know with certainty whether this represents a continuity with or deviation from pre-Hispanic patterns.[55] However, the crisis in recruitment of specialists that characterized the colonial period must have increased the tendency of individuals to perform a number of roles.

By adapting in a variety of ways, the role of the native specialist was revitalized as the protagonist of the renewed indigenous religious system. Native beliefs and rites had adapted as well in order to resist the attack of Christianity. Even as late as the third decade of the eighteenth century, the native synthesis still encompassed the public sphere. But this reaffirmation of the native sense of reality, through collective ceremonies of worship, was increasingly circumscribed. First, it was ever more restricted to the most marginalized communities; second, within those communities, it was ever more confined to clandestinity; and third, even within these bounds, its competence was ever more compromised. There was no area within the supernatural world over which it exercised an uncontested monopoly.

However, within these restrictions, the intellectual and metaphysical framework within which native beliefs and rites were located (however much these had been transformed) had not been abandoned. The fate of the individual, the community, and the deities had not been atomized but remained intertwined. Although anxiety about the efficacy of native rites had grown, this was manifested as anger, confusion, and despair rather than as indifference or complete disbelief. It was as if a deep sense of betrayal had forced individuals to resort to the alien religious system as an act of revenge or retaliation. Thus the sphere of competence of native deities had been increasingly circumscribed, but it had not been eliminated. Native Andeans may have lost their trust in the ability of native deities to protect them, but they had not abandoned their faith in their very existence. This irreducible and ineradicable faith in native sacred entities was the clearest evidence that the "disenchantment" of the native religious world sought by the Extirpation had not occurred. Indeed, the faith in their own Christian sacred entities that the Spanish priests sought to inculcate in the Indians may well have reinforced belief in their Andean counterparts. The attempt to dismiss all Andean sacred entities as "things" may well have failed because such materialistic reasoning was incompatible with the mysteries of the Christian faith.[56]

Six: IDOLATRY REDISCOVERED

A priest forces the attendance of children
at the *doctrina.*

*If . . . the penitent has no error of understanding or desire to give
divine worship to creatures, but . . . only did materially what he
saw others do or what his parents taught him . . . this is not formal
idolatry or apostasy but only material in appearance. Of this third
type of idolater I consider most of the Indians to be, whose mental
powers are so small that they do not know or understand what their
sacrifices and offerings mean.*
—Alonso de la Peña Montenegro, Bishop of Quito, *Itinerario* (1668)

*All the Indians of the village of Pachangara have committed the
crime of idolatry . . . because they have rendered the worship due to
Our God to diabolical huacas.*
—Pedro de Celís, Visitor-General of Idolatry, *Idolatrías* (1725)

I

IN JANUARY 1725, THE NEW ARCHBISHOP OF LIMA, DIEGO Morcillo Rubio de Auñon, appointed the first Visitor-General for the extirpation of idolatry since the campaigns of the mid-seventeeth century.[1] Pedro de Celís y la Bega was, like his predecessors, an ordinary doctrinero.[2] The decree that nominated him extended his responsibilities throughout the entire archbishopric. Yet the investigations he conducted under this commission were limited to a handful of doctrinas within the province of Cajatambo and, as far as can be deduced from the existing documents, were of such limited duration that after 1725 no further traces are to be found. Even Celís's fate after this date is unknown. Nor, despite the continued existence of isolated trials afterward, is there evidence of any further campaigns elsewhere in Cajatambo or in other provinces. Hence there is an essential paradox, even contradiction, to be resolved. If concern for the "persistence" of native religious practices was so great that a campaign of extirpation was revived, why did it so quickly fade into oblivion?

The sudden emergence of the renewed campaign and its equally precipitous disappearance were closely related to Morcillo's short tenure as archbishop. Having been elected to the see in 1723, following the death of Archbishop Antonio de Soloaga the previous year, Morcillo had only been able to take up his miter in 1724, six months before Celís's appointment. This delay undoubtedly resulted from the prolongation until 1724 of his tenure of the office of viceroy, which he had assumed in 1720.[3] The first serious indications of the persistence of native religious practices were reported to the archbishopric in April 1723 by Toribio de Mendizábal, the priest of Santiago de Carampoma in the province of Huarochirí.[4] Although preliminary investigations were initiated, the transformation of these inquiries into a campaign of idolatry proper took place only after the accession of the new archbishop to the see. The "idolatries" uncovered by Celís in October 1724 led to his appointment as Visitor-General in early 1725. The resumption of the campaigns of idolatry in the third decade of the eighteenth century depended as much on the personal initiative of Archbishop Morcillo as the initiation of the campaigns of the early and mid-seventeenth century had depended on Lobo Guerrero and Villagómez. It is less easy, however, to demonstrate the reasons for the sudden end to the idolatry investigations. Morcillo's death in 1730 may have deprived the inquiries of a necessary patron. But the question remains why the investigations apparently ended in 1725, several years before the archbishop's death. There must be profounder reasons for the paralysis of the campaign.

We cannot conclude that the campaign faltered because the Church no longer took seriously the threat of religious deviance. The rapidity of Celís's appointment, following hard on the lightning progress of his investigations, can leave no doubt about the seriousness with which the Church considered the persistence of native religious practices. Thus if the wave of repression during 1724 and 1725 was short-lived and extremely limited in geographic extent, it still merits the epithet "campaign of extirpation." The revival of the title of Visitor-General conferred on its recipient all its attendant powers. Celís was authorized not only to take depositions but also to absolve the accused or pass sentence and administer punishment without further consultation. All priests and vicars were instructed not to offer any obstacles to the exercise of his authority; any who did so could receive legal penalties at the Visitor's discretion. The only restriction imposed on his jurisdiction was the requirement that all the accused should be sent to Lima for final determination of sentence.[5]

Celís's methods echoed those of earlier campaigns of

extirpation. He traveled with his extirpatory team of notaries and assistants and conducted his inquiries according to the regulations established by Arriaga and Villagómez. Denunciations were elicited by the familiar device of issuing a carta de edicto. The auto de fe was employed to provide a ritual context for the expression of contrition. For example, more than two hundred villagers of Pachangara were absolved en masse in a public auto held in their village church. The punishments administered resembled those of the mid-seventeenth century in their severity. The major ringleaders were banished to obrajes while the ordinary male villagers received forty lashes in public and the old men twenty-five.[6]

But what, above all, characterized these events as a true revival of the campaign of extirpation was the ideology that underlay them. Celís was nominated "Visitor-General for the extirpation of idolatry throughout the archbishopric," with the power to investigate, try, and absolve those guilty of "idolatry, superstition and hechicerías."[7] The appointment derived from Morcillo's conviction that many Indians of the archbishopric had "relapsed into the sin of idolatry, maintaining the rites and ceremonies of their heathen ancestors." Three conclusions may be drawn from the wording of this edict: first, that even by the 1720s, the ecclesiastical authorities were seriously concerned by the continued existence of native religious beliefs and rites; second, that the phenomenon was still perceived to be not localized but widespread, contaminating the entire archbishopric; and third, that religious deviance was still perceived within the classic framework of idolatry and hechicerías. The archbishop's edict reveals a strong continuity of ideas from the seventeenth to the eighteenth century.

The continued close identification of the sins of idolatry, superstition, and hechicerías is evident in the cartas de edicto issued by Celís on arrival at Indian villages. The

Indians were ordered to denounce all those who were
"brujos, sortílegos, idólatras o hechiceros." To some extent the edicts distinguished between these categories.
Idolaters were presumably (though it is not explicitly
stated) those who offered sacrifices of animal blood to
huacas in secret or public places. Under the category of
brujos and hechiceros fell those who cast spells by utter-
ing certain words or names or by manipulating certain
substances (such as a colored earth called *anaipullo*, little
toads named *guacanpache*, or small stones called *conopas*).
Then there were those who practiced "other superstitions." By far the greater part of the practices condemned
by the edicts fell into this subdivision. There were those,
for example, who summoned storm clouds or threw
stones in water when it began to rain; those who performed prohibited dances when going to the mita or to
clean their irrigation canals; those who, at sowing time,
poured chicha or spread coca on their crops and ab-
stained from meat and ají in the belief that only through
such ceremonies would they achieve more abundant harvests; and those who performed such "ridiculous" actions as removing their eyelashes and blowing them into
the wind or piling up stones to secure good fortune. Classic idolatry—the rendering of worship to huacas—was
understood to continue exactly as in pagan times, with
the ancient rites and ceremonies conserved and valued
above the worship of the Christian god. The offenders
were understood to be guilty not only of the act but also the
intent to give worship. Because the same intent was perceived to underlie the other categories of offenses—which
strictly speaking were hechicerías or superstitions—they
became idolatrous by association. Thus the veneration of
huacas represented only one type of offense, hardly distinguishable from the others. Even the act of removing
the eyelashes and blowing them into the wind was considered to be as idolatrous (or as superstitious) as the

adoration of idols. All these offenses were grouped together with no attempt to distinguish degrees of idolatry or superstition, or to differentiate between idolatría and hechicería. As late as the 1720s, then, the Indians were understood to attribute divinity to the objects of their ceremonies. There had been no redefinition of the sin of idolatry, nor was there a greater tolerance of Indian "superstitions."[8]

The same language of idolatry and apostasy determined the wording of the charges brought against individual offenders. The villagers of Pachangara were condemned by Celís for the sin of idolatry because they had substituted for God diabolical huacas as objects of worship.[9] The same ideological framework prevailed when the accused were brought to Lima for hearings before the promotor fiscal, Matheo Salazar y de la Serna. Juan de Rojas and Francisco Libiac Condor were accused of "heresy, apostasy, and idolatry" for worshiping sacred stones to which they had attributed "divinity and omnipotence." The sin was not merely one of idolatrous actions but also one of idolatrous intent. The accused had genuinely believed that by worshiping these stones and sacrificing animals, chicha, and coca to them, they could maintain and increase their livestock. The implicit veneration of ancestors, from whom the sacred stones had been inherited, constituted not only *adoración vana* (vain adoration) but also idolatry. Both of the accused were to be condemned for their evangelizing activities in that they had encouraged other Indians of the village to gather and worship the stones, preaching to them that they would preserve their lives and increase their livestock. Last, having already been punished for such offenses, they were guilty of relapse into idolatry.[10]

The deviant religious practices of the defendant Pedro de la Cruz (or Quiñones) were classified not only as idolatry but also, since he was a baptized Christian, as heresy and apostasy. Cruz had shown intent to worship idols of stone by making offerings of animal and human blood in the belief that an abundance of crops could be secured and good fortune ensured for the *lactacamayoc* (village steward). He had also encouraged his fellow Indians to participate in idolatrous ceremonies. Equally important was the defendant's insincerity and lack of repentance. It has been demonstrated above that many defendants succeeded in undermining the charges against them by affirming their lack of conviction in their own actions and confessing that they were motivated by base material needs. Like Juan Vásques before him, de la Cruz revised his testimony to portray himself as a trickster rather than an idolater; unlike Vásques, however, de la Cruz failed to convince his interrogators because his excuses were not accompanied by genuine contrition. Furthermore, his statements were hopelessly inconsistent. Whereas he had confessed to Celís that he had officiated for nine years over "brujerías y idolatrías," he denied this earlier confession when he was brought before the promotor fiscal. It was true that an Indian woman had taught him to consult a stone in her house to learn if there would be good harvests, but, of course, the stone had never replied. He knew well that stones could not talk. If he had led the Indians to believe the contrary, it had been mere trickery. When reminded of his testimony to Celís, he admitted that he was, after all, the principal minister in the worship of the stones, but he insisted that he had been motivated purely by financial reward. To maintain appearances, he had impersonated the voice of the apus while hiding in a spot apart from the Indians and had lied in the replies he gave in order to deceive them. He denied ever officiating at human sacrifices and said he could not remember having previously testified that he had been present at the sacrifice of an old man. The promotor questioned de la Cruz closely about his role in the ritual sacrifices made by Juan Batista to the "omnipotent" Apu Quichunque to recover from an illness. De la Cruz acknowledged that Batista had questioned him about his illness but denied attributing it to the anger of the apu or advising him to perform any sacrifice; rather, the sick man himself had resolved to do it and for this purpose had availed himself of the services of the accused, who had cut the cuy's throat for him and anointed the stone with blood. He had not genuinely believed that by means of this sacrifice he would achieve a remedy for the illness and had done it only with the intention of continuing his deception. Shrewdly, then, de la Cruz portrayed himself as merely acquiescent in the demands made of him by Batista, rather than the initiator of the idolatrous sacrifices.[11]

But far from exonerating himself, his retraction of his earlier confession became another serious charge against him. The fiscal declared that his argument that the earlier deposition had been extracted from him under duress was false and malicious, since the punishment he had been given had not amounted to six lashes. His original confessions should be upheld because according to all authorities on criminal law, the first confession was that which should condemn or free a prisoner. The second deposition made by de la Cruz, in which he denied what he had declared in the first, was premeditated and designed purely to release himself from punishment; in any case, even in this confession he implicated himself in various offenses of idolatry. His transparent insincerity cast doubt on his statement that he had merely sought to deceive the Indians for financial reasons. But his greatest sin was his stubborn denial of the "implicit and explicit pact with the Devil" that he had maintained by speaking with his idols. To oblige him to declare the whole truth and reveal his accomplices, the promotor recommended subjecting him to torture. Even more than his idolatries, his failure to offer his full cooperation and genuine contrition earned him severe punishment by the authorities.[12]

It is clear that the renewed campaign of 1725 was stillborn not because the ecclesiastical authorities did not take seriously the "persistence" of "idolatry" but rather because idolatry prosecutions fell victim to certain contradictions in the ideology and methods of the Extirpation. There were two principal contradictions that undermined the foundations of the idolatry prosecutions and acted to subvert the charge of idolatry. The first lay in the uncertainties concerning the status of the accused as true apostates; the second, in the unresolved significance of testimony motivated by malice.

The campaigns of extirpation rested on the intellectual conviction that its victims were idolaters and apostates. The language of the prosecution framed the accusation in these terms. But increasingly the Indians' defense chose to contest their status as apostates. In the mid-seventeenth century, as has been illustrated, the role of the defense had been little more than a formality; but from the 1690s and especially by the 1720s, the defense became more professional. The increasing frequency of idolatry trials heard in Lima contributed significantly. The arguments presented by the defense could be so convincing that they might result in the absolution of the accused or, at least, a significant reduction in sentence. Above all, by disputing that the accused were apostates, the charge of idolatry was subverted.

Since most defendants invariably confessed their native religious practices, the charge of idolatry could not be explicitly denied. Instead, the defense argued that no real apostasy could have been committed in a state of ignorance of the faith. For example, the procurador de los naturales, Francisco De Avila y Torres, rejected the promotor's qualification of de la Cruz and Francisco Bartolomé as genuine apostates on the grounds of their inadequacy, their coarseness, and their relative ignorance of the faith. De la Cruz was demonstrably ignorant of the creed and of the Lord's commandments; therefore, if he was unaware of the laws of God, he could not commit apostasy by breaking them. With true knowledge of the mysteries and precepts of the faith, he would not have committed his offenses (which, contradicting himself, the procurador referred to as "apostasy"). The most effective remedy was not punishment but further instruction. A similar argument was advanced in favor of Bartolomé. Although he could apparently recite his prayers and was familiar with at least part of the Christian doctrine, he still suffered from appalling ignorance as he only reproduced it without understanding what he had learned. With true knowledge, he would not have committed "idolatry."[13]

In defense of Rojas and Libiac Condor, Carvajal pleaded that their ignorance and their willing cooperation during the trial entitled them to mercy. It was true that they had confessed and incriminated themselves, but as "new Christians," recently converted, they merited less severity on account of their feeble reflective abilities. They were, after all, fully repentant of their crimes and would be best served by instruction in the faith to avoid repetition of their errors. The charge of idolatry was effectively subverted by these arguments as the punishment imposed on Libiac Condor by the provisor, Pedro de la Peña, was extraordinarily lenient in relation to the seriousness of the accusation. He was not to be banished or imprisoned; instead, he would undergo a public whipping every day for four days and would pay a fine of twenty-five pesos. This restraint derived from the accused's repentance and his promise to live as a better Christian. As in the seventeenth-century trials, defendants who cooperated under interrogation could expect relative benevolence.[14]

What is especially noteworthy is that nearly two hun-

dred years after the conquest and more than one hundred
years after the first campaigns of extirpation, the Indians
could still be presented as "new Christians" or recent
converts. A paradoxical dichotomy still prevailed in the
ideology of the Extirpation. The Indians s ʼod guilty on
the charge of idolatry, through both act and intent; even
the procurador could not help but continue to refer to his
clients' offense as "apostasy" at the same time as he denied it ("with true knowledge of the mysteries and precepts of the faith they would not have committed apostasy"). Yet their responsibility was reduced on account of
their ignorance and poor instruction. This defense had
never been consistently developed or applied before; indeed, it was in direct contradiction to that offered for
other defendants. The counsel for Juan Vásques, for example, had argued that his solid knowledge of the faith
indicated that he could not be a heretic. Yet now the
procurador wished to maintain that ignorance of the faith
was equally incompatible with heresy. Both arguments
were weak, but the latter was particularly subversive and
threatened to undermine the whole edifice of idolatry trials. If the offense of "idolatry" or "apostasy" could not be
committed with true knowledge of the faith, then, by definition, practitioners of native rites were not "idolaters"
because their crimes proved their lack of true knowledge.
If this argument was to be accepted, any Indian would be
able to practice native religious rites without becoming
an apostate, remaining instead a poorly instructed Christian. Thus the arguments advanced by the defense acted
to undermine the foundations on which the ideology of
extirpation was constructed.

The issue was further complicated by the ambiguities of
testimony proven to originate in enmity for the accused.
The increasing professionalization of the trials, which accompanied their transferral to Lima, exposed ever more
clearly the malicious motives behind much of the evidence

offered in prosecutions. But these motives proved counter-productive, since the origin of an accusation in enmity was contested. The manipulation of idolatry trials by communities to settle their own internal disputes threatened to undermine their effectiveness both as a means of eliminating hated rivals and as a means of eliminating indigenous rites. They became "self-unfulfilling."

The two extirpation trials in Carampoma of 1723 and 1730 (which incidentally both preceded and postdated the campaign of 1724–25) originated from the factional divisions of the community. As in the seventeenth-century trials, the profound cleavages between the protectors of native rites and their opponents had reached a crisis. Two successive caciques segundas personas, Lorenzo Batista Canchocapcha and his successor Francisco Julcarilpo, had attempted to interfere with the traditional religious practices of their communities. The latter was an equivocal protector of native rites who was prepared to testify against the community's religious specialists; and the former was an unambiguous opponent of indigenous ceremonies. The enmity both had earned within Carampoma was the principal determinant of the idolatry trials, provoking the prosecution in the first place but also itself invalidating the charge to which it had given rise.[15]

The confrontation between Batista and the nativists had burst into violence and exposed the existence of clandestine rites. One night, in an unspecified year before 1723, Batista had caught the Indians red-handed in their native rites. Supervised by the native religious specialist Juan de Rojas, they had stoned and beaten the cacique with such violence that he had subsequently died from his wounds. This attack had provoked an idolatry investigation in which Rojas had been publicly punished. Since no record of this earlier trial remained, the prosecuting priest of 1723, Toribio de Mendizábal, was unable to establish for certain the identity of those responsible for the actions of that night. But Batista's successor, Francisco Julcarilpo, testified to the notoriety of Rojas's father as a brujo and confirmed that Rojas had already been publicly whipped for his offenses. This testimony, together with that of other witnesses, was sufficient to have Rojas transferred to Lima.[16]

It was clear that Julcarilpo had, possibly unwillingly, aligned himself with the opposition. His intervention in Rojas's trial must have left his position dangerously ambiguous in the eyes of the nativists. His own patronage of native deities could be used against him to secure his removal. Thus, in 1730, Julcarilpo became the victim of a new idolatry trial. In revenge, the cacique provided a detailed account of the collective rites he knew the Indians of his village practiced. If he had failed to denounce these "idolatries," it was through fear that he would suffer the fate of his predecessor, Batista. However, in a subsequent confession, he denied any knowledge of idolatry and declared that, out of fear and believing they would free him, he had told stories of what he had heard had occurred in the past but had no reason to believe were true any longer. His fear of the seriousness of the punishment awaiting him now exceeded his wish to wreak vengeance on the nativists.[17]

Julcarilpo attempted to disqualify the evidence against him by alleging that the chief witness, Juan Mango, was his capital enemy. This plea seems to have been based in fact. Julcarilpo claimed that the enmity arose from Mango's conviction for the theft of some of his mules. But there were additional grounds for resentment. In the investigation of 1723 against Rojas, Mango had been accused of superstitious cures and making a diabolical pact, which gave him further reason to resent Julcarilpo, whose intervention had been crucial. Finally, Mango's wife believed herself to have been bewitched by Julcarilpo's wife. After a violent fight between the two women, Mango's wife had been mysteriously confined to bed in inexplicable pain. As a practicing specialist himself, Mango could not have been unaware of Julcarilpo's patronage of native rites. His opportune "discovery" of Julcarilpo's "idolatries" was for the benefit of the extirpators and derived from his suspicion that the cacique's hostility had been expressed in black magic against him.[18]

Julcarilpo extended his allegations of enmity to include the lieutenant corregidor, Manuel Márquez, who was prosecuting the case. Referring to the depletion of his goods, which had been placed under embargo, he accused Márquez of acting in collusion with his capital enemy in a conspiracy to take possession of his property. Furthermore, the lieutenant had fabricated evidence: some of the witnesses supposed to have made depositions before Márquez had denied doing so. On the grounds of the lieutenant's corruption and lack of competence to hear the case, Julcarilpo appealed for his judgment to be considered null and void.

The final sentence against Julcarilpo is missing, so it is impossible to determine with certainty the impact this accusation of enmity had on the case. The promotor fiscal, Juan de Pernia, conceded the enmity of Mango for the accused but insisted that this was not sufficient to invalidate his testimony.[19] Since previous accusations had collapsed under the discovery of malicious motives, there is little reason to suppose that this case was different.

The frequency of such an outcome reveals a fatal flaw in the Extirpation that had always existed but that by the eighteenth century, with the increasing professionalization of the trials, had become more conspicuous. This flaw lay in two fundamental differences in procedure between the Extirpation and the Inquisition. First, the Holy Office disqualified the testimony of known enemies; second, the accused was not informed of the identity of his accusers. To ensure the exclusion of malicious testimony,

the accused was required to submit a list of potential enemies whose evidence should not be admitted. Under the
early Extirpation, especially as conducted by local Visitors-General, witnesses were allowed to know the identity
of those who had incriminated them, and known enemies
were to be exploited, not excluded. What did it matter if
the accusation was that of an enemy if it brought to light
otherwise hidden religious deviance? The fact that the
witness was hostile to the defendant did not necessarily
mean that what he said was not true. Indeed, the confrontation of witness and suspect was a tool employed
precisely to extract information in a spiral of mutual denunciation.[20] This practice provided an excellent lever to
open up cracks in the testimony of declarants who were
reluctant to cooperate, but it had one great disadvantage.
It removed an essential safeguard. A victim of the Inquisition could not add names to his list of enemies retro-
spectively. If testimony against him derived from a source
omitted from his list, he could not contest the evidence on
the grounds of enmity. A victim of the Extirpation, however, could attempt to disqualify any witness against him
as soon as he learned his identity. The charge of capital enmity was extremely hard to contest, especially as it became increasingly clear that a principal motive behind denunciations was indeed the desire to attack one's enemies.

The few idolatry trials of the early eighteenth century
were more professional than their predecessors of the
seventeenth century. Rather than allowing the cases to be
conducted locally and transferred to the center merely
for confirmation of the sentence, by the 1720s the detailed investigation of idolatry accusations occurred in
Lima under the watchful eye of both the fiscal and the defense. The professionalization itself undermined the Extirpation by highlighting its unresolved contradictions:
first, failure to settle the status of the Indians as apostates;
and second, failure to provide legal safeguards against

the invalidation of accusations by the testimony of enemies. In the end, what function could the idolatry trials serve if they had merely become the instrument of internecine Indian struggles?

II

If the Extirpation failed to destroy the native religious system, it was because it was unable to substitute the essential role of the religious specialist, especially his vocation as curandero, attending to the physical health of his community, or as shaman, maintaining the essential bond between deities and humanity. Even by the late eighteenth century, the role of this specialist remained intact, indeed even grew stronger.

The religious specialists of the village of Yura, in the province of Arequipa, were tried by their village priest in 1788 precisely because they had so effectively maintained and propagated among their community the shamanic traditions of their ancestors. The principal defendant, Pascual Mamani (or Guamani), ensured the reproduction of his livestock by "speaking under the *llacolla*" with mountain spirits. Beneath a form of enclosure constructed out of llacollas, or typical square cloaks used by the Indians, he could enter an ecstatic state and communicate with a large bird that enveloped him in its wings. Afterward, he emerged with enormous energy and sped through the mountains at such a rate that nobody could catch him. Those who did lay hands on him were left motionless. Mamani's experience resembles those of shamans from the Amazon when they return from their spiritual "travels." The shamans of the Conibo-Shipibo Indians of the Ucayali region of eastern Peru take the hallucinogenic drug *ayahuasca*, prepared from the vine *Banisteriopsis*, to permit the flight of the soul from the body in the form of a bird. They are thus enabled to travel to kill a distant person or enact into reality the aggressive impulses of their

clients. Similarly, among the Jívaro of the Ecuadorean
Amazon, the bewitching shaman enlists the aid of supernatural *wakani* birds as spiritual helpers in his assault on
a victim.[21]

Mamani was not a solitary practitioner; on the contrary, he stood at the apex of a hierarchy of practitioners
who themselves were at the center of village life. These
specialists shared the classic experience of initiation by
means of the lightning bolt that had traversed their bodies while they had been in attendance to Mamani at the
llacolla. Some neophytes were not allowed inside the llacolla on account of their inferior status; nor were they all
able to understand the mountain spirits when they addressed Mamani in Quechua. These rankings testify to
the preservation of a well-developed shamanic tradition.
Furthermore, Mamani revealed that participation in native rites was not restricted to these specialists but extended to the majority of the Indians living on the *es-
tancia* (outlying estate) of Cañagua. It is not implausible
that such large numbers should have been involved in
shamanic practices. In various modern tribal societies of
the Amazon, the widespread consumption of drinks prepared from hallucinogenic drugs permits a very considerable number of members of society to participate in the
shamanic trance experience.[22]

The bond between the shamans and their spirits had
survived persecution with renewed vigor. Although Mamani had previously been tried and imprisoned for native rites, he had been fortified in his resistance by the
spirits themselves. Vowing, while incarcerated, to burn
all the instruments of his practices, he had been dissuaded by the voice of the mountains threatening him
with the death of his llamas and his own violent death if
he forsook his protectors and obeyed the "inquisitors." It
is certain that the trial of 1788 was equally ineffective in
suppressing the practice of native rites, since the same

village of Yura was subjected to idolatry investigations more than a generation later, in 1821, which exposed the continued function of a shamanic sect communicating with the mountains under the llacolla. One of the accused was even called Pascual Mamani. Even if he was not the Mamani of 1788 (which is not impossible), the repetition of the name suggests the continuity of the shamanic tradition.[23]

Mamani's strength derived not only from the spiritual assistance of native deities but also from the political power he wielded as alcalde of Los Altos de Yura. Several of his assistants also held important positions within the village power structure. His brother, Andrés Mamani, was also an alcalde of Yura, and Miguel Quispe was formerly the alcalde of Cañagua. Mamani's combination in his own person of both religious and political authority converted him into a significant threat to some of his colleagues on the cabildo. It was the alcalde of Yura, José Zegarra, who denounced him to the priest Juan de Urizar in 1788 and who physically took him to prison. The earlier accusation, for which he had spent a month in prison before being released with nothing more than a minor reprimand, had also emanated from his enemies on the town council. To avenge himself and to deter further denunciations, Mamani had prevailed on the mountain spirits to punish those responsible for his incarceration. Within a short time all of them, including the principal witness and member of the cabildo, Isidro de la Cruz, his son, Martín de la Cruz, and another Indian who had been alcalde at the time of Mamani's arrest, had died inexplicably. The fate of these witnesses was a fearful tribute to Mamani's powers, but it was insufficient to prevent the subsequent denunciation of 1788. His enemies were determined to persevere until they secured his removal from a position of authority. Indeed, the main consequence of the later trial was to deprive Mamani of his post of alcalde of Los Altos de Yura and to replace him with another candidate. The rivalries within the cabildo had provoked the repeated accusations of idolatry.[24]

The political and religious authority wielded by Mamani exceeded even that of the kuraka of Yura, Diego Quespi. Indeed, by 1788 the power of the kuraka seems to have diminished considerably. In the light of the fate of earlier kurakas, Quespi's extremely ambiguous position in relation to the practice of native rites might easily have made him a conspicuous victim of an idolatry accusation. On the one hand, Quespi was among the first to bring evidence of Mamani's practices to the attention of the priest. On the other, one witness claimed that Quespi had entered the llacolla in the company of Mamani. But if this was true, it is curious that Quespi was not named by Mamani as one of his companions. Even his denunciation of Mamani to the priest failed to provoke any counteraccusation against him. Since the evidence that Quespi advanced against Mamani proved insufficient, in the opinion of the priest, to uphold an accusation of idolatry, it is likely that the kuraka sought to appear cooperative while, at the same time, depriving the investigation of convincing proof. Quespi, like Julcarilpo and others before him, was playing the traditional double game. But unlike his predecessors, and despite testimony that incriminated him, Quespi was never himself accused of idolatry.

If Urizar failed to accuse Quespi, it was because the kuraka no longer presented the greatest threat to his authority. The native lord was unable, for example, to prevent the imprisonment of a large number of the native dignitaries of Yura and offered no resistance to the stripping of Mamani's office. Urizar was aware that the strength of the nativist movement lay not in the protection of the kuraka but in their grasp over the cabildo. Millones has argued that the alcalde de los naturales had replaced the kuraka at the nexus of village power by the beginning of the nineteenth century. Indeed, the rise of the alcalde was proportional to the decline of the kuraka, whose functions, including collection of tribute, he had assumed in the aftermath of the Tupac Amaru revolt of 1780. Like the kuraka before him, the alcalde found himself in the contradictory position of community leader and functionary of the Spanish government. Indeed, his need to legitimize his authority in the eyes of the community was even greater since it depended even more on forces external to the community. Patronage of the huacas remained the most comprehensible means of reinforcement of authority. Thus, as late as 1821, members of the cabildo were still sponsoring the practice of native rites.[25]

However, insofar as the balance of power had shifted away from the kuraka to the alcalde, it had also tilted in favor of the priest. As the case of Urizar illustrates, the decline of a powerful protector of native rites left the priest greater freedom of action. As a result, it is possible that the recourse to idolatry accusations was becoming increasingly unnecessary. Only when the protection afforded by members of the power structure was a strong threat to the priest's authority (if, for example, a religious specialist like Mamani was integrated into that structure) would the priest need to resort to idolatry accusations as a means of asserting his control.[26]

The sharply decreasing occurrence of idolatry trials derived not only from shifts in the balance of power within native communities but also from changes in the classification system applied by the ecclesiastical authorities to the practice of indigenous rites. These changes came very late. The trial of 1788 may be contrasted with its predecessors primarily on account of the clear distinction between the offenses of idolatry and superstition. Ever since its beginnings, the Extirpation had been characterized by a failure to separate these two sins. As has been demonstrated above, even as late as the third decade of the eigh-

teenth century, practitioners of native rites were accused
of the indistinguishable offenses of idolatry and superstition, with no attempt to establish degrees of seriousness.
Celís's edicts considered the act of blowing one's eyelashes into the wind to be as idolatrous as the adoration
of huacas as both shared the *intent* to worship. Even in
1788 Mamani was accused of classic idolatry. But, at the
same time, a dichotomy emerged between idolatry and
superstition. Whereas some of his offenses merited the
label idolatry, his other less serious offenses were categorized as superstition. The beginnings of this phenomenon may be observed half a century before. A rudimentary distinction was drawn between the two offenses in
the trial against Domingo García in 1741. Whereas the act
of making offerings and giving worship to stones on his
knees was classified as idolatry, the spreading of llama
blood on the floor of a church was classified as superstition.[27] However, in this case, there was no discussion of
the relative seriousness or significance of the two offenses. It was only in the case of 1788 against Mamani
that the distinction became crucial in the classification of
native religious practices and in the significance attributed to their continued observance.

By clearly distinguishing between idolatry and superstition, for which he offered unusually precise definitions,
Urizar gave expression to a significant change in the classification of native religious practices, sharply at variance
with his seventeenth- and even early eighteenth-century
predecessors. Mamani's communication with the mountain spirits under the llacolla constituted idolatry because
his intent to harm his enemies through maleficio could
only be achieved by means of an explicit pact with the
Devil. But his use of conopas to protect his livestock was
distinguished as the lesser offense of "false observances,"
which only constituted superstition. These activities
would have been condemned as idolatrous by earlier in-

vestigators. Mamani's practices resembled those so
strongly censured by Celís's edicts. So, for example, he
rubbed the bodies of llamas that were about to give birth
with small stone conopas in the shape of these beasts and
strew the ground on which they trod with coca and
chicha to secure the successful delivery of the newborn
kid. He preserved the llamas from attack by ferocious animals by keeping a stone puma that was lame in one leg,
and he guarded against water shortage by casting his
conopas into the water where the animals used to drink.
But whereas Celís and his predecessors would have
damned these practices as pagan idolatries, Urizar's conclusion was very different. Since there was no evidence
of an explicit pact with the Devil, Mamani was guilty
only of false observances. While acknowledging that
false observances were normally considered to involve
an implicit pact, Urizar insisted that *in the case of the Indians* they could be attributed to "invincible ignorance" because of their lack of instruction and correction. These offenses were classified as superstitions, defined by Urizar
as "residual customs," preserved since time immemorial.
Thus whereas idolatry remained assimilated to devil
worship, superstition was clearly demarcated from it
through the absence of an explicit pact with the Devil. Although the language of the diabolical pact was preserved, the activities to which it was applied were more
narrowly circumscribed.[28]

This departure from the traditional classifications of
the Extirpation was carried a step farther when the hearings were transferred to Arequipa. The protector de los
naturales, Agustín de Valverde, exploited the distinction
between idolatry and superstition to exclude the former
entirely as a charge against his clients.

Under the name of superstition are included many offenses
and it is not sufficient to call them all idolatry, because even
idolatry admits of its divisions and it should first be deter-

mined if it is internal or external, with regard to intention or to effect, or finally if it is feigned. From the accusation it is not clear which type of idolatry is attributed to the Indians and the autos do not elaborate on the state of mind [*animo*] or belief in which these ignorant people committed their nonsensical deeds.[29]

Thus not only were the accused guilty of superstition rather than idolatry but even this charge was open to dispute because the prosecution was unable to prove the state of mind in which they had committed the offense. To constitute genuine superstition, belief and knowledge must be demonstrated; in their absence, superstition became little more than venial sin, which merited guidance rather than punishment. The very fact that the accused were, after all, Indians was sufficient to prove that their deeds arose more from ignorance, stupidity, and accident than from malice or clear intention. When committed by Indians, superstition could not be considered a serious offense. It originated in ignorance that should be reduced by repeated instruction, preaching, and good example.

By failing to address the central issue of the distinction between idolatry and superstition, the promotor implicitly acknowledged the merits of the protector's argument. Despite an early reference to the great inclination of the Indians toward "idolatry," he accused Mamani of relapse into "superstition." At the same time, he conceded that the offense might not have been committed with full intention and due deliberation, on account of his natural coarseness and savagery. He concluded that he could be excused from the ordinary penalties. Instead, all the instruments of his "superstitions" should be publicly burned in the main square and his punishment restricted to a whipping and instruction in the faith under the supervision of his priest. Since the evidence against the other Indians accused was inconclusive, he recommended that they should be absolved. The definitive sentence followed these recommendations, and the punishment proposed was decreed.[30]

The arguments of the protector and the promotor are remarkable, first, for their similarity to each other and, second, for their divergence both from the conclusions of Urizar and from the ideology of the Extirpation. Urizar had differed from his predecessors by distinguishing superstition from idolatry; the promotor and the protector went further by substituting the charge of superstition for that of idolatry entirely. The prosecution abandoned the framework of both idolatry and the diabolical pact and accepted what had been rejected many times before, the defense's apology for the accused on the grounds of ignorance. Whereas the Extirpation had perceived the Indians as willful and scheming apostates, by 1788 they were no longer considered responsible for their deeds. Their action might be reprehensible but their intention was not wicked; they were poor, brutish peasants whose mere status as Indians was sufficient explanation for their religious deviance.

The ideology of the Extirpation that had derived from the works of Acosta and Arriaga no longer determined the understanding of the significance of native religious rites. The arguments advanced by the counsel in the trial of Mamani resemble instead the perception of indigenous practices embodied in the *Itinerario para párrochos de indios* (1668) of the seventeenth-century bishop of Quito, Alonso de la Peña Montenegro (1653–87). This work ran to five editions in the first century of its publication and exerted an important influence in Peru. Although there is no explicit evidence that either the promotor or the protector had read the work, their theological arguments resemble those of de la Peña. Returning, to some extent, to Thomist roots, and in contrast to Acosta and Arriaga, de la Peña recognized a clear distinction between idolatry and superstition, by classifying the former as a subcate-

gory of the latter. Whereas superstition was defined as
false religion, idolatry (worship rendered to creature instead of creator) was classified as one of its three subdivisions, alongside magic and maleficio. Since idolatry was
explicitly defined as a branch of superstition, not all superstition could constitute idolatry.[31]

Idolatry itself was subdivided into three types. The
first type, which de la Peña called "perfect, consummate,
and complete idolatry," exhibited three characteristics:
error in understanding, intent to give worship, and the
act of adoration itself. But this was neither the only nor
the most common kind among the Indians of Peru. The
second type possessed two of the above properties but
lacked error in understanding. This type was typical of
the Indians who had been baptized, since, despite their
awareness that the huacas were not divine, they still offered them sacrifices to honor and propitiate them. The
third type lacked both error of understanding and the intent to give worship. The sin lay only in exterior actions
of worship that were little more than mimicry of what the
other Indians did or what the elders had taught. Although this was still a mortal sin, it was not formal idolatry or apostasy, "but only material in appearance." It
was into this third category, de la Peña believed, that the
majority of Indians in Peru fell.

Thus many practices condemned by Celís's edicts as
idolatrous—including hair-cutting ceremonies, leaving
stones on mountain summits as a relief from fatigue,
abandoning clothes or herbs used to cure the sick in the
belief that passersby would take away the illness, washing
in rivers to cleanse oneself of sin, throwing maize or chicha onto the fire to placate its anger, howling at eclipses—
were classified by de la Peña as false observances, a mere
subcategory of superstition. If an express pact with the
Devil was always a mortal sin, those who performed superstitious acts without attributing them any efficacy

would only be guilty of venial sin. Thus an offender should always be asked about the state of mind in which he committed an act. The absence of genuine intent to worship signified only the existence of an implicit pact with the Devil, which could be attributed to invincible ignorance.

De la Peña's tolerance of most Indian religious practices originated in a pessimistic assessment of Indian character. He considered most of the Indians to be only "material idolaters" since their mental powers were so small that they did not understand what their sacrifices signified. Their diminished mental capacity conferred on them less free will than other men. Therefore, they sinned with imperfect knowledge and should be treated with mercy. It was true that ignorance did not excuse the sin of idolatry, since, with natural reason alone, it was possible to apprehend the existence of the One True God. After all, a man had only to use his own eyes to appreciate that stones and mountains were not alive, and to pretend to be blind in such an obvious matter was crass and culpable ignorance. However, the case of the Indians was an exception to the judgment of the learned fathers, such as Augustine, on account of their *corta capacidad*, or imperfect mental capacity. For although God could be perceived by natural light alone, in reality, as Aquinas observed, such perception required the ability to philosophize, which the Indians, through poor instruction and education, demonstrably lacked.

De la Peña concluded that a distinction should be drawn, on the one hand, between those Indians who had been baptized and always lived among Christians under the instruction of a priest and, on the other, those baptized in their infancy but who had grown up and lived in the mountains without teaching. These latter might be credited with "blameless ignorance" in that the idolatry they committed was motivated by the example of their forefathers. Whereas a distinction between baptized and nonbaptized Indians had been traditional, based on questions of natural law and the limited spiritual jurisdiction of temporal princes, de la Peña was advocating an original and radical differentiation *among* baptized Indians.

This resolved the issue that had always divided the Extirpation and its opponents: could baptized but poorly instructed Indians be called idolaters and heretics? De la Peña was certain that they could not. Mamani and his colleagues were excellent examples of Indians who had been baptized but had grown up without constant exposure to Christian teachings. Since idolatry investigations had always taken place in distant and inaccessible locations, its victims were by definition likely to fall into this category. Thus resolution of the status of Indians in this category was essential for interpreting the significance of "persisting" native rites. By 1788, the investigators of native religious practices, sharing de la Peña's understanding of the Indian character, had adopted the bishop's distinction and had finally opted to tolerate them.

It is important to recognize that this new tolerance did not characterize idolatry investigations until the second half of the eighteenth century. De la Peña's categories did not determine the ideology and practices of extirpation at the time that he wrote. Taking de la Peña's work as representative of the mid-seventeenth century, Kubler suggested that, *after 1650,* many indigenous rites, which had previously been the object of campaigns of extirpation, were redefined as relatively inoffensive superstitions.[32] But, first, it is clear that there was no *redefinition* of idolatry and superstition since both de la Peña and Mamani's judges had reverted to the established Thomist categories. Therefore, it would be more correct to speak of a *reclassification* of native practices within these preexisting categories, whereby the assimilation of idolatry and superstition, which had been characteristic of the ideology of the Extirpation, was rejected.[33]

Second, Kubler was incorrect to attribute this change to the mid-seventeenth century; the Church was clearly *not* satisfied by the 1660s that idolatry no longer existed in Peru. The writings of de la Peña were not necessarily representative of the Church as a whole; ecclesiastical opinions were by no means monolithic. In 1706, Diego Ladrón de Guevara, the bishop of Quito (1704–18), was clearly at odds with de la Peña when he informed the king that idolatry was so firmly rooted among the Indians of the province that Spaniards and "other people" had become contaminated with "the vice of superstition and magic."[34] Even as late as the second half of the eighteenth century, in the province of Cajamarca, there were at least three trials for superstition, whose procedures were based on the *Instructions* of Lobo Guerrero and Villagómez. The investigating priest bore the title and functions of Visitor-General of Idolatry, to which was also added the title Commissary of the Holy Tribunal of the Inquisition.[35]

The debate over the existence and significance of native religious practices continued during the first half of the eighteenth century, and hence it would be a mistake to conclude that by the mid-seventeenth century indigenous religious practices had become "acceptable" or that the ecclesiastical authorities were no longer interested in their prosecution. Although de la Peña reverted to Thomist classifications as early as the 1660s, the practice of idolatry trials was not altered until the late eighteenth century; only by the end of that century were the authorities truly satisfied that "idolatry" no longer existed.

CONCLUSION

Indian "superstitions."

I

THE CHALLENGE THAT CONFRONTED THE EXTIRPATORS OF indigenous religion in colonial Peru was nothing less than the wholesale uprooting of the old Andean sacred universe and its replacement by a new Christian one, to which native Andeans could transfer their spiritual loyalties. The principal imperative in this struggle was the denial of the efficacy of the opposing religion and its consignment to impotence in the eyes of its followers. By assimilating native religious leaders to the category of hechicero, the colonizers sought to devalue their status by means of the weapons of skepticism and incredulity. Traditional religion would be subverted by delegitimizing its defenders and spurning its authority.

The devaluation of the native shaman is not contradicted by the equation of indigenous religion with devil worship. It is true that the origins of religious deviance were traced to diabolical intervention and that indigenous deities were identified with Satan. Some observers have concluded from this fact that by associating native deities with the mighty figure of the Devil, Spaniards unwittingly invested native religion with supernatural power and furnished a natural ally for Andeans in their struggle against the alien Christian god. Michael T. Taussig argued that black slaves on the Colombian Pacific coast in the sixteenth and seventeenth centuries appropriated their enemy's enemy and took to devil worship. By acknowledging fear of the slaves' spiritual powers, the credulous Spanish inadvertently delivered a powerful instrument to their bondsmen.[1] Similarly, according to Taussig, "the credulous Spaniards were fearful, not scornful, of Indian deities"; the remorseless extirpation of idolatry actually bestowed power on its victims and credited native deities with invincibility. "Insofar as the Indians assimilated Christianity they also assimilated the Devil, who ratified the nature spirits whom they persistently worshiped as their 'owners' and as their source of identity."[2]

The problem with this interpretation is that far from being credulous, educated Spanish clerics, particularly extirpators of native religion, manifested great skepticism regarding the claims of individual Andeans to enjoy privileged communications with deities. If, in abstract theological terms, Spaniards sought a metaphysical explanation for the existence of religious deviance by reference to a Manichaean vision of the universe in which fallen angels fought for souls in perpetual rebellion against the True God, they did not, in general, deduce from this that individual Indians were consorting with the Devil in their everyday lives. Certainly there was considerable ambiguity concerning a genuine diabolical presence in native religious ceremonies. But even in the rare instances in which satanic intervention was implicitly accepted, the role of the Devil lay not in conferring power on his followers but, on the contrary, in deceiving his adepts and making them believe in acts that were false and imaginary.[3] More frequently, Spaniards rejected the thesis of demonic intervention, accusing native religious leaders of simple fraud. Therefore, there is no reason to believe that the Extirpation empowered Indians by associating native religion with devil worship. Furthermore, there is no evidence in the idolatry trials that individual defendants either interiorized the Christian understanding of the Devil or perceived him as a potential ally against the Christian religion.

It is also misleading to argue, as some have, that Spaniards interpreted native religion in the light of the European witch craze and identified native religious practitioners with European witches. Irene Silverblatt has argued that contemporary demonological theories and, in particular, the example of the witch hunt determined how Spaniards perceived native Andean religious specialists: "The European experience [of witch hunts] profoundly influenced its Andean counterpart: the ideology of the demon hunters in Europe shaped the ideology of the extirpators in the New World";[4] "the Spanish conquest of Peru thus transported the Devil, and his ally, the witch, to the Andes."[5] She has also written, "Spanish clerics unearthed witchcraft in Peru, claiming that the most dangerous of all witches were poor, native women. No doubt Spanish priests and administrators were predisposed to finding poor women witches, for they came to Peru fresh from the European witch hunts which damned women (particularly the indigent) for heresy and susceptibility to diabolic influence. This stereotype, transported to the colonies, molded the Andean witch hunts—the seventeenth-century campaigns to extirpate idolatry."[6] Taussig also implicitly made the connection when he wrote, "Along with their lust for gold and silver, the Spaniards brought to the New World their fear of the Devil—the Prince of Darkness, the active principle of all evil, cruelty, filthiness, and folly, whose triumph was unleashed in the witch craze of seventeenth-century Europe."[7]

But, as has been demonstrated, it is not true that the demonology of Jakob Sprenger and Heinrich Kramer, the authors of the *Malleus maleficarum*, was transposed to New World native religious practitioners. Although the cases of Juana Icha and Inés Carva do exhibit some characteristics typical of European beliefs about witches (including sexual contact with the Devil), they were the exception that proves the rule. Silverblatt's argument is misleading because it fails to recognize that the paradigm was not the brujo, or classic witch, but the hechicero; this was a paradigm that did not empower the victim but disempowered him (or her). The appropriate comparison for the treatment of the Andean practitioner is not the witch hunt but the Spanish Inquisition's treatment of the hechicero, since the skepticism and incredulity with which inquisitors treated this figure were transferred to the native religious specialist.

It is also questionable whether Spaniards expected native religious specialists to be women. It is certainly true that hechicería was understood to be a typically female activity. In the second half of the seventeenth century, the Inquisition in Lima prosecuted many more females than males for the offense. Only 11 out of 120 men who appeared before the Tribunal were accused of hechicería, whereas 49 out of 64 women were charged with the offense.[8] But it is open to doubt whether this cultural prejudice was transposed to native religious leaders. In fact, Spaniards do not seem to have been blinded to the fact that men and women participated equally as leaders of Andean religion. Arriaga's handbook of extirpation did

not single women out as especially susceptible to demonic temptation. When describing the different sorts of
religious specialists, the extirpator made it clear that men
and women shared the office and that, in his view, men
occupied the principal role: "All these offices and min-
istries are common to men and women, even that of confession, since there are also important female confessors.
But it is most common for men to hold the principal offices. . . . [T]he less important tasks, such as divination
and making chicha, are performed by women."[9] Even
those whom he described as "true witches" (as opposed
to hechiceros)—the *cauchus*—were represented as male,
not female.[10] Silverblatt has convincingly argued that
Spanish chroniclers (including Arriaga here) tended to
underestimate women's participation in religious rites,
attributing to them only a minor role as assistants when,
in fact, they also served as the principal officiants. But it
was precisely this prejudice about gender roles that prevented Spaniards from characterizing women as the principal offenders. Despite his reference to Eurocentric categories, Arriaga was sufficiently conscious of the native
reality to appreciate that in Peru religious specialists were
of both sexes.

There is no evidence to support Silverblatt's contention
that women were singled out as victims of campaigns of
extirpation. Indeed, in the idolatry trials preserved in the
Archivo Arzobispal de Lima (AAL), men and women appear as victims in about equal proportions, with, if anything, a slight predominance of males. Two scholars have
observed that the preservation of traditional religion could
not be considered a specifically feminine act of resistance
since "a similar number—if not more—men were tried
for idolatry."[11] This is certainly the impression with which
one is left after close exposure to the sources held in the
AAL. Since a rigorous breakdown of these idolatry trials
according to the gender of the victims has not been con-

ducted, at the very least it must be concluded that the argument for clear gender differentiation remains unproven.

The detailed evidence left by the extirpator Rodrigo Hernández Príncipe from his visitation to the village of Recuay (in the province of Huaylas) and its district in 1622 permits analysis according to gender of the religious specialists that he persecuted. Although he punished more women than men for native religious practices, the difference between the two sexes was not so great as to suggest a profound differentiation. As Silverblatt herself points out, the list of practitioners described by the extirpator includes both male and female ministers.[12] For example, the ayllu Hecos enjoyed the services of ten male ministers and twelve female ministers; the ayllu Híchoc, twelve male ministers and twenty female ministers; the ayllu Caquimarca, six male ministers and eleven female ministers; the ayllu Allauca, eight male and twelve female ministers; the ayllu Picos, eight male ministers and sixteen female ministers; and the Chaupis, ten male ministers and eleven female ministers.[13] Although there is a preponderance of women in all these examples, in some instances it is only by a small margin. It is surely insufficient evidence to argue that extirpators saw women as especially prone to diabolic temptations; indeed, on the contrary, it shows that this Visitor-General did not single women out for punishment on grounds of their gender. Both sexes were represented among the victims of extirpation.

Silverblatt insists that the supposed equation of native priests with witches determined not only how Spaniards sought to repress native religion but also how Andean religious leaders came to perceive themselves. According to her interpretation, gender differentiation was a key factor in the response of Andean religion to the experience of repression. The marginalization of women as "witches" by colonial society conferred on them a special role as representatives of Andean traditions and leaders of native ritual; thus women began to hold offices in indigenous religious organizations largely denied to them during the pre-Columbian period. Furthermore, because of the male bias of colonial economic, political, and religious institutions, Andean women tended to turn to those traditional practices that were interpreted by the colonial regime as diabolic, thus appropriating a weapon with which they could resist Spanish hegemony.[14]

There are many problems with this interpretation. For one thing, it is difficult to assess with any degree of certainty women's role in native religious rites in pre-Columbian times since our sources are precisely those Spanish male chroniclers whose patriarchal bias, as Silverblatt so rightly stresses, probably made them insensitive to the significance of the female role in the pre-Hispanic period. It is thus almost impossible to measure whether women's role in religious rites increased in the colonial period.

Although Silverblatt is right to restore women to equal status with men in the preservation of native religion in the seventeenth century—women were often the principal officiants in the worship of outlawed cults—there is no evidence in these documents that they became identified as the upholders of traditional Andean culture. The more mundane truth is that both men and women performed this role. As Millones has stressed, the need to legitimize authority by native standards drove many kurakas to continue their patronage of native rites, proving that men were not disqualified by participation in colonial power structures. The colonial system obliged men equally with women to take an important role.

If Spaniards did not seek witches, they cannot have unwittingly conferred power on Andean women by identifying them as such; nor is there any convincing evidence that Andean women appropriated the category of witch and exploited it to turn diabolical power against the Spaniards. Indeed, if the Spaniards possessed a bias on matters of gender, it was not to fear women's diabolic powers but, on the contrary, to belittle them. Silverblatt is not convincing when she writes, "While Spanish gender norms may have rendered women invisible, they also transformed them into witches. The Spanish provided native women with an ideology of rebellion."[15] Probably much closer to the truth is Ruth Behar's observation, "The inquisitors of Spain and Mexico viewed women's power as illegitimate in the sense that it was a delusion and therefore not really a form of power at all."[16] It was this interpretation of female "power" that was transposed by extirpators to Andean women. If Spanish gender norms made women "invisible," the field of sorcery was no exception. As Deborah A. Poole and Penelope Harvey have observed, that women acted as ritual specialists for their communities may have been simply an "involuntary effect" of "social invisibility." Female participation in local religious duties "cannot be considered, therefore, as a conscious decision to resist Spanish authority on gender lines."[17] Silverblatt probably exaggerates Andean women's awareness of the significance of their acts as a manifestation of collective cultural resistance.

In short, Spanish extirpators of native religion did not seek the Devil and Andean women did not seek to ally with him. Nor did Spaniards confer power on native religious practitioners by associating them with diabolism, precisely because they devalued their status and refused to acknowledge a real diabolical presence. If anything, Spaniards erred, not by attributing too much power to native religion, but by attributing too little to it.

II

Despite their intermittence, the campaigns of extirpation, may be considered a distinct movement, demonstrating consistency of objectives and methods from the early seventeenth century until well into the eighteenth century. Of course, the investigations of the eighteenth century never attained the ambitious scale of those of the early and mid-seventeenth century. The designation "campaign of extirpation," if justified in terms of consistency of ideology and intent, may be inappropriate in terms of results, on account of the limited geographic scope and the absence of numerous Visitors. There was only one short-lived campaign of extirpation in 1724–25 and only one Visitor-General, Pedro de Celís. But the stillbirth of this campaign derived more from a change of circumstances than a change of attitudes. The peculiar interaction of center and locality that had given rise to the earlier campaigns was rarely replicated by the eighteenth century.

The initiation of idolatry trials required a local priest whose authority was under such threat that only the resort to extraordinary powers could tip the balance in his favor. If the conflicts of local society threw up very few extirpators in the eighteenth century, this derived from changes in the relationship between native and colonial sources of authority (between the kuraka or cabildo and the priest). By the eighteenth century, the conditions that had encouraged priests or members of native society to advance legal charges of idolatry had changed. Above all, the decline in the role of the kuraka had led to a strengthening of the position of the priest.

At the same time, the circumstances at the center had also changed. Both Melchor Liñán de Cisneros and Diego Morcillo de Auñón took the charges of idolatry seriously enough to promote organized trials. But these trials did not necessarily take the form of campaigns of extirpation. It is possible that investigations conducted by overmighty local priests had become discredited as the most effective means of countering native religious deviance. The period between the 1690s and the 1720s was characterized by the assertion of more direct jurisdiction over idolatry investigations. Instead of delegating jurisdiction to local representatives, cases were increasingly summoned to Lima to be heard by the lawyers and judges directly responsible to the archbishopric. One principal consequence was to decrease the incentive for local priests to denounce alleged idolaters, since they would no longer be granted the powerful commission of Visitor-General. Thus added to the fact that these powers may have become increasingly unnecessary was the fact that they were increasingly unlikely to be granted. The balance between center and locality had shifted largely in favor of the former.

Another principal consequence of increased central control was the greater professionalization and formalization of the trials. This was most clearly reflected in the more significant role accorded to the defense. Whereas in the seventeenth century, the defense had been little more than a symbolic formality, often executed by a member of the Visitor's own entourage, by the 1720s the protection of Indian interests had been permanently entrusted to a professional representative. Since the hearings in Lima were presided over by lawyers rather than priests, greater weight was given to legal than to theological arguments. There was no speculation about the possible metaphysical role of the Devil in the accused's actions; instead, the emphasis lay exclusively on the rational assembling of empirical evidence. The priority of the defense was not to serve the Visitor but to construct the best case for his client. Thus the eighteenth-century trials were characterized by the elaboration of complicated and sophisticated legal arguments designed to secure the release of the accused. The effectiveness of this approach is revealed by the fact that many Indians fled from prison in their own villages and moved to Lima in the belief they would be tried more fairly there.[18]

The emphasis on empirical evidence and on legal formalities encouraged an increasingly explicit rejection of denunciations motivated purely by personal enmity. Whereas the most zealous Visitors of the seventeenth century, such as Sarmiento and Noboa, had been indifferent to the motives of witnesses as long as idolatry was uncovered, the authorities in Lima were increasingly unprepared to convict on testimony clearly rooted in malice. Unlike the Visitors of the seventeenth century, the archbishop's officials had no vested interest in proving the existence of idolatry to justify their enterprise and reap the rewards. The rejection of evidence inspired by personal enmity undermined the foundations of the idolatry trials, which were failing even to convict offenders, let alone reform them. As these trials were becoming increasingly ineffective in securing their purpose, it is not surprising that they were abandoned as a means of suppressing native religious practices. Idolatry trials disappeared not because their advocates had lost interest in idolatry but because they did not work.

Measured by the standard of its own objectives, it is doubtful whether the Extirpation can be called a success. It is impossible to determine the impact of the mass destruction of many thousands of sacred objects, since the total numbers of such objects existing in the viceroyalty are unknown and incalculable. In any case, the work of the Extirpation was qualitative as well as quantitative. Its objective was not simply the physical elimination of sacred objects but the prevention of acts of religious deviance. The failure of this goal is suggested by the high incidence of recidivists uncovered. A large number of defendants admitted that having already been punished by a previous Visitor, they had relapsed into the same offense. Some of the accused had even been tried on two or more occasions.[19]

Possibly even more significant than backsliding was

the insistence of many offenders that they had genuinely put their faith in the ceremonies and rites they had employed. Hernando Ticssi Mallqui confessed that despite punishment on an earlier visitation, he had returned to his native practices, "believing them to be true and the Christian faith to be a lie." His sincere conviction was representative of many native practitioners. If these defendants sought to avoid punishment, insistence on the efficacy of native rites was a strange strategy, since the Extirpation punished according to belief as well as practice. The defendants had nothing to gain and everything to lose by confessing their true beliefs. Their stubborn defense of their actions also flew in the face of the skepticism of their interrogators, who expected them to deny belief. It is clear that these defendants were not practicing meaningless vestiges of a dead religion but that their ceremonies were sustained by a living, genuine belief. Persecution had eliminated neither belief nor rite.[20]

Indeed, it seems, ironically, that idolatry trials could be counterproductive. The subjection of a native practitioner to persecution, far from putting an end to his activities, could, on the contrary, further enhance his reputation among his fellows as an effective mediator with the supernatural world. The very fact that he had challenged the Christian hegemony sufficiently to provoke the wrath of the Visitors may have convinced his potential clients that he was a force to be reckoned with. Thus the attempt to expose the specialist to the stigma of infamy could backfire. Furthermore, a religious specialist who became notorious after punishment in an idolatry trial became a ready target for further denunciations. The public fame he had acquired qualified him as the first suspect when maleficio was suspected on a subsequent occasion. He became a scapegoat for the community, a sacrificial victim of whose guilt subsequent Visitors would be convinced simply on the grounds of his appearance at a previous trial. Thus the idolatry trials tended to feed on themselves; rather than *eliminate*, they *created* a class of official religious deviants. Persecuting those they had already identified as deviants, they only increased the respect these individuals inspired in their communities.[21]

If the Extirpation failed to achieve its objectives it was partly because of its ideological inconsistencies, partly because of its institutional inadequacies, and partly because the task it set itself was simply beyond it. In terms of ideology, the Extirpation never resolved the fundamental contradictions that underlay it. Whereas, on the one hand, native religious specialists were labeled heretics and apostates, which should have demanded severe penalties, on the other, they were also designated hechiceros, who, by common consent, were not heretics but charlatans. This inconsistency subverted the association of idolatry with heresy and of native practitioners with both. And whereas the decision to profess Christianity was recognized to be a voluntary choice, the Extirpation used repression to force the Indians to be good Christians. Acosta had already warned about seizing idols by force. Arriaga and his colleagues did recognize that preaching and education were the key, yet they still advocated repression. The weakness of the Extirpation was that it never persuaded its opponents, who were well aware of its contradictions, of the validity of the instrument of repression. Lacking widespread support, the Extirpation relied on powerful patrons to breathe life into it. It remained a collection of individuals rather than a collection of institutions. Ideologically developed, it was institutionally retarded. It was always a fundamentally amateur organization.

This amateurishness was particularly noticeable in its failure to resolve certain points of practice that its model, the Inquisition, had satisfactorily settled. The most important weakness was the failure to exclude the testimony of known enemies. The Inquisition refused to consider such testimony because its source would be suspect, and, most important, it would undermine a conviction. The victim of the Holy Office was allowed to compile a list of his mortal enemies whose testimony would be disallowed. An inevitable corollary was that the accused could not know the names of his accusers since, by adding their names to his list, he could have disqualified any evidence against him. The Extirpation was not so punctilious. The early Visitors exploited enmities so as to secure denunciations of individuals. Convinced of the collective guilt of all Indians, they accepted evidence from any source. The accused in the idolatry trials was allowed to know the name of his or her denunciator and, indeed, was often physically confronted with the accuser, since, by experience, the extirpators found that through this method, they could obtain mutual denunciations of accuser and defendant. As a legal device, however, this procedure was inadequate. If Indians were allowed to know their accusers, they could simply claim that they were mortal enemies and that their testimony should be disallowed. Indeed, by definition, he who was willing to bring an idolatry charge was most certainly a mortal enemy!

The legal professionalization of the idolatry trials after the 1690s rendered such testimony invalid. But by this time the Indians had already learned that they could use these trials to attack their enemies. The failure to forbid this type of evidence earlier had allowed the Indians themselves to pervert the original purpose of the trials. Such a problem had not been entirely unanticipated. Those who had opposed the subjection of the Indians to the Inquisition had based their objections precisely on the fact that since the Indians were so tempted to lie and avenge themselves on their enemies, they would use the institution for these purposes and the Tribunal would be overwhelmed with denunciations based on hatred. This is exactly the fate that befell the Extirpation, a fate from which it could have been saved by more professional rules. Thus, in one sense, a fundamental weakness of the Extirpation was that it failed to model itself sufficiently on the Inquisition.[22]

However, the Extirpation was weakened not only because the model of the Inquisition was poorly applied but, more profoundly, because it was not entirely appropriate for the different task that lay before the repressor of Andean religion. The most fundamental difference between the Inquisition and the Extirpation was the identity of their victims. The Inquisition functioned mainly in towns and pursued individuals (Spaniards, mestizos, blacks, mulattos) who, by definition, were already substantially integrated into Spanish culture. As a percentage of the total population, their numbers were small and hence controllable. As a considerable minority, they comprised a "natural" class of religious deviants, whom it was relatively easy to isolate from the mainstream of their society. The small numbers of unrepentant heretics (those who denied, boasted of, or relapsed into their activities) could be liquidated to prevent the contamination of the bulk of good Christians; the contrite offenders (including hechiceros) could be rehabilitated. Bartolomé Bennassar has indicated that the power of the Inquisition lay less in the severity of its physical punishments than in the psychological weapons it could employ. The most potent elements of its armory were the use of secrecy, the threat of misery (the *threat* of deprivation of life and material goods was more effective than its *application*), and the memory of infamy.[23] The bestowal of infamy exploited the offender's fear of exclusion from society and became a powerful incentive to conform. At the same time, it clearly demarcated the deviant from the nondeviant and established social sanctions for crossing the divide. Because offenders had departed from the norms generally accepted by their fellows, they were reviled by the general population; although their fate might excite curiosity as a public spectacle, it aroused little sympathy. The public punishment of an offender acted as an exemplary warning to others not to stray from the religious practices prescribed by elite society. Thus the status of the heretic as outcast both encouraged him to return to the fold before it was too late and discouraged others from falling into religious deviance. The success of the Inquisition lay in the fact that its norms were recognized both by the elite that imposed conformity and by the society of which the offender formed a part.

These conditions were not replicated in the context within which the Peruvian Extirpation was forced to operate. First, the Extirpation differed from the Inquisition in terms of the sheer numbers of its potential victims. Almost the entire native population of the viceroyalty practiced some form of native religious ceremonies, and thus, paradoxically, every Indian was a religious "deviant." Thus, attempting to replicate the stark opposition of heretic and Christian community, the Extirpation was forced to drive a theoretical cleavage between the mass of the Indians and the figure of the hechicero. But this figure was a Spanish invention, and his abstract differentiation from the rest of his community did not reflect Andean realities. Whereas the heretic in peninsular Spain was a genuine outsider, reviled by society, the Andean religious specialist lay at the center of his community.[24] Subjection to an idolatry trial did not provoke the ostracism by the community that was characteristic of the treatment given to the victim of the Inquisition. Indeed, the victim's reputation might only be enhanced. Thus, by contrast with Spain, where the punishment of the heretic evoked rejection of the nonconformist, in Peru, the punishment of the native specialist evoked a sense of identification with the victim. Designation as an outcast by the dominant elite did not imply rejection by the offender's peers, since the victims of the Extirpation did not share the cultural norms of their persecutors.

The Extirpation differed fundamentally from the Inquisition in that it primarily persecuted individuals who inhabited rural communities and who, by definition, were not culturally integrated. Thus the persecution suffered by its victims (which in itself was never as harsh as that of the heretical victims of the Inquisition) was negated, or at least counterbalanced, by the spiritual sustenance provided by the solidarity of the community with the individual offender. Whereas the victim of the Inquisition suffered twice over, first from the rejection of the elite and second from that of his peers, the victim of the Extirpation suffered while being fortified by the moral support of his society. Indeed, it was better to break the norms of the alien elite than those of one's own community, for which the consequences, in terms of both human and divine wrath, were infinitely more terrifying. For these reasons, the technique of infamy, so effective for the Inquisition, was not a weapon that could be easily employed in the Andean context. The alternative cultural inheritance of the victims of the Extirpation conferred a communally accepted validity on their religious behavior that was not available to the victims of the Inquisition. The failure of the Extirpation lay, then, in the fact that the norms of the Spanish dominant elite and of Indian society did not coincide but contradicted one another. If the victims of the Extirpation chose to conform to the norms of their own society, it could hardly be otherwise when, in reality, it was the Spaniards who were the true religious "deviants" in Peru, not the Indians.

The strength of Andean religious norms not only neutralized the effectiveness of the weapon of infamy but also eliminated the weapon of secrecy. The Visitors abandoned inquisitorial scruples about naming accusers and allowing denunciations of enemies precisely because they were aware that native religious practices were not the preserve of an isolated few but were widespread among the indigenous population. In a sense, the Extirpation could not afford these scruples if it was to uncover the "true" extent of departure from Christian norms.[25] Moreover, failure to replicate the inquisitorial model also forced the Extirpation to rely exclusively on the third technique of the Holy Tribunal, that of the threat of misery. But although the threat of severe punishment, such as loss of worldly goods, banishment, or physical suffering (and even death), was effective in eliciting confessions, exclusive recourse to this method only laid bare more clearly the inconsistency at the heart of the movement: how could repression and the threat of force be reconciled with the voluntary renunciation of idols?

Finally, the Extirpation failed because it had simply set itself a task that, however well organized and consistent it had been, it could not have achieved. The "disenchantment" of the native religious world was an objective that was well beyond its competence. The physical destruction of huacas did not prevent their "posthumous" survival in purely spiritual form, or through association with those indestructible repositories of divine power that lay in natural phenomena. The Jesuit Francisco de Patiño highlighted the dilemma when he recounted how an Indian inquired of him, "Father, are you tired of taking our idols from us? Take away that mountain if you can, since that is the God that I worship."[26] Mountains have remained until this day receptacles of irresistible forces, whether benevolent or hostile, whether of Andean or Spanish origin. The sacred Andean landscape could not be obliterated.[27]

In any case, the last redoubt of the native religious system lay not in the purely physical world but in the imagination. It was the failure of the Extirpation to breach this fortress that ensured the failure of their enterprise. By conceptualizing Andean religion as a collection of "objects" that had to be destroyed, the extirpators left entire areas of the native religious experience unexplored and hence unassailed. Their lack of interest in the importance of dreams and their failure to explore the role of hallucinogenic drugs and the ecstatic experience precluded an effective assault on the mystery of the Andean world. It is worth remembering that the disenchantment of the native religious universe could not take place without the transfer of "mystery" to other spheres, in particular, the rites of the Church. The construction of a new sacred universe to compensate the fading of the old one was a task that was beyond the scope of the Extirpation.

If the native religious system refused to be reduced to a collection of mere "objects," it was because native specialists consciously chose to locate the battleground within the abstract sphere. This in itself is sufficient proof that the indigenous system was the intellectual equal of the Christian system, capable of resisting persecution. Salomon and Urioste have written of the resilience of local native religion, "If *huaca* priests had retained the loyalty of people officially bound to Christianity, it was in all likelihood because they had succeeded, under the adverse conditions of clandestinity and church hegemony, in presenting *huaca* religion as comparable in cogency with the church's teachings." Thus native religion was remobilized and reconceptualized as an "alternative faith" whose overall claims and dimensions could bear comparison with those of the imposed Church. Native priests made conscious efforts "to match Catholic priests in the breadth of their claims while at the same time maintaining distinctness from Catholicism."[28] Indeed, the failure of the Extirpation to destroy the Andean concept of the reality of the universe is most evident in the inability to exorcise the power of these native practitioners, a power that was only affirmed in the colonial period and that has survived until the present day.

Ironically, that the Indians continued to denounce curanderos to colonial authorities itself indicates that native
communities had not lost faith in their own religious specialists. The resort to denunciation signified fear and resentment of the native practitioner that could only result
from a strong belief in his powers. Many of the accusations against curanderos were made by their own clients,
who believed themselves or their relatives to be bewitched.
There may be compelling psychological reasons to explain this behavior. The consultation of a curandero in a
life or death matter created a relationship of fear and de-
pendency between the client and practitioner that could
only breed resentment. If the cure failed to work or, worse
still, resulted in the death of the patient, this resentment
could easily become a furious hatred. By attributing the
failure to malice, the client could justify his feeling of hostility. Bringing legal action both gave vent to these feelings in a retaliatory act and reasserted a sense of control.
Even today, practicing shamans of modern South America may be accused of witchcraft by resentful clients. In
his research among the Jívaro of the Ecuadorean Amazon, Michael J. Harner observed that a shaman who was
unable to identify the witch responsible for the death of a
patient was himself accused of responsibility by the family of the dead man. The power he exercised over the fate
of the patient gave rise to a strong current of suppressed
resentment that was released by his sudden impotence.
Accusations of idolatry against curanderos in the colonial period served an analogous purpose to accusations
of witchcraft against their modern counterparts. They
were acts of revenge.[29]

Although the curandero was the most frequent victim
of idolatry trials, he has survived into the present day
with the significance of his role renewed and reshaped.
This may derive from the peculiar ability of the curandero to adapt to cultural change. Claude Lévi-Strauss ar-

gued that shamanic healing rites actively sustain the myths
central to a society's culture. Through the interaction of
healer and patient, the structure of ideas immanent in a
culture is actively elaborated and brought to consciousness.[30] This is as true today as in former times. In the
large cities of modern Latin American society, far from
losing his significance, the curandero has acquired a new
vitality.[31] It is no surprise, then, that in the colonial period, he occupied a special place in the native response to
the intrusion of a new intolerant religion. It was precisely
the clash of two religious systems that may have revitalized his role by making him the agent of accommodation.

One student of modern Peruvian folk healers, Douglas
Sharon, has interpreted the curandero as "the nexus between the traditional and the modern." An individual
confronting a society in the process of cultural change
would be profoundly disturbed if forced suddenly to
abandon his ancestral principles and traditions. The function of the curandero is to diminish the force of this blow
and to provide a means of adaptation to it: "He provides
a beginning, an entrance, an opening in a smooth fashion
toward the society to which one is going to adapt." Thus
he functions as "a shock absorber" between both social
fields, the link of amalgamation, the connection between
what is behind and what is ahead. He is "a bridge in the
social field," whose primary purpose is to restore equilibrium.[32] As the technician of the sacred, he works to re-
constitute a disrupted holy universe. In the colonial period, his ability both to accept and to design and effect
changes in the categories of the sacred conferred a dynamic flexibility on the native religious system. The enduring vitality of the curandero, the mediator between
the human world and the supernatural realm, ensured
the survival of that alternate reality in the native imagination.

One function of the curandero as "bridge" was to allow

the native system to absorb Christian elements. Gruzin-ski has demonstrated that in colonial Mexico the inter-vention of curanderos enabled Christian entities to slide into the indigenous system of the interpretation of illness and, by adoption, become "native" powers in their own right, as effective as fire, sun, or water. It was by the same means that the concept of the Christian afterlife was in-troduced. Curanderos admitted that after death souls risked the fires of purgatory or Hell. The notions of the soul, sin, grace, eternity, and posthumous punishment progressively invaded the indigenous world, without the curandero losing his pivotal role; on the contrary, he strengthened his powers by absorbing supernatural com-ponents of the competing system. The syncretism of In-dian and Christian religious forms through the agency of the curandero was functional and highly adaptive.[33]

However, the native system did not capitulate to Chris-tianity. Although Christian symbolism is woven into the entire fabric of the contemporary shaman's mesa, con-temporary native beliefs appear to be rooted in an archaic pre-Columbian substratum.[34] As Taussig has stressed, if the Spanish conquest stripped indigenous religion of its formal institutional coverings, it by no means destroyed its basis in thought. Its numinous force passed "under-ground" into the realm of healing magic. "It befalls con-temporary folk healers and shamans to sustain this sys-tem of thought, linked to the precolonial past as much as it is mixed with the religion of the conquerors.... [U]nder-lying the accretion of added elements and transforma-tions, something essential in the precolonial structure of ideas continues, not as a mere survival or relic from an ir-retrievable past, but as an active force mediating his-tory."[35] Thus modern recourse to healers is not a survival of "primitive instincts" but represents the expression of an ancient belief that interpersonal tensions have mater-ial effects. In this sense, Peruvian folk healers manipulate

a coherent system of symbolic communication. The shamanism of modern healers is "new foliage on a very old
tree."[36]

The process of adaptation and containment undertaken
by native religious specialists was slow and painful. In
the beginning, it was by no means coherent. Arriaga was
aware of this when he highlighted two contradictory yet
coexistent responses of native religion to the threats and
persecutions of Christianity. The first asserted the radical
separation between the world of the Spaniards and the
world of the Indians; the second affirmed the compati-
bility of Christian and indigenous rites (for example,
using the same material to make the mantle of the Virgin
and a shirt for the huaca). These two responses coexisted
from very early after the conquest and nestled uneasily
against each other until a new native synthesis was
achieved.[37]

The first response was most clearly manifested in the
Taki Onqoy movement, which advocated the "unlearn-
ing" of ties to colonial society and the vindication of *exclusively* Andean loyalties, relationships, and values. Of
course, in practice, even Taki Onqoy exhibited acculturation to Christianity and, by making borrowings from it,
implicitly acknowledged the alien religion's supernatural
power. But this power was understood to be effective
solely for Spaniards; only the Andean system could sustain the existence of the Indians. Although Taki Onqoy
was suppressed, the insistence on exclusivity remained
in the consciousness of many religious practitioners. Since
tolerance of Christianity would have been more characteristic of a tradition that allowed the incorporation of
new deities into its firmament, this amounted to a cataclysmic transformation in the Andean tradition.[38]

The second response, which matured gradually, can be
seen in the achievement of Juan Vásques, who accomplished the articulation of the native system to the Chris-

tian system by means of the subordination of one religion to the other. Individuals such as Juana Icha and Fernando Carvachin had clearly perceived the antagonism between the clashing cultures, and their spiritual crisis—or state of nepantlism—derived from their inability to find a compromise and reinterpret one religion in terms of the other. Theirs was an experience of painful incongruity: their universe had become destructured and atomized, without a corresponding restructuration. Vásques's response represented a more sophisticated, restructured, holistic approach. The holy became whole once again.[39]

The evidence of the idolatry trials reveals a process of synthesis within the native tradition that paralleled that within the Christian tradition. It is possible that the Catholic synthesis had taken its crystallized form among acculturated Indians by the late seventeenth century. The idolatry trials cannot demonstrate the truth of this hypothesis because they only reflect the most marginalized sections of society where, by definition, this synthesis had either taken hold incompletely or not at all. The participants in these trials were deficient in their understanding of the basic tenets of Christianity: only one God who was the Creator of all things; the interrelationship of the three persons of the Trinity; the redemptive mission of Christ; the significance of the sacraments of baptism and confession; the content of the Ten Commandments or the four basic prayers (Pater noster, Credo, Ave María, and Salve Regina). Even if Marzal is right that by the middle of the seventeenth century the majority of the native inhabitants of Peru were aware of these tenets, it was not true of the majority of the victims of the Extirpation. Millones is probably correct to suggest that the new religious universe took its modern form toward the end of the colonial period.

The documentation of the idolatry trials is inappropriate as a basis for such conclusions because it is impossi-

ble to determine how representative it is.[40] These documents do reveal, however, the transformations that the
native system underwent in the process of forming a new
synthesis. Marzal is right to point out that it is impossible
to chart with exactitude the evolution of individual beliefs and rites of Andean popular religion.[41] But it is clear
that whereas gradually the worship of local huacas and
mallquis disappeared, the worship of Pachamama and
the apus was conserved. In present Andean society, the
apu remains the personification of the landscape, the
tutelary deity intervening directly in the material world
and requiring propitiation through regular, formal offerings. A large part of the South Andean region (from
Huancavelica to Puno) is characterized by offerings to
the earth and livestock (*pago a la tierra* and *tinka al ganado*),
and the Aymará region celebrates a thanksgiving rite for
the harvest (*mamatan urupa*). The apu remains typically
Andean in its ambivalent nature: it can be cruel and
capricious, yet its protection is critical to the livelihood of
the peasant. It remains the *runa micheq*, the "shepherd of
men."[42]

These modern beliefs about Pachamama and the apus
have not remained static, any more than the beliefs of the
colonial period. Although the apu is understood to be a
generic primordial forebear, it no longer functions as the
paqarina, or mythical place of origin of a specific kin
group. Similarly, although the term "huaca" has survived, its significance has changed considerably. In Kuyo
Grande, huacas are hills and rocks of strange shape where
men rarely or never go, places inhabited by malevolent
beings who make people or animals disappear.[43] In effect, the significance of the term has changed from "object
of reverence" to "place of danger or malevolent power," a
dramatic narrowing of meaning. The ambivalence of the
huaca, its most typical Andean characteristic, has been
lost in that it has shed its protective and benevolent func-

tions; it is now located squarely in "the evil sphere," its power marginalized and confined to isolated places, far from the center of the life of the community. As Michael J. Sallnow has shown, the numinous force of the huacas has largely passed into the cult of the saints, the new honorary patrons of the Andean community, whose rites are frequently associated with eternally resonant sacred loci within the Andean landscape. The numinous force has forsaken the huaca for other abodes.[44]

The worship of mallquis disappeared because Spaniards were effective in locating their resting places and consigning them to oblivion. Although mallquis were successfully concealed well into the second half of the seventeenth century and were even preserved "posthumously" by symbolic association with stone huacas or with the fast-flowing rivers into which their charred remains had been hurled, ultimately their numinous significance ebbed until even the last faint echoes were silenced.[45] Thus the worship of mallquis does not form part of the modern Andean native religious complex. Furthermore, although the cult of the dead is still an important part of present-day religious observances, it is qualitatively different from the pre-Hispanic and colonial veneration of mallquis. In contemporary Andean communities, ancestors are held in reverence and are believed to possess a direct influence over the material well-being of their descendants in this world. The souls of the dead maintain a bond with the living, afford protection, and act as intermediaries with God, and their propitiation is still the collective responsibility of the entire community, performed by means of communal offerings and celebrations. The ceremonies enacted on the Christian feast days of All Saints and All Souls date back to the pre-Hispanic celebration of Pariacaca when the dead were sent to their repose in the next life. But it is significant that today veneration is limited to this one feast rather than occurring regularly during the year. Furthermore, since the Christian custom of burial under the earth, in contrast with colonial times, is universally accepted, the cult of the dead is confined to offerings at gravesides and in the home rather than to the actual physical remains of the deceased. Finally, it is restricted to immediate rather than distant forebears, who are almost exclusively held in fear, even revulsion. Those mummified remains of mythical ancestors, called *machu tullu*, that are found in pre-Inca stone burial chambers, or *chullpas*, in dominant places all over the Bolivian Altiplano are objects inspiring repugnance and are to be avoided lest they cause sickness or death. Modern rites for the recently departed serve not only to see the dead on their way but also to protect the living from them; as a result of evangelization, their spirits are implicitly associated with devils. Indeed, little in attitudes toward the dead today suggests a continuation of the "worship" of the colonial period; in fact, the dead are considered fundamentally antithetical to the living.[46]

The displacement of huacas and mallquis has been effected because Christianity offered a substitute that represented a more efficacious source of supernatural power. In contrast, the worship of apus and Pachamama has been maintained because the Christian religion failed to furnish an alternative ritual support for the agricultural and stock-breeding activity of the peasants, or an effective medical resource for the preservation of the health and well-being of both the individual and the community. These essential areas of native life remained a half-moon outside the overlapping jurisdictions of the two religious systems. The ever-reducing limits of the competence of the native system were, to a large extent, set by the ability of the alien system to adapt itself to the new environment and respond to the needs and realities of the native world. Because Christianity was highly adaptive, it succeeded in conquering the public sphere, but, in the private sphere, the native system revalidated itself. Devotion to this sphere, largely unassailed by Christianity, became the raison d'etre of the new native religious synthesis. The two religious systems have remained discrete but mutually interactive parts of a greater whole until the present day.[47]

The greatest achievement of the native synthesis was that the new religious forms that it developed during the colonial period were still firmly enclosed within the logical structure of Andean thought. The persecution of huacas was insufficient to restructure the criteria whereby the Andean interpreted the symbols, ceremony, and sacred personages offered by the new religion. Ironically, the extirpators were unable to destroy native faith in the logic of their own religious world since it was *only* this logic that could make sense of the shock of the arrival of Christianity. In this sense, the old cultural matrix was not obliterated but itself adapted to contain and domesticate the alien religious system within itself and to make use of foreign elements so as to continue to offer its own answers.[48]

NOTES

In citing work in the notes, short titles have been used. Archives have been identified by the following abbreviations:

AAL   Archivo Arzobispal de Lima
AGI   Archivo General de Indias, Sevilla
AHN   Archivo Histórico Nacional, Madrid
ARSI   Archivum Romanum Societatis Iesu, Roma
BN   Biblioteca Nacional, Lima
RAH   Real Academia de la Historia, Madrid

Introduction

1. See Gruzinski, *La colonisation de l'imaginaire*. "Imaginaire" is the ability to represent and interpret the real.

2. The anthropologist Victor Turner stressed the "polysemy" or "multivocality" of symbols. See Turner, *The Forest of Symbols*, 50. Developing this idea in the context of the clash of Christianity and native Andean religion, Joseph W. Bastien pointed out that one symbolic system can be expressed by, and give expression to, another symbolic system. This polysemic property allows an impositional symbol to take on the meaning of an indigenous symbol and vice versa and thus may satisfy a conquering people with one meaning even as it refers to another meaning within the culture of the conquered people. See Bastien, *Mountain of the Condor*, 69.

3. See Silverblatt, "Peru," 315–16. See also Earls and Silverblatt, "La realidad física y social." References to the symbol of the serpent in Andean culture abound in a variety of sources. The Augustinian missionaries in Huamachuco reported it was very common to find the image of a serpent painted on buildings, especially around Cuzco and Huamachuco. In ancient times, a huge serpent called Uscaiguai used to appear to the Indians and was the object of veneration. To eliminate this cult, the missionaries insisted that the Indians should cease to paint the image of serpents. See Augustinians, *Relación de la religión,* 39. The chronicler Alonso Ramos Gavilán recounted how a live serpent unfurled itself from a representation of the deity Copacati (a stone figure encircled by snakes, held sacred by the Yunguyos Indians of the Lake Titicaca region) and slid around beside it in full view of the priest and villagers. Crying that the serpent was the Devil, the priest beat and stoned it to death. Ramos Gavilán, *Historia del celebre santuario,* 167.

4. See Taussig, *The Devil,* 171.

5. The classic account of the evangelization of Peru is still Armas Medina, *Cristianización del Perú.*

6. For a definition of *huaca,* see the Glossary. As for the official Cuzqueño religion, even imperial Inca beliefs and rites may have endured to a greater extent than is often allowed. See Marzal, *La transformación,* 274; and Duviols, *La lutte,* 346–47.

7. Salomon and Urioste, *The Huarochirí Manuscript,* 4.

8. Stern, *Peru's Indian Peoples,* 67.

9. The extent of the movement has probably been exaggerated. Rafael Varón has argued that it probably did not spread outside the jurisdiction of Huamanga, thanks to the prompt and effective action of Albornoz. Gabriela Ramos has pointed out that early accounts of the movement do not mention that it was widespread. Varón, "El Taki Onqoy"; Ramos, "Política eclesiástica," 145. See also the introduction by Luis Millones in Millones, *El retorno,* 25–29; Urbano and Duviols, *Fábulas y mitos,* 129; and Stern, *Peru's Indian Peoples,* 51–55.

10. The tension in Christian thought between voluntary conversion and forced baptism has been explored in the Peruvian context by Sabine MacCormack. She argues convincingly that, in Peru, coercion prevailed over persuasion. See MacCormack, "'The Heart Has Its Reasons,'" esp. 446. See also Mills, "The Limits of Religious Coercion."

11. The primary sources quoted in the latter work all refer to the province of Cajatambo. For comments on Duviols's work, see Acosta, "La extirpación."

12. Duviols, *La lutte,* 348. George Kubler concluded that by the 1660s, the colonial Church was satisfied that genuine idolatry no longer existed in Peru and that the Catholicization of the Quechua had been achieved. Kubler, "The Quechua," 340, 400–403.

13. The exceptions are the interesting analysis in Spalding, *Hua-*

rochirí, 263–69, and the work of Millones, for example, "Los ganados del señor" and "Religion and Power in the Andes."

14. MacCormack, *Religion in the Andes*, 5. MacCormack's work is not, of course, primarily a study of extirpation.

15. Apart from the existence of a few isolated cases in other archives, the bulk of the sources for the Extirpation lies in the AAL under the section Procesos de hechicerías e idolatrías. Some of the documents date from the period before 1640, but the vast majority fall within the second half of the seventeenth century (particularly the 1650s, 1660s, and 1690s) and, to a much lesser extent, the early eighteenth century. The chronology of this book reflects the richness of the documentation for this later period.

As Duviols has pointed out (*La lutte*, 212), the number of documents surviving in the AAL from any given period is no indicator of the real frequency of the trials. Whereas the Archivo General de Indias furnishes a great deal of information concerning the political history of the campaigns of 1609 to 1622 and indicates extensive extirpation in these years, almost no records remain in the AAL of the details of the visits and trials themselves. Conversely, plenty of documentation exists in the AAL for the trials of 1649 to 1670, despite an almost complete dearth of references to the political history of these campaigns in the AGI. To a certain extent, then, the various archives must complement one another. Even so, it is dangerous to conclude, for example, that the small numbers of cases that have survived from the later seventeenth century or early eighteenth century must necessarily indicate declining interest in native religious practices on the part of ecclesiastical authorities, since it is impossible to know what percentage of documents have survived from any given period.

The geographic range of this work has also been determined by the sources. The small number of references to trials outside the archbishopric of Lima has confined the focus largely to the archdiocese. Within these confines, however, the existing material is extremely rich, and I have chosen to draw upon trials from a variety of different geographic regions. Duviols, in *Cultura andina*, showed that research into the Extirpation will also benefit from local studies, for which the province of Cajatambo is the ideal candidate, since the vast majority of the surviving sources record the trials in this province. Using Duviols's published transcriptions, Kenneth Mills recently published a study of idolatry investigations in San Pedro de Acas, Cajatambo; see Mills, *An Evil Lost to View?* Some years earlier, Ana Sánchez published a transcription of documents from investigations in Chancay; see Sánchez, *Amancebados*.

16. For more detailed exposition of these categories, see pp. 48–55 for idolatry and superstition and pp. 68–70 for hechicería and brujería.

17. Stern, *Peru's Indian Peoples*, 66–67. It should be noted that Ramos has questioned Stern's interpretation, arguing that these phenomena may be less evidence of genuine acculturation than further proof of

the long reach of the official Christian discourse. The notion of possession of the taquiongos by the huacas might owe more to the Christian tradition of diabolical possession than to an accurate representation of Andean realities. It is also questionable whether taquiongos were known by Christian names, since this is suspiciously reminiscent of cases of religious deviants punished in Spain and in urban white and mestizo Peru. It should not be forgotten that the accounts of Taki Onqoy written by Cristóbal de Albornoz and Cristóbal de Molina themselves form part of the Christian discourse imposed on Andean expressions of the supernatural. The revivalist movement was not simply "discovered" but was "constructed" (even "invented") by colonial ecclesiastics. No mention was made of Taki Onqoy at all in Albornoz's *Información* of 1569. The first description of the movement did not appear until the *Información* of the following year, and the most elaborate and detailed account only emerged in that of 1584. It differs so greatly from the account of 1570 that Ramos refers to it as "conjured up by Catholic preachers." Furthermore, in the earliest account, the most characteristic element of the movement—the "possession" or invasion of participants' bodies by the huacas—was entirely absent. The testimony given by Molina in the *Información* of 1577 also omitted reference to dancing or possession, in startling contrast to his *Relación de las fábulas y ritos de los Incas* (1574). Ramos hypothesizes that either the *Relación* was composed somewhat later than the date traditionally assigned to it or the section on Taki Onqoy was added to the end of it at a later date. In any case, the *Relación* appears to be the "official" ecclesiastical account of the revivalist movement, coinciding with the development of a harsher approach toward evangelization. It is also significant that the elaboration of Taki Onqoy by its "discoverers" developed in direct proportion to the growth of their ambitions within the Cuzqueño church hierarchy. Ramos, "Política eclesiástica," 140–41, 145–46, 154–58. These observations on Taki Onqoy are important because they emphasize that representations of native religion remain the cultural and intellectual constructs of Christians and demonstrate that it is not so easy to distinguish evidence of genuine acculturation from the Christian discourse in which they are embedded. Even so, they do not fundamentally undermine the thesis of early cross-cultural exchange between Christianity and native religion.

18. Taussig, *The Devil*, 173.

19. For the two religions as mutually exclusive alternatives, see Farriss, *Maya Society*, 293.

20. Klor de Alva, "Spiritual Conflict and Accommodation," 351–52. The model is devised for Mesoamerica, but it applies with equal relevance to the Andes.

21. Diego Durán noted the use of the Nahuatl term *nepantla*, meaning "in the middle," to describe the religious status of the colonial Nahua. See Durán, *The Book of the Gods*, 410–11.

22. Nutini, *Todos Santos*, 78.

23. Wachtel, *Vision of the Vanquished*, 152–58.

24. Taussig, *The Devil*, 173. Despite using the word *juxtaposition*, Taussig emphasizes the interaction of the two religious traditions. See note 30, below.

25. Marzal, *La transformación*, 440.

26. The first quote is from Madsen, "Religious Syncretism," 369, 378–79. Madsen takes this definition from Barnett, *Innovation*, 49, 54. The second quote is from Nutini, *Todos Santos*, 16.

27. Marzal, *La transformación*, 55, 61.

28. Herskovits, *Man and His Works*, 553–57.

29. Gruzinski, *Man-Gods*, 3; Zemon Davis, *Society and Culture*, 192; Farriss, *Maya Society*, 295–99; Herskovits, *Man and His Works*, 529. The term "transculturation" was first coined by the Cuban F. Ortiz, in preference to "acculturation," since the latter implied the acquiring of the dominant culture by the dominated rather than a true process of cultural exchange.

30. This concept is adapted from Taussig, whose original quote is, "The folding of the underworld of the conquering society into the culture of the conquered should be understood not as an organic synthesis or 'syncretism' of the three great streams of New World history—African, Christian and Indian—but as 'a chamber of mirrors' reflecting each stream's perception of the other." Taussig, *Shamanism*, 218.

31. Bastien, *Mountain of the Condor*, 58 and 63.

32. Madsen, "Religious Syncretism," 388; Redfield, *Folk Culture of Yucatán*, 104–8.

33. Durkheim, *Elementary Forms*.

34. Bastien, *Mountain of the Condor*, 69.

35. Lockhart, *The Nahuas after the Conquest*, 260. Likewise, in the modern Tlaxacala region, "the pre-conquest style ritual specialists are held carefully apart from the Christian specialists and rites, even though the two complement each other within an overall system." See also Nutini, *Todos Santos*, 338.

36. An apu was (and still is) the spirit believed to inhabit lofty snow-capped peaks of the Andes. For further details, see the Glossary.

37. M. Mauss posited a dichotomy between religion and magic, distinguishing between secret practices and public practices. See Marcel Mauss, *General Theory of Magic*. See also Bernand and Gruzinski, *De l'idolâtrie*, 44. Magic is distinguished from religion by its lack of the communal or ecclesiastical dimension. Although magic resembles religion in that it constitutes a body of beliefs and practices concerning the sacred, it lacks a community of adepts and, hence, there is no "magical Church." Whereas religion partakes of a social and institutional dimension and consists of cults and rituals, the essence of magic is the manipulation or diversion of the forces of nature. See Marzal, *La transformación*, 305.

38. Spalding, *Huarochirí*, 256.

39. Ibid., 263. The increasing clandestinity of native rites creates a methodological problem for the historian of the Extirpation. As Millones has observed, clandestinity is both the prime characteristic of Andean religion and, at the same time, the greatest obstacle to its analysis, "like studying a protagonist who hardly ever appears on stage and whose existence is only known from the summary of the plot of the play." Millones, "Los ganados del señor," 140.

40. For the unsatisfactoriness of clandestine rites and Christian dominance of the public sphere, see Farriss, *Maya Society*, 299–300.

41. Cobo, *Historia del nuevo mundo*, 116.

42. For this observation, see Gruzinski, "Le filet déchiré," 412; and Marzal, *La transformación*, 299.

43. Kubler argued that the proliferation of witchcraft was a colonial phenomenon. Kubler, "The Quechua," 398.

44. Wolf, "Types of Latin American Peasantry," 460. Quoted in Sharon, *The Wizard*, 24.

45. For research that throws Wolf's conclusions into doubt, see, for example, Robinson, "Indian Migration in Eighteenth-Century Yucatán."

46. See Evans, "Migration Processes in Upper Peru," 63, 71; Cook, "Migration in Colonial Peru," 56; Wightman, ". . . residente en esa ciudad," 86, and *Indigenous Migration and Social Change*, vii, 3–6, 57, 59, 72. Wightman has indicated that the process of migration was not simply a one-way movement from country to city; there was also an urban-to-rural outflow as urban natives moved into depopulated lands in the countryside.

47. See Marzal, *La transformación*, 309; and Cobo, *Historia del nuevo mundo*, 167.

48. This was also true of Mesoamerica. See Gruzinski, "Le filet déchiré," 356. Farriss identifies as a principal shock of conquest the realization by the Maya that the Christian god was not merely to take precedence over their own gods but to replace them altogether. Farriss, *Maya Society*, 287.

49. See Bastien, *Mountain of the Condor*, 173–81; and Harris, "The Dead and the Devils."

50. MacCormack, *Religion in the Andes*, 433.

51. Among others, see Bastien, *Mountain of the Condor;* Casaverde Rojas, "El mundo sobrenatural"; Condori and Gow, *Kay Pacha;* Gow and Gow, "El alpaca"; Núñez del Prado Béjar, "El mundo sobrenatural de los quechuas"; Sallnow, *Pilgrims of the Andes;* Sharon, *The Wizard;* and Urton, *At the Crossroads.*

52. Farriss, *Maya Society*, 8–9.

53. Marzal argues that the two religious systems became almost superimposed on one another, except for two small "half-moons" representing aspects of the Catholic system that never managed to insert themselves into the native world (for example, the priesthood) or aspects of

Andean religion that never managed to become Christianized (for example, the worship of Pachamama). Marzal, *La transformación*, 440.

Chapter One

1. Since the eradication of native Andean religion was a judicial process, the principal sources for its study are records of trials. Judicial documents are problematical historical sources in that they document a conflict between two adversaries. They do not record a free flow of information between two parties but rather the results of a forcible interrogation, during which testimony might have been elicited under duress. The evidence of both the accuser and the accused must be treated with great reservation, since both are determined by the exigencies of the case.

The accuser may be the best source of evidence for the historian, since he is not necessarily concerned to avoid incriminating himself, but his motive may be suspect. Enmity toward the defendant may encourage him to depict his adversary in the most unfavorable light. The accused is, by definition, on the defensive. His evidence may be incomplete, as facts that will not serve his case will be suppressed, and there is the obvious danger that the testimony may be false, or only part of the truth. The accuser, for example, may be a worse idolater than the accused. The frequent similarity between depositions (observed by Duviols in *Cultura andina*, xxxvii) may reflect concerted cooperation between declarants so as to present an impenetrable united front against the judicial process.

Another restriction is that the information available for research has already been preselected by the questions the interrogator chose to put to the accused. More significant, the *form* in which his questions are expressed determines the response of the defendant. The testimony of both accuser and accused (but especially the latter) will be expressed in a manner likely to win the approval of their interlocutors. This may determine, for example, the terminology and vocabulary employed. This problem is exacerbated when, as in idolatry trials, the participants were poorly acculturated or highly unacculturated Indians. Many, possibly most, of the defendants were monolingual, and their testimony had to pass through the filter of an interpreter. This interpreter might be an Indian or a Spaniard, whose knowledge of the native language could be inadequate. In addition, he was not necessarily favorable to the accused, nor was he concerned to present an accurate translation. In most instances the original words of the declarants are rarely recorded, either in Spanish or in Quechua, so it is often impossible for the historian to distinguish the content from the form in which it is recorded. See Millones, *Historia y poder*, 179–80.

2. Las Casas, *Del único modo*; Acosta; *De procuranda*, 2:261.

3. For the regulations established by the Lima councils and Toledo's visitation, see Duviols, *Cultura andina*, xxviii-xxx.

4. In 1571, Philip II formally removed the Indians in the Spanish colonies from the jurisdiction of the Holy Office. However, an Indian Inquisition continued to operate in Mexico under an institutional framework quite similar to that of the formal Inquisition. See Greenleaf, "Historiography of the Mexican Inquisition," 261. See also Klor de Alva, "Colonizing Souls," 3–22. For the grounds for Indian exclusion from inquisitorial jurisdiction, see Duviols, *La lutte*, 217; Solórzano Pereira, *Política indiana*, 364; and Medina, *Historia del Tribunal*, 1:27–28.

5. It is possible that the death penalty may have been employed on rare occasions. A letter of the bishop of La Plata, Alonso de Granero, in 1582, recommended that those hechiceros and idolaters who were not to be burned, "as has been done with others," should be punished with confinement. As Duviols indicates, it is ambiguous if "others" refers to native specialists or to prisoners of the Inquisition. However, it seems likely that the latter interpretation is correct. See Duviols, *Cultura andina*, xxxi. Although some Visitors threatened the Indians with the death penalty (and even killed them during interrogation), there is no evidence that it was applied as an official judicial punishment.

6. For Albornoz's statistical bias, see Millones, *El retorno*, 13.

7. This title will hereafter appear as Visitor-General, or simply Visitor.

8. Between them, the three Visitors were to investigate the provinces of Huarochirí, Canta, Checras, Tarma, and Chinchacocha. See Duviols, *La lutte*, 156.

9. For the powers of the Visitor-General, see Duviols, *Cultura andina*, xlvii–xlviii.

10. For a detailed account of the method of procedure of the Visitor in the field, see Duviols, *La lutte*, 201–10. Duviols's account is largely based on Arriaga, *La extirpación*, 240–56.

11. Duviols, *La lutte*, 221.

12. For the number of prisoners at the House of Santa Cruz, see Arriaga, *La extirpación*, 260. Whereas this institution was frequently used in the early seventeenth century (it was overflowing with prisoners between 1620 and 1626), and to some extent also in the mid-seventeenth century, as time passed it became an increasingly infrequent feature of the Extirpation. It ceased to function by the end of the seventeenth century. Duviols, *La lutte*, 198–200.

13. Duviols, *Cultura andina*, xxxii–xxxiii, and *La lutte*, 156.

14. Duviols, *Cultura andina*, lxxiii, and *La lutte*, 221–24.

15. Eymerich, *Directorium inquisitorum*. See Duviols, *Cultura andina*, lxvii–lxviii.

16. AGI, Lima 302, Campo to the king, 8 October 1626.

17. AGI, Lima 332, Avendaño to the king, 5 August 1653. The debate over the Indians and the Inquisition was long-standing. As late as 1686, Sancho de Andrade, the bishop of Huamanga (1682–87), wrote to Pope Innocent XI requesting that as more than one and a half cen-

turies had passed since preaching had begun in Peru, the Indians should no longer be considered neophytes and should be subjected to the jurisdiction of the Inquisition along with the Spaniards. See Vargas Ugarte, *Historia de la Iglesia*, 3:13, 319–20.

18. Duviols, *La lutte*, 226.

19. Arriaga gave details of the missionary work of the Jesuits and discussed the need of both Visitors and Jesuit priests to persuade the Indians to surrender their idols. Arriaga, *La extirpación*, 242.

20. Villagómez, *Carta pastoral*, 180.

21. AGI, Lima 303, Villagómez to the king, 28 August 1654.

22. For the "pedagogy of fear," see Bennassar, "Modelos de la mentalidad inquisitorial."

23. Duviols, *La lutte*, 157.

24. The fact that many documents have survived from the province of Cajatambo does not necessarily indicate that this region was a unique reserve of native religious rites, nor should the lack of documentation for any other province be interpreted as reflecting the absence of these practices. It is not surprising that most documents refer to provinces geographically close to Lima. Thus not only Cajatambo but also Checras, Chancay, Huarochirí, Jauja, and Huaylas are all heavily represented. Geographic proximity and the relative ease of communications account for the place of these provinces at the forefront of the campaigns. News of native practices could be communicated more quickly (priests from these provinces went to Lima more frequently than those of distant provinces) and visitations could be organized at less expense.

Nor is it surprising that these same provinces were also subject to *repeated* idolatry visitations. Cajatambo, for example, which witnessed the idolatry trials of Bernardo de Noboa between 1656 and 1658, had already been visited in the years 1617 to 1622 (Duviols, *Cultura andina*, xi–xii). Once an area had been identified as "contaminated by idolatry," it would inevitably become a prime candidate for subsequent investigations, if only to ensure that the fruits of previous labors had not been overturned. Thus the initial visitation set off a chain reaction and the search for idolatry tended to be self-fulfilling. The frequency of visitations, therefore, did not necessarily represent an empirical higher incidence of native religious practices in these areas.

25. For more information on some of these Visitors, see Arriaga, *La extirpación*, 227–28.

26. Before his arrival in Lima, Lobo Guerrero had been the archbishop of Santa Fe (1599–1608). See Egaña, *Historia de la Iglesia*, 2:505, 508. There he had already "discovered" idolatry, at least a decade before Avila's revelations in Huarochirí, and had personally conducted idolatry trials. The Jesuit account of these trials strongly resembles the language of Lobo Guerrero's later correspondence from Lima with the king. ARSI, Nuevo Reino de Granada y Quito 14, fols. 1–17v, Descrip-

ción del Nuevo Reino de Granada . . . , [undated but concludes in the year 1598 in which Lobo Guerrero was appointed archbishop of Santa Fe], especially fol. 10, with references to *la extirpación de idolatrías*. For references to Lobo Guerrero in Santa Fe, see Duviols, *La lutte*, 176; Vargas Ugarte, *Historia de la Iglesia*, 2:298–99; and Castañeda Delgado, "Bartolomé Lobo Guerrero," 83.

27. Duviols, *La lutte*, 321.

28. AGI, Lima 302, Arias to the king, 27 May 1632 and 13 May 1633.

29. For Arias's biographical details, see Egaña, *Historia de la Iglesia*, 2:289.

30. Duviols, *La lutte*, 163.

31. Indeed, Villagómez's work lacked originality, especially the *Instrucción* or second part, where huge sections, even entire chapters, were lifted almost word for word from Arriaga's work. For example, chapter 42 of the *Instrucción*, *De las cosas que adoran los indios, en que consiste su idolatría* . . . , is more or less entirely totally copied from Arriaga's chapter 2; chapter 43, *De los ministros de la idolatría*, is a virtual reprint of Arriaga's chapter 3; and chapter 44 on indigenous feasts is hardly distinguishable from Arriaga's chapter 5. All the chapters in Villagómez's work describing Indian beliefs and practices or prescribing measures and procedures to be taken against them were entirely copied from, or very heavily based on, Arriaga's work.

32. The documentary sources are very uneven in what they reveal of the activities of these Visitors. There is far more information about the efforts of Noboa and Quijano (and the later Visitor of the 1660s, Juan Sarmiento de Vivero) than those of Jurado and Gamarra, for example, and virtually nothing at all about Osorio and Recio de Castilla. It is hard to determine if the frequency of references to certain individuals signifies greater zeal on their part or simply the disproportionate survival of documentation of their activities. The emergence of these individuals (especially Noboa and Sarmiento) as significant in other documentary sources (for example, legal proceedings brought by Indians against the exactions of their Visitors) suggests greater zeal.

For further details of these campaigns, see Duviols, *La lutte*, 164–65. For further background, see Vargas Ugarte, *Historia de la Iglesia*, 3:1–34. Felipe de Medina wrote a report of his visitations to Chancay in 1650, accompanied by the Jesuits Lorenzo de Tapia and Jerónimo de Herrera. See AGI, Lima 303, Relación que hizo Felipe de Medina, 25 March 1650. It was printed in Medina, *La imprenta en Lima*, 2:215–21.

33. AGI, Lima 59, Villagómez to the king, 10 July 1658. See Vargas Ugarte, *Historia de la Iglesia*, 3:8; and Marzal, *La transformación*, 219–21.

34. For early Jesuit objections to participation in idolatry visitations, see Arriaga, *La extirpación*, 242. Villagómez had already complained to the king of the difficulty of persuading the Jesuits; see AGI, Lima 303, Villagómez to the king, 28 August 1654, fols. 5v–6. Jesuit priests accompanied the Visitors on expeditions to Cajatambo in 1660 and be-

tween 1664 and 1666; see ARSI, Peruana Litterae Annuae V 1651–74, Annual Letter for 1660–61, fols. 69v–70, and Annual Letter for 1664–66, fol. 107v.

35. Acosta, "La extirpación," 185. In two letters to the king, Villagómez asked him to change his mind and allow the Visitors to charge the Indians for their upkeep; AGI, Lima 303, 28 August 1654, fols. 2v–5, and AGI, Lima 59, 10 July 1658, fol. 3.

36. The only real (and very perceptive) consideration of the eighteenth-century material is that of Karen Spalding, but even she exaggerates official disinterest when she writes that the continued maintenance of traditional ceremonies "was never followed up by the religious authorities." Spalding, *Huarochirí*, 263–69.

37. In Mexico, control over Indian orthodoxy was placed under the care of the *provisor* (vicar-general) of each diocese and archdiocese. A bureaucracy of officials was created and tribunals and *juzgados* (courts) were established for Indians. But these routine functions never escalated into fully fledged "campaigns of extirpation." See Greenleaf, "Historiography of the Mexican Inquisition," 261.

38. Bernand and Gruzinski, *De l'idolâtrie*, 153, 170.

39. Ibid., 6. The authors describe how the early chroniclers of America interpreted native religions in terms of the concept of "idolatry."

40. Saint Thomas Aquinas, the greatest authority of the Middle Ages on the questions of idolatry and superstition, drew heavily on the work of Saint Augustine for his definitions. See Aquinas, *Summa theologiae*, 2a2ae 92.1; 92.2; 94.1. Also see Augustine, *On Christian Doctrine*, 2.20. I have found useful analyses in Glenn, *Tour of the Summa*, 247; and Monahan, *Moral Theology*, 3:9–21. For definitions of superstition and idolatry, see also Castañeda Delgado and Hernández Aparicio, *La Inquisición de Lima*, 363–64.

41. Aquinas, *Summa theologiae*, 2a2ae 94.4.

42. Ciruelo, *Reprobación*, 5, 16, 18.

43. Ibid., 5–6, 25–26, 31.

44. Acosta, *Historia natural*, 217, 231, 235, 255, 278.

45. Ibid., 219.

46. Ibid., 225–228, 234, 271.

47. Acosta, *De procuranda*, 2:255–59, 269–71.

48. Arriaga, *La extirpación*, 195–96, 198, 205, 215–16, 218, 244–46. For the reference to the mother's milk, see Acosta, *De procuranda*, 2:255.

49. Duviols, *La lutte*, 148, 221.

50. AGI, Lima 301, Manifestación que hicieron todos los indios de un pueblo. See also Duviols's analysis of this visitation in Duviols, "La visite des idolâtries," 497–510.

51. AGI, Lima 301, Lobo Guerrero to the king, 20 April 1611, fol. 2.

52. Constituciones sinodales del arzobispo Lobo Guerrero, Lima, 1614, lib. 1, tit. 1, cap. 6. Reprinted in Duviols, *Cultura andina*, 511–14.

53. Bernand and Gruzinski, *De l'idolâtrie*, 156. Even so, the extirpators could not help recognizing the cultural origin of this behavior; Arriaga, for example, agreed with Acosta that the inclination was imbibed with the mothers' milk. This betrayed a fundamental unresolved contradiction at the heart of extirpation ideology: how far could a culturally determined trait be an act of choice?

54. Las Casas, *Apologética historia sumaria*, 1:381, 387, 440. David Brading has emphasized the polarization between Acosta and Las Casas. Whereas the Jesuit defined Satan as the fountainhead and source of pagan religion, the Dominican elaborated an essentially naturalistic argument, tracing the origin of idolatry to human fears and ambitions, which were the effect of Man's fallen nature, with the Devil merely intervening to take advantage of this weakness. See Brading, *The First America*, 192.

55. Bernand and Gruzinski, *De l'idolâtrie*, 114–15; Molina, *Relación*; Durán, *Historia de las Indias*, 1:55.

56. Arriaga, *La extirpación*, 194, 225.

57. AGI, Lima 302, Campo to the king, 8 October 1626.

58. AGI, Lima 325, de la Serna to the king, 9 May 1622. For discussion of the letter, see Duviols, *Cultura andina*, xlv–xlvi. AGI, Lima 302, de la Torre to the king, 30 October 1626.

59. AGI, Lima 310, *cabildo eclesiástico* to the king, 8 May 1623. For the secret investigation against the Visitadores, see AAL, Idolatrías 1 (4.7), Idolatrías 1 (2.6), and Idolatrías 1 (6.5)

60. AGI, Lima 98, Audiencia of Lima to the king, 30 October 1626.

61. AGI, Lima 305, Perez de Grado to the king, 18 March 1623. AGI, Lima 38, Cabrera to the congress of the Company of Jesus, 9 July 1618.

62. AGI, Lima 309, Perea to the king, March 1620.

63. AGI, Lima 307, Constituciones synodales del obispado de Trujillo del Perú, acción primera, sec. 1, cap. 6, fols. 4v, 12. The bishop referred to instructions he had drawn up to enable the priests to distinguish "idolatry" from "superstition," but no trace of these seems to have survived. It is important to observe that the distinction was considered significant by figures of authority at the height of the early Extirpation.

64. AGI, Lima 308, Verdugo to the king, 20 April 1621, 2 February 1626. By a royal decree of 22 August 1620, the king had ordered the appointment of Visitors to look into idolatry and reduce the Indians to the faith, as well as the personal involvement of prelates in eliminating idolatry. It is not entirely clear if the Visitors whom Verdugo had suspended were the ordinary ecclesiastical Visitors or specially appointed for the extirpation of idolatry. The constitutions of the synod of Huamanga of 1629 discussed the need for better-quality priests and preaching and made no reference to the elimination of idolatry. AGI, Lima 308, Constituciones synodales del obispado de Huamanga, lib. 1, tit. 1, const. 6, 5 August 1629.

65. Letters of Juan Alonso Ocón, bishop of Cuzco, and of the Jesuit Francisco Patiño to Archbishop Pedro de Villagómez, 14 October 1648, in Villagómez, *Carta pastoral*, 273, 277, 283. Ocón's perception of the nature of idolatry was no doubt determined by his earlier tenure of the bishopric of Yucatán where he had uncovered numerous "idolatries." For the reference to Duviols, see Duviols, *La lutte*, 173.

66. AGI, Lima 308, Godoy to the king, 10 July 1656.

67. AGI, Lima 308, *carta de edicto* issued by Francisco de Godoy, 15 June 1652.

68. AGI, Lima 308, Godoy to the king, 15 July 1652, 10 July 1656, 18 June 1657.

69. Letters of Juan Alonso Ocón, bishop of Cuzco, to Archbishop Pedro de Villagómez, 14 October 1648 and 14 December 1648, and of the Jesuit Francisco Patiño to Archbishop Pedro de Villagómez, 14 October 1648, in Villagómez, *Carta pastoral*, 275, 286.

70. Bernand and Gruzinski, *De l'idolâtrie*, 167–68.

71. AGI Lima 38, Esquilache to the king, 23 March 1619. See Duviols, *La lutte*, 210.

72. Letter of Francisco Patiño to Archbishop Pedro de Villagómez, 14 October 1648, in Villagómez, *Carta pastoral*, 279.

73. Letter of Juan Alonso Ocón to Archbishop Pedro de Villagómez, 14 October 1648, in Villagómez, *Carta pastoral*, 274.

74. AGI, Lima 306, Relación de la visita que hizo Manuel de Mollinedo, obispo de Cuzco, 20 November 1674.

Chapter Two

1. A *huanca* was not the same as a *huaca*. The latter was an "object of reverence" in general, including large stones; see the Glossary. The former, a more limited term of reference, was a large stone driven into the ground, commemorating some tutelary ancestor of the *ayllu* (kin group) or group of *ayllus*, a primordial populator or hero of the distribution of fertile lands or of agricultural practices. It demarcated the limits of land that could be cultivated and was believed to be occupied by the soul of the legendary hero.

2. AAL, Idolatrías 2 (6.8), fols. 1–2v.

3. Ibid., fol. 13v.

4. Ibid., fols. 14v, 17v–18v.

5. In general terms, *brujo* or *bruja* may be translated as "witch" and *hechicero* or *hechicera* as "sorcerer."

6. Lisón Tolosana, *Brujería*, 48–50. That this distinction existed in the peasant mind may be construed from the examples of accused who admitted that they were hechiceras while denying being brujas.

7. The theologian Pedro Ciruelo defined a bruja as a woman who had made a pact with the Devil. Ciruelo, *Reprobación*.

8. Blázquez Miguel, *Hechicería y Superstición*, 111; Caro Baroja, *Las brujas*, 112.

9. Contreras, *El Santo Oficio*, 687. See also Blázquez Miguel, *Hechicería y Superstición*, 5.

10. Lisón Tolosana, *Brujería*, 21.

11. Caro Baroja, *Vidas mágicas*, 389; del Río, *Disquisitionum magicarum*, 87; Vitoria, *De la magia*, 1226, 1274.

12. Castañega, *Tratado*, 33–35. See also Caro Baroja, *Vidas mágicas*, 391.

13. García Cárcel, *Herejía*, 247–48; Caro Baroja, *Las brujas*, 125; and see Eymerich, *Directorium inquisitorum*.

14. Vitoria, *De la magia*, 1237, 1283, 1288.

15. Castañega, *Tratado*, xii.

16. García Cárcel, *Herejía*, 244.

17. Ibid., 245. Caro Baroja, *Las brujas*, 153–61; for del Río, see Caro Baroja, *El Señor Inquisidor*, 171–96.

18. García Cárcel, *Herejía*, 244; Caro Baroja, *Las brujas*, 137–48.

19. See Monter, *Frontiers of Heresy*, 256; and Caro Baroja, *Brujería vasca*, 16–17.

20. Reguera, *La Inquisición española*, 193–94. See also Goñi Gaztambide, "El tratado *De superstitionibus.*"

21. Caro Baroja, *El Señor Inquisidor*, 186.

22. Caro Baroja, *Las brujas*, 67–68, 86–88, 109. However, it should be noted that Augustine himself remained uncertain about the real powers of demons. See MacCormack, *Religion in the Andes*, 227 n. 10; Augustine, *City of God*, 18.16–18.

23. Lisón Tolosana, *Brujería*, 22.

24. Caro Baroja, *El Señor Inquisidor*, 194–95. He dismisses the work as atypical of both Spaniard and Jesuit.

25. Reguera, *La Inquisición española*, 197; Caro Baroja, *Vidas mágicas*, 20.

26. Caro Baroja, *Vidas mágicas*, 20–21; Caro Baroja, *El Señor Inquisidor*, 194–95; Lisón Tolosana, *Brujería*, 45. Kamen points out that as the number of inquisitors with legal training on the Supreme Council increased, so the demand for satisfactory legal proof increased. See Kamen, "Notas sobre brujería," 232.

27. Caro Baroja, *Las brujas*, 233–39; Henningsen, *Witches' Advocate*.

28. Monter, *Frontiers of Heresy*, 260–61.

29. Lisón Tolosana, *Brujería*, 18–20, 27, 45.

30. Reguera, *La Inquisición española*, 210.

31. Lisón Tolosana, *Brujería*, 19.

32. Reguera, *La Inquisición española*, 206–7.

33. Blázquez Miguel, *Hechicería y Superstición*, 11. See also Guilhem, "La Inquisición," 199, 203–4.

34. Caro Baroja, *El Señor Inquisidor*, 194–95.

35. Blázquez Miguel, *Inquisición*, 101.

36. Lisón Tolosana, *Brujería*, 25.

37. AHN, Inquisición Lima, Lib. 1031, fol. 338.

38. AHN, Inquisición Lima, Lib. 1032, Causa de Petrona de Saavedra, 1695, fols. 458–65.

39. AHN, Inquisición Lima, Lib. 1032, Causa de Melchor de Aranibar, 1692, fols. 398v-404v.

40. AHN, Inquisición Lima, Lib. 1031, Causa de Ana María de Contreras, 1646, fols. 332–33; Causa de Luisa Vargas, 1647, fols. 349v-50.
AHN, Inquisición Lima, Lib. 1032, Causa de Francisca de Bustos, 1667,
fol. 116; Causa de Francisca de Benavides, 1691, fols. 406v-408. The
documents yield more examples. Antonia de Abarca admitted chewing coca and other superstitions but denied that she was a bruja or
that there was any intention in her hechicerías, insisting that they
were tricks to earn a living; AHN, Inquisición Lima, Lib. 1031, Causa
de Antonia de Abarca, 1655, fols. 378–81. Anna Ballejo denied naming
the Devil in any of her spells or performing them on his behalf, and
she insisted she had had no other intention than that of earning her
keep; AHN, Inquisición Lima, Lib. 1031, Causa de Anna Ballejo, 1655,
fols. 389–91. Inés de la Peñalillo, condemned for hechicería, pleaded
poverty and maintained that she had never believed that her superstitions could be effective and therefore she had had no implicit or explicit pact with the Devil; AHN, Inquisición Lima, Lib. 1032, Causa de
Inés de la Peñalillo, 1689, fol. 423v.

41. AHN, Inquisición Lima, Lib. 1031, Causa de Josepha de Baides,
1660, fols. 460–68; Causa de Juliana Gutiérrez, 1661, fol. 487; Causa de
Ana de Arala, 1662, fol. 495; Causa de Juana de Morales, 1662, fol.
495v.

42. AHN, Inquisición Lima, Lib. 1032, Causa de Juan Romero, 1693,
fols. 411v-416v.

43. For the severity of punishments administered by the Inquisition
of Lima, see also Castañeda Delgado and Hernández Aparicio, *La Inquisición de Lima*, 372. As Behar has pointed out for colonial Mexico,
the outcome of a case hinged less on the question of whether a person
was guilty or not than on subtler distinctions between "repentant and
unrepentant sinners, between accidental and deliberate sinners, between knaves and fools." See Behar, "Sex and Sin," 36; she takes the
quote from Monter, *Ritual, Myth and Magic*, 72.

44. Farriss observed, "Some of the more "enlightened" curates in
the later colonial period, influenced by general intellectual trends
among the educated elite in Europe and America, even came to be
skeptical of the shamans' supernatural powers and to regard anyone
who claimed control over the spirit world as a charlatan rather than a
witch." Farriss, *Maya Society*, 289. My contention is that this was not a
late development but an integral part of the ideology of the hechicero.

45. Vargas Ugarte, *Los Concilios Limenses*, 1:21–22, 73–74.

46. For references to the Second Council, see Vargas Ugarte, *Los
Concilios Limenses*, 1:254. For the royal decree of 1575, see Duviols, *Cultura andina*, xxxix. The Third Council of Lima (1583) had little new to

say about hechiceros. It largely confirmed the constitutions of the previous council, identifying hechiceros and dogmatizadores as "the plague of the faith," "monstrous ministers of the Devil . . . whose evil lies were such that in one day they could destroy everything God's servants had achieved in one year." See Duviols, *Cultura andina,* xxviii–xxix.

47. Albornoz, *Instrucción,* 172–73. Even if the distinction of first discovery of the Taki Onqoy movement belonged to Luis de Olivera, a priest in the doctrina of Parinacochas in the bishopric of Cuzco, it was the writings of Albornoz that were to constitute the major influence on the ideology of the Extirpation. Albornoz's *Instrucción* was the prototype of the manual of extirpation, the model for the subsequent works of Arriaga and Villagómez.

48. *Información de 1570,* in Millones, *El retorno,* 93, 95.

49. *Información de 1570; Información de 1584; Relación de la visita de extirpación de idolatrías;* all in Millones, *El retorno,* 147, 225, 257.

50. *Información de 1570,* 65, 83, 100, 133; *Relación de la visita de extirpación de idolatrías,* 259.

51. *Información de 1577,* 181.

52. *Información de 1570,* 147–48.

53. *Información de 1584,* 226; *Relación de la visita de extirpación de idolatrías,* 259–60. See also Urbano and Duviols, *Fábulas y mitos,* 150.

54. *Información de 1584,* 227. For the further identification of hechicería and idolatry, see *Relación de la visita de extirpación de idolatrías,* 256, 280. See also Molina, *Relación,* 62–66: "The provinces had hechiceros of many types."

55. Guaman Poma, *Nueva corónica,* 1:247–251, 253, 257; 2:638. Guaman Poma possibly drew directly on the *Relaciones de visitas* of Albornoz but not the texts that later formed *Instrucción.* See Urbano and Duviols, *Fábulas y mitos,* 146.

56. Acosta, *De procuranda,* 1:375, 451; Acosta, *Historia natural,* 236, 260, 264–65.

57. See Arriaga, *La extirpación,* 205–209, 249, for the different types of religious specialists. For the use of the term "hechicero" as a catchall label, see Bernand and Gruzinski, *De l'idolâtrie,* 186. They argue that *hechicero* was used as a necessity of language, a justification of extirpation in the name of the fight against the Devil. As MacCormack observes, although Andean beliefs, myths, and rituals provided the raw materials to be molded by Europeans, the categories that Europeans recognized as definitive could not be modified. MacCormack, *Religion in the Andes,* 386. The category of the hechicero was the most definitive of all.

58. Molina had cast doubt on the claim of the hechiceros that they genuinely relayed the huaca's messages to the Indians. However, he also seems to have accepted the alternative possibility that demons might provide the hechiceros with information for their prognostications.

Molina, *Relación*, 62–66. See also Vitoria, *De la magia*, 1237: "Although some of the works of magicians are illusory and a fiction of the senses, others have a real existence," for which proposition he quoted the authority of Saint Augustine. MacCormack discusses Spanish ambivalence toward the question of the real demonic presence at oracles in *Religion in the Andes*, 55–58, 251.

59. Arriaga reproduced this account of the hechiceros of Peru in the Annual Letter of the Jesuits for 1618. RAH, Jesuitas, Letras anuas, Perú, 1618, fol. 391; published in Duviols, *Cultura andina*, 456.

60. Arriaga, *La extirpación*, 214, 224, 226–27, 232, 238, 244, 249–50, 274, 276.

61. Ibid., 250.

62. Cobo, *Historia del nuevo mundo*, 224–25.

63. Ibid., 227–30.

64. See the opening paragraph of this chapter.

65. AAL, Idolatrías 2 (4.13), Causa de idolatría contra Don Tomás de Acosta, cacique de segunda persona de este repartimiento de Checras, Santiago de Maray, 1647, fols. 3v–4.

66. AAL, Idolatrías 6 (7.3), Causa contra Don Leandro Pomachagua, governador de cinco repartimientos, por hechicerías, 1666, fol. 9.

67. Juan Pariavilca testified that his father had been accused of hechicería because he had made sacrifices to a stone in his house; AAL, Idolatrías 4 (6.14), Causa de hechicero contra Diego Caxa Guaman, San José de Chorrillo, 1659, fol. 3. Raphaela de los Rios denounced some Indians as hechiceros because they knew about huacas and had entered one in a trance state; AAL, Idolatrías 6 (5.7), Causa de hechicería contra los indios del pueblo de San Gerónimo de Sallan, 1662, fol. 1. Cristóbal Yaguas was charged as an hechicero idólatra because he had been seen worshiping and performing pagan ceremonies in the ancient village of his people; AAL, Idolatrías 7 (1.3), Causa contra Cristóbal Yaguas, Huamantanga, 1664, fol. 1. María Llano was accused of being an hechicera idólatra for revering huacas in order to secure good crops; AAL, Idolatrías 7 (5.12), Causa de hechicería, Ihuari, 1665, fol. 13. Juana Yanca and Angelina de Salamanca were hechiceras because they went to worship the stone Sorimana, and Pedro Alpacai was an hechicero because he offered chicha to an idol, Vilcatambu; BN, B1701, Declaraciones sobre la práctica de la hechicería e idolatría por los indios del pueblo de Chichas, 1671, fols. 2, 5, 6. Some Indians from the village of Santiago de Maray were accused of being hechiceros idólatras after they spoke to their huaca as their creator and asked him to intercede for their health and to help them avoid the mita; AAL, Idolatrías 1 (4.10), Causa contra indios sobre idolatría, Santo Tomás de Auquimarca, 1644, fol. 3v.

68. For further examples, see AAL, Idolatrías 5 (1.1), Causa de hechicería contra María Magdalena Angelina, San Francisco de Ancor, 1660, fol. 8; AAL, Idolatrías 5 (3.1), Causa de hechicería contra Isabel

Choqui, San Lorenzo de Quinti, 1660, fol. 1; Idolatrías 5 (2.17), Declaración de Pedro Villanga, San Pedro de Pilas, 1660, fol. 6v.
   69. See Bernand and Gruzinski, *De l'idolâtrie*, 238.
   70. For example, María Ticllaguacho was defined as an hechicera
sacerdote because she had been a maestra de huacas for five years, and
her colleague Catalina Llacsa was classified as an hechicera idólatra
because she had made sacrifices to huacas; AAL, Idolatrías 3 (2.11),
Causa de hechicería contra Rodrigo de Guzmán Rupachagua, Huamantanga, 1656, fols. 11v, 15. Francisca Cochaquillay was considered
an hechicera for her sacrifices of guinea pigs at the village huaca; AAL,
Idolatrías 3 (4.18), Denuncia que hace Don Juan Tocas contra Alonso
Ricari, San Francisco de Cajamarquilla, 1656, fol. 2v.
   71. Inés Carvachumbi and Juana Icha were accused of being hechiceras because they had been seen invoking their apus on mountains.
Icha's propitiatory offerings to a spring were classified as hechicería
and the idolatry of her presumed express pact with her apu, whom
she held to be her Father and Creator, was deemed the strongest
grounds for the charge of hechicera; AAL, Idolatrías 2 (2.10), Causa de
hechicería contra Inés Carva, Pomacocha, 1650, fols. 1–2, 8v, 30v. Juana
Chauca and her husband were denounced as hechiceros because they
worshiped mountains, offering coca and chicha, so that they would
receive good crops and lands; AAL, Idolatrías 5 (1.1), Causa de hechicería contra María Magdalena Angelina, San Francisco de Ancor,
1660, fol. 2. Juan Chapa was classified an hechicero idólatra since he
made sacrifices to Pataacaca, a mountain worshiped by his ancestors,
to increase his livestock. Juana Tunque was considered an hechicera
since she made sacrifices to a mountain worshiped by her ancestors;
AAL, Idolatrías 5 (1.2), Acusación hecha contra Juan Chapa por hechicería, San Pedro de Pilas, 1660, fols. 5–10v. Francisca Mayguay was accused of being an hechicera idólatra for offerings she had made to a
mountain called Cotoni; she herself denounced Francisca Ianac as an
hechicera for offering maize and chicha to the mountain Maguaca;
AAL, Idolatrías 5 (2.18), Causa de hechicería contra Francisca Mayguay, San Pedro de Pilas, 1660, fols. 4, 18. Magdalena Sacsacarva was
called an hechicera idólatra because she made sacrifices to Sunivilca,
a mountain that she begged for good health; AAL, Idolatrías 5 (2.26),
Causa de hechicería contra Magdalena Sacsacarva, San Bartolomé de
Tupe, 1660, fol. 2. Juan Payco was denounced as an hechicero because
he worshiped on a mountain called Chanqui. Juana Choquiticlla had
a reputation as a great hechicera because she went to worship a mountain called Sacsuma; AAL, Idolatrías 5 (4.32), Causa de hechicería contra María Pomaticlla, San Lorenzo de Huarochirí, 1660, no fol. nos.
   72. Bernand and Gruzinski, *De l'idolâtrie*, 120.
   73. Duviols argued that the absence of the death penalty in Peru was
evidence that the idolatry trials were not inspired by the contemporary Spanish Inquisition but by the former medieval Inquisition, which

had been more "humane." This distinction is not necessary. The Extirpation was inspired by the contemporary Inquisition in its approach to the hechicero. It is precisely in this aspect that it can most clearly be understood as "the Bastard Child of the Inquisition." See Duviols, *La lutte*, 223.

Chapter Three

1. Marzal, *La transformación*, 260.

2. Lewis, *Ecstatic Religion*, 51. See also Hultkrantz, "Aspects of Shamanism."

3. For this account of the functions of the shaman, I have drawn on the following sources: Eliade, *Shamanism*, passim; Lewis, *Ecstatic Religion*, passim; Furst, *Flesh of the Gods*, ix; Harner, *Hallucinogens and Shamanism*, xi, 16; Harner, *Way of the Shaman*, 20, 42–44; Sharon, *The Wizard*, 8; and Taussig, "Folk-healing," 236–37. The term "altered state of consciousness" is used in preference to "trance" to avoid association with the Western mediumistic experience or the West African, Brazilian, or Caribbean possession cults, which are characterized by amnesia and a loss of control of one's faculties. The shaman, by contrast, is the "master of spirits"; he or she possesses them, rather than the reverse. See Doore, "Ancient Wisdom," 15; and Lewis, *Ecstatic Religion*, 51.

4. Doore, "Ancient Wisdom," 8. See also Noll, "The Presence of Spirits," 49.

5. Casaverde Rojas, "El mundo sobrenatural," 212–24. Núñez del Prado Béjar, "El mundo sobrenatural de los quechuas," 104–8.

6. For further details of Andean religious specialists, see Sharon, *The Wizard*, 76–85; Marzal, *La transformación*, 53; Tschopik, "Aymara of Chucuito," 218–31; Labarre, "Aymara Indians," 211–23; and Buechler and Buechler, *Bolivian Aymara*, 94–103.

7. AAL, Idolatrías 6 (5.8), Causa de hechicería contra los indios de San Gerónimo de Sallan, 1662, fol. 10.

8. For the testimony of María Ticlla, see AAL, Idolatrías 5 (1.2), Acusación contra Juan Chapa por hechicero, San Pedro de Pilas, 1660, fol. 10. For the testimony of Pedro Villanga and Juana Conoa, see AAL, Idolatrías 5 (2.17), Declaración de Pedro Villanga, San Pedro de Pilas, 1660, fols. 5v and 6v, respectively.

9. AAL, Idolatrías 7 (5.12), Causa de hechicería, Ihuari, 1665, fol. 13v.

10. For Santiago Poma and Sebastian Quito, see AAL, Idolatrías 6 (5.7), Causa de hechicería contra los indios de San Gerónimo de Sallan, 1662, fols. 28v and 31v, respectively.

11. AAL, Idolatrías 5 (4.29), Declaración de Juana Aycro, San Pedro de Pilas, 1660, fol. 1.

12. AAL, Idolatrías 5 (1.1), Causa de hechicería contra María Magdalena Angelina, San Francisco de Ancor, 1660, fol. 8.

13. AAL, Idolatrías 5 (4.28), Causa contra Pablo Ato, San Pedro de Pilas, 1660, fol. 1.

14. AAL, Idolatrías 5 (1.2), Acusación contra Juan Chapa, fol. 9.

15. AAL, Idolatrías 6 (5.7), Causa de hechicería contra los indios del pueblo de San Gerónimo de Sallan, fols. 19v, 23, 57.

16. For the first three defendants, see AAL, Idolatrías 6 (5.8), Causa de hechicería contra los indios de San Gerónimo de Sallan, fols. 5, 21v, and 27, respectively. For the last two defendants, see AAL, Idolatrías 5 (4.28), Causa contra Pablo Ato, fol. 3.

17. Vitoria, *De la magia*, 1256–57.

18. Vargas Ugarte, *Los Concilios Limenses*, 1:255. Aguirre Beltrán has emphasized the rationalist bias of the Western medicine that Spaniards introduced into America and its failure to address the role of subjective reality in the healing of illness. Aguirre Beltrán, *Medicina y magia*, 255. This rationalist bias encouraged the Spanish authorities to believe that they could separate the natural and the magical connotations of native medicine. Such an aim was futile because it ignored the fundamentally different concept of the relation between illness and humans that characterized native society. The ceremonies and the herbs formed an inseparable psychosomatic and psychotherapeutic complex that could not be unraveled. See Marzal, *La transformación*, 300.

19. Guaman Poma, *Nueva corónica*, 2:769.

20. Arriaga, *La extirpación*, 238.

21. Villagómez, *Carta pastoral*, 268.

22. AAL, Idolatrías 5 (1.1), Causa de hechicería contra María Magdalena Angelina, fols. 10–11v.

23. AAL, Idolatrías 6 (5.5), Declaración de Don Diego Pacha en razón de las idolatrías del paraje de Cañas, San Gerónimo de Sallan, 1662, fol. 1v.

24. AAL, Idolatrías 6 (7.1), Causa de idolatría en Santiago de Lunahuana, 1661, no fol.

25. AAL, Idolatrías 5 (2.26), Causa de hechicería contra Magdalena Sacsacarva, San Bartolomé de Tupe, 1660, fol. 2.

26. AAL, Idolatrías 5 (2.18), Causa contra Francisca Mayguay, San Pedro de Pilas, 1660, fol. 4.

27. AAL, Idolatrías 3 (2.11), Causa contra Rodrigo de Guzmán Rupachagua, Huamantanga, 1656, fols. 2r–4v.

28. AAL, Idolatrías 9 (5.15), Causa de idolatría, Santiago de Maray, 1677, fol. 50.

29. AAL, Idolatrías 4 (4.23), Causa contra Francisco Malqui, San Pedro de Caras, 1659, fol. 7.

30. AAL, Idolatrías 3 (2.11), Causa contra Rodrigo de Guzmán Rupachagua, fols. 2r–4v.

31. AAL, Idolatrías 6 (5.8), Causa de hechicería contra los indios de San Gerónimo de Sallan, fols. 13v–16v.

32. AAL, Idolatrías 5 (2.18), Causa contra Francisca Mayguay, fols. 4–5.

33. AAL, Idolatrías 6 (6.18), Causa contra Juana de los Reyes, Asunción de Ambar, 1662, fol. 2.

34. AAL, Idolatrías 9 (4.40), Causa contra Francisca Tomasa, Lima, 1670, no fol.

35. AAL, Idolatrías 5 (4.24) Causa de hechicería contra Isabel Concepción, San Lorenzo de Quinti, 1660, no fol.

36. AAL, Idolatrías 7 (4.36), Causa contra María Sania, Santo Domingo de Cochalaraos, 1667, fols. 2v–4r.

37. AAL, Idolatrías 9 (4.38), Causa contra Pasquala de Salsedo, Lima, 1669, fols. 1, 4v, 12.

38. AAL, Idolatrías 6 (5.7), Causa de hechicería contra los indios del pueblo de San Gerónimo de Sallan, fols. 33v–38v, 57v–58r.

39. AAL, Idolatrías 6 (5.8), Causa de hechicería contra los indios de San Gerónimo de Sallan, fol. 58v.

40. AAL, Idolatrías 6 (3.3), Causa contra Agustín Carbajal, León de Huánuco, 1662, no fol. Like Carbajal, Luis de Aguilar had been remonstrated less for his supposed healing abilities than for deceiving others about his alleged powers; AAL, Idolatrías 5 (4.28), Causa contra Pablo Ato, fol. 4v.

41. AAL, Idolatrías 6 (5.8), Causa de hechicería contra los indios de San Gerónimo de Sallan, fols. 16, 57.

42. AAL, Idolatrías 8 (7.6), Causa contra Juana de Mayo, Lima, 1668, fols. 1r–2v.

43. AAL, Idolatrías 2 (2.10), Causa de hechicería contra Inés Carva, Pomacocha, 1650, fol. 5. AAL, Idolatrías 2 (4.14), Causa contra Juana Icha de hechizos y pactos expresos con un demonio Apu Parato, Pomacocha, 1650, fols. 6–10.

44. Ginzburg, *Night Battles*.

45. Ibid., preface and pp. 10–12, 100–101, 107–9, 137–38. See also Duviols, *Cultura andina*, liv–lv, for a brief consideration of the relationship between the shaman of the Benandanti and the hechicero of Spanish demonology. What makes the context of the Benandanti particularly apposite for the treatment of religious deviance in Peru is Ginzburg's claim that on account of elements such as trances, professed healing abilities, journeys in the form of animals, and participation in processions for the dead, there are real, not merely analogical, connections between the Benandanti and shamans. Ginzburg, *Night Battles*, 32.

46. AAL, Idolatrías 2 (2.10), Causa de hechicería contra Inés Carva, fol. 5; AAL Idolatrías 2 (4.14), Causa contra Juana Icha, fols. 6–10.

47. AAL, Idolatrías 2 (4.14), Causa contra Juana Icha, fol. 2.

48. Ibid., fol. 9.

49. Ibid., fols. 6v, 9. On the significance of Supay, see Taylor, "Supay," 47–63; Duviols, *La lutte*, 37–39; and MacCormack, *Religion in the Andes*, 254–57.

50. AAL, Idolatrías 2 (2.10), Causa de hechicería contra Inés Carva, fols. 4v–5v.

51. AAL, Idolatrías 2 (4.14), Causa contra Juana Icha, fols. 9, 10, 17v.
52. Ibid., fols. 16, 18v, 29.
53. AAL, Idolatrías 6 (5.8), Causa de hechicería contra los indios de San Gerónimo de Sallan, fols. 10–11v.
54. AAL, Idolatrías 4 (4.23), Causa contra Francisco Malqui, fol. 7v.
55. AAL, Idolatrías 3 (2.11), Causa contra Rodrigo de Guzmán Rupachagua, fols. 11–12.
56. Silverblatt, *Moon, Sun and Witches*, 184.
57. AAL, Idolatrías 6 (5.8), Causa de hechicería contra los indios de San Gerónimo de Sallan, fols. 10–13v, 57–58v.
58. AAL, Idolatrías 6 (5.7), Causa de hechicería contra los indios del pueblo de San Gerónimo de Sallan, fols. 1v–2, 18v–19r.
59. AAL, Idolatrías 7 (4.36), Causa contra María Sania, fols. 12–16v.
60. AAL, Idolatrías 3 (2.11), Causa contra Rodrigo de Guzmán Rupachagua, fols. 17–18.
61. AAL, Idolatrías 6 (5.7), Causa de hechicería contra los indios del pueblo de San Gerónimo de Sallan, fol. 57v.
62. AAL, Idolatrías 5 (4.28), Causa contra Pablo Ato, fol. 4v; AAL, Idolatrías 5 (1.2), Acusación contra Juan Chapa, fol. 23.
63. Ginzburg, *Night Battles*, 94–95.
64. AAL, Idolatrías 3 (2.11), Causa contra Rodrigo de Guzmán Rupachagua, fols. 6, 11–12, 16. The guardian spirits of modern South American shamans are often "power animals," spiritual beings that not only protect and serve the shaman but also become another identity or alter ego for him. These spirits are characterized by animal-human duality. Among the Jívaro Indians of the Ecuadorean Amazon, a guardian spirit usually appears first in a vision as an animal and then in a dream as a human. See Harner, *Way of the Shaman*, 43–44.
65. Eliade, *Shamanism*, 33, 84–85, 103. See also Sharon, *The Wizard*, 112–15, on the connection between shamanic power and ecstasy.
66. AAL, Idolatrías 2 (4.14), Causa contra Juana Icha, fols. 7v–8v, 16.
67. AAL, Idolatrías 6 (5.7), Causa de hechicería contra los indios del pueblo de San Gerónimo de Sallan, fols. 1v–2, 18v–19r. Such ecstatic experiences are typically shamanic; particularly the entering of the earth, visits to sacred lakes or bodies of water, and the assistance from benevolent supernatural beings. See Sharon, *The Wizard*, 47.
68. AAL, Idolatrías 3 (2.11), Causa contra Rodrigo de Guzmán Rupachagua, fol. 16.
69. Ibid., fols. 4v–6.
70. AAL, Idolatrías 3 (6.11), Denuncia que hace Don Juan Tocas contra Hernando Hacas Cristóbal Poma Libiac, 1656, fols. 8–9. A useful analogy with colonial Mexico may be drawn from the work of Gruzinski. He has described the relationship between the Nahua tutelary deities and the "Man-God" (*ixiptla*) or exteriorization of the numen, who acted as the deity's "skin, bark or envelope." Whereas we should say that the Man-God possessed the force *teotl*, the Nahua believed

that the "Man-God" *was* teotl: "In him the god arises." This bond was formed by means of "paths of ecstasy" and of hallucination, whereby the protective numen—*altepetl iyollo*—or "heart of the people" undertook to grant privileged access to the world of the gods and lend his efficacious protection to the people who revered him. Gruzinski, *Man-Gods*, 21–22.

71. AAL, Idolatrías 3 (2.11), Causa contra Rodrigo de Guzmán Rupachagua, fols. 5–6, 11–12; AAL, Idolatrías 2 (4.14), Causa contra Juana Icha, fol 9.

72. AAL, Idolatrías 3 (2.11), Causa contra Rodrigo de Guzmán Rupachagua, fols. 11–12. Gruzinski has suggested that the "counter-acculturation process" in central Mexico had similarly come under the influence of what it strove to drive out, in respect not only of methods but also of objectives. The Man-God Andrés Mixcoatl evinced the same mobility, the same exclusivity, the same determination to eliminate the "other," as his enemy, the Franciscan missionary with his peripatetic dissemination of the word of God. "It was almost as if, beyond the difference of culture and religions, the two religious strategies were exact copies of each other and had become one." See Gruzinski, *Man-Gods*, 61.

73. AAL, Idolatrías 3 (2.11), Causa contra Rodrigo de Guzmán Rupachagua, fol. 5; AAL, Idolatrías 6 (5.7), Causa de hechicería contra los indios del pueblo de San Gerónimo de Sallan, fols. 1v–2, 18v–19r. Once again an analogy may be drawn with the Benandanti, some of whom experienced a similar inner struggle. In 1676, one member of the sect had a vision of a guardian angel who begged him not to go to the sabbat. After a struggle, he decided that "he wanted his soul to be with God," and the visions troubled him no more. See Ginzburg, *Night Battles*, 144.

74. AAL, Idolatrías 2 (4.14), Causa contra Juana Icha, fols. 10v–13. See Silverblatt, *Moon, Sun and Witches*, 183–90.

75. AAL, Idolatrías 11 (2.32), Causa contra Francisca Huaylas y María de la Cruz, Lima, 1691, fols. 1, 13, 20, 22, 26. Unfortunately, because the final sentence and punishment are missing, it is impossible to know if de Estela's arguments were successful in reducing the sentence.

The lack of sentences is a phenomenon that is not peculiar to idolatry trials. Marzal found that in eighty-five cases of denunciations brought by Indians against their local priests in the second half of the seventeenth century, only approximately 15% contained a final sentence. See Marzal, *La transformación*, 374.

There is no obvious explanation for why so many of the idolatry trials documented in this study lacked a final sentence. If final verdicts *were* reached in these cases, it is strange that they were not recorded. If the cases were dismissed without resolution, this outcome should have been noted as well. It is possible that some trials became so interminable that they were lost to the record. The suspension of a trial after the death or escape of the defendant (not an uncommon occurrence) might have passed undocumented. The frequent dismissal or abandonment of trials would suggest fundamental flaws and grave doubts about their efficiency. In the absence of clear explanations, however, this important issue cannot be resolved.

76. AAL, Idolatrías 10 (1.8), Causa contra María de la Cruz, Hananhuanca, 1691, fols. 1, 28, 33, 36. Rather disingenuously, the procurador argued that the fact that the cacique had suffered no ill effects was sufficient to prove that the women had not conspired to kill him.

77. AAL, Idolatrías 12 (4.47), Causa de hechicería contra Juana Augustina, San Luis de Huari, 1697, fols. 1–11v.

78. The effect of her contrition on the final sentence is unknown since the archbishop's decision is missing. It is interesting to observe that whereas the practitioners of the mid-seventeenth century, such as Icha and Carva, had spoken of their tutelary deities as apus, Augustina referred to her guardian spirit by the Christian term "angel." This may suggest a greater level of acculturation by the end of the century.

79. AAL, Idolatrías 13 (3.6), Causa contra Juan Vásques, Lima, 1710, fols. 1, 24–29, 31–33.

80. It is interesting to compare Vásques's clairvoyant abilities with those of the curing shamans of the Peruvian and Ecuadorean Amazon. By ingesting the psychotropic beverage *ayahuasca,* prepared from the vine of the genus *Banisteriopsis,* contemporary shamans in the Peruvian Amazon are able to "see" inside the body of patients. Like Vásques, these specialists believe that their skills and knowledge have been imparted to them by the spirits of plants, which are referred to as *doctores* or *vegetales que enseñan*—plants that teach. See Luna, *Vegetalismo,* 14–15, 63, 161. The shamans of the Jívaro are able to see into the body of the patient "as though it were glass." See Harner, *Hallucinogens and Shamanism,* 23.

81. AAL, Idolatrías 13 (3.6), Causa contra Juan Vásques, fol. 32.

82. Ibid., fols. 34–38.

83. Ibid., fol. 40v.

84. Ibid., fols. 40–42, for the arguments of the prosecution.

85. Ibid., fols. 44–46.

86. Ibid., fols. 47–49. The experts called on were Dr. Francisco Bermejo y Roldán, professor of medicine at Lima University and *protomédico;* Dr. Joseph de Avendaño, also a professor of medicine; and Juan Calderón, examiner in pharmacology.

87. Ibid., fol. 80.

88. The Bethlehemites were a hospital order, suggesting that the authorities wished to encourage Vásques's medical talents but in a purely Christian context.

89. Ibid., fol. 40v.

Chapter Four

1. Acosta, "La extirpación," 174.

2. Ibid., 177–78, 181–83. See also Acosta, "Los clérigos doctrineros," 118–41. For Peruvian doctrineros as "priest-entrepreneurs" who used their posts to enhance commercial interests, see Lockhart, *Spanish Peru*, 52–55; and Stern, *Peru's Indian Peoples*, 46.

3. Guaman Poma, *Nueva corónica*, 2:561. By *Padre*, Guaman Poma meant priest in general, not specifically a priest of the Society of Jesus. Elsewhere he praised the Jesuit priests who did not become involved in lawsuits (p. 603).

4. See the biography of Avila by Duviols in Avila, *Dioses y hombres*, 151–68; and Duviols, *La lutte*, 149.

5. Apart from Avila, those Visitors involved in legal cases included Avendaño, Hernández Príncipe, de Mora y Aguilar, Osorio, Delgado, Antolínez, Estrada Beltrán, and de los Ríos. Some were even delegated to investigate and adjudicate complaints against their colleagues. See Acosta, "La extirpación," 177–78, 181–83; Acosta "Los doctrineros," 69–109; García, "Apuntes para una biografía," 241–61; Guibovich Pérez, "La carrera de un visitador," 170–71, 174.

6. See Avila, *Dioses y hombres*, 151–68; and Acosta, "La extirpación," 183–84. Guibovich Pérez concludes that Avendaño's participation in the campaigns of idolatry was the determining factor in his rise within the ecclesiastical hierarchy; Guibovich Pérez, "La carrera de un visitador," 182.

7. Guaman Poma, *Nueva corónica*, 2:580.

8. Acosta, "La extirpación," 184–90.

9. Spalding, *Huarochirí*, 217.

10. For example, see the case of Diego Yaruparia cited below.

11. See Spalding, "Social Climbers," 60–61.

12. Farriss, *Maya Society*, 291.

13. AAL, Idolatrías 10 (4.42), Causa contra los indios idólatras del pueblo de San Francisco de Guantan, 1680, fols. 1–6.

14. AAL, Idolatrías 12 (1.13), Causa contra Pedro Vilcaguaman, Santa María de Jesús de Huarochirí, 1700, fols. 1–7, 10v. Macuychauca was no longer alcalde at the time of the idolatry trial but had been so three years before, at the time of the events he described.

15. AAL, Idolatrías 12 (4.49), Causa de hechicería contra Gerónimo Pumayauri, Santa María de Jesús de Huarochirí, 1700, fols. 1v–4.

16. There is intriguing evidence that the rivalry among village officials may have taken the form, not of a Christian faction against a nativist one, but of two hostile nativist factions. This is suggested by the testimony of Vilcaguaman's wife, a principal witness against him, that her husband frequented the house of Macuychauca's wife, "a notorious bruja." It is difficult to be sure how to interpret this accusation. It is possible that Vilcaguaman's wife was simply fabricating charges,

exploiting the powerful resonance of the accusation of bruja. Alternatively, it may point to a rift between Macuychauca and his wife with regard to their patronage of native religious practices. Finally, it could suggest that if Macuychauca shared his wife's leanings, he was manipulating the idolatry charge cynically as a weapon of disqualification against Vilcaguaman whose ability to do harm to him he genuinely feared. Whatever the truth, it is undeniable that the idolatry trial was a powerful means of resolving quarrels between the hostile factions within community life. AAL, Idolatrías 12 (1.13), Causa contra Pedro Vilcaguaman, fols. 1–7, 10v.

17. Duviols, *La lutte*, 231; Hernández Príncipe, "Relación de la visita."

18. Arriaga, *La extirpación*, 222.

19. Ibid., 239.

20. Stern, *Peru's Indian Peoples*, 65. Stern points out the ambivalent stance adopted by kurakas toward the Taki Onqoy movement in the 1560s.

21. Millones, "Los ganados del señor," 107–8; Millones, "Religion and power," 243–63; Millones, *Historia y poder*, 177–78. The mutual interdependence of kuraka and religious specialist was so great that Millones has spoken of a relationship of "symbiosis."

22. Guaman Poma, *Nueva corónica*, 2:580.

23. BN, B612, Testimonio del expediente sobre la denuncia de incesto, idolatría y otros excesos cometidos por el cacique de Santiago de Aija, Diego Yaruparia, Santiago de Aija, 1672, fols. 1–4.

24. Ibid., fols. 11–13, 18v.

25. AAL, Idolatrías 12 (5.27), Cartas de Don Martín Sosa y de Don Antonio Ilario de Sosa, principal del pueblo de Vichaycocha del repartimiento de Pacaraos, 1697, fol. 5.

26. Ibid., fol. 53.

27. BN, B612, Testimonio del expediente sobre . . . Diego Yaruparia, fols. 35–36. No final decision or sentence appears in the case. For consideration of the question of missing sentences, see Chap. 3, n. 75.

28. AAL, Idolatrías 12 (5.27), Cartas de Don Martín Sosa, fols. 23v–24.

29. AAL, Idolatrías 7 (4.35), Causa contra Leandro Pomachagua, governador del pueblo de Pachas, acusado de permitir idolatrías a Luis Guánuco, 1667, fols. 3–4; see also AAL, Idolatrías 7 (3.4), Pleitos y causas de hechicerías que sigue Don Luis de Villavicencio, cura de la provincia de Pachas, contra Don Leandro Pomachagua, governador del repartimiento de la doctrina, acusado de favorecer a los indios hechiceros, 1667; and AAL, Idolatrías 6 (7.3), Causa contra Don Leandro Pomachagua, governador de cinco repartimientos, por hechicerías, 1666, fols. 1, 9.

30. AAL, Idolatrías 7 (4.35), Causa contra Leandro Pomachagua, fols. 9, 19.

31. AAL, Idolatrías 7 (3.4), Pleitos y causas de hechicerías . . . contra Don Leandro Pomachagua, fol. 1.

32. For native willingness to use Spanish justice, see Stern, *Peru's Indian Peoples*, chap. 5, especially 132–33.

33. AAL, Idolatrías 4 (5.6), Causa de idolatría contra los indios idólatras hechiceros del pueblo de San Francisco de Mangas, 1662, fols. 28v, 94–97. For the incorporation of the accusation of idolatry into the discourse of political disputes, see Acosta, "La extirpación," 187.

34. Stern, *Peru's Indian Peoples*, chap. 5, especially 132–33.

35. AAL, Idolatrías 2 (6.8), Autos hechos por Juan Gutiérrez de Aguilar, cura de Pira y Cajamarquilla contra indios por idolatría, San Gerónimo de Pampas, 1646, fols. 10, 17v, 26v, 45, 76, 85–91. For full details of the charge, see the opening section of chap. 2.

36. AAL, Idolatrías 2 (4.13), Causa de idolatría contra Don Tomás de Acosta, cacique de segunda persona de este repartimiento de Checras, Santiago de Maray, 1647, fols. 1–4, 10–11, 57, 61–64.

37. Ibid., fol. 77.

38. AAL, Idolatrías 12 (2.33), Causa contra Don Miguel Menacho y Don Juan de Guzmán, caciques principales del repartimiento de Huamantanga, 1696, fol. 3. See also BN, B1400, Por las preguntas siguientes se examinan los testigos que fueron presentados por parte de Don Juan de Campos Vilcatapayo, principal del pueblo de San Pedro de Quipan del repartimiento de Huamantanga, en los autos que sigue con Don Juan de Guzmán y Don Miguel Menacho sobre el cacicazgo y gobierno de dicho repartimiento, Lima, 1695. The existence of this case indicates an investigation of the cacicazgo before the idolatry trial of 1696. One of the central questions was for the witnesses to verify if Juan de Campos had always been the principal of Huamantanga.

39. AAL, Idolatrías 11 (5.25), Causa contra Domingo Capcha y Francisco Guaman, Huamantanga, 1696.

40. AAL, Idolatrías 8 (6.24), El fiscal contra Don Francisco de Vergara, cacique del repartimiento de Santo Domingo de Ocros, 1665, fols. 1, 11, 13, 20; see also AAL, Idolatrías 9 (2.31), Pleito contra Don Francisco de Vergara, governador del pueblo de Santo Domingo de Ocros, 1669, fols. 9, 21–23.

41. AAL, Idolatrías 9 (5.14), Auto contra Don Juan Soclac y Doña María Chumpi, 1676, fols. 3, 4, 9v.

42. AAL, Idolatrías 11 (7.19), Causa contra Juan Picho, cacique principal y governor del repartimiento de Hurinhuanca en el valle de Jauja, 1691, fols. 1, 3, 31, 41, 53v; see also AAL, Idolatrías 10 (1.9), Proceso contra Pedro Guaman, Diego Yacan and Juliana, indios, 1690, fols. 7, 10v.

43. AAL, Idolatrías 10 (1.8), Causa contra María de la Cruz, Hananhuanca, 1691. For the references in this case, see fols. 1, 20, 36, 41, 59v–60, 70v, 73, 101, 107–8, 146–48, 172, 181, 183v–84, 274.

44. Juan de Blancas Coloma was the priest of the doctrina of Yauli in Nuevo Potosí before being appointed Visitor-General of Idolatry. He replaced Martínez in the Picho case in June 1691 and in the Apoalaya

case in August 1691. See AAL, Idolatrías 10 (1.8), Causa contra María
de la Cruz, fols. 99–101.

45. AAL, Idolatrías 7 (1.3), Causa contra Cristóbal Yaguas, Huamantanga, 1664, fols. 1, 23, 31, 35; see also AAL, Idolatrías 3 (2.11), Causa
contra Rodrigo de Guzmán Rupachagua, Huamantanga, 1656, fol. 3v.

46. AAL, Idolatrías 9 (4.41), Auto y pleito contra Don Lorenzo
Guaraca, cacique del pueblo de Mangas, 1671.

47. AAL, Idolatrías 1 (4.5), Causa contra Juan Caxaatoc, San Miguel
de Ullucmayo, 1617.

48. BN, B612, Testimonio del expediente sobre . . . Diego Yaruparia.

Chapter Five

1. Bernand and Gruzinski, *De l'idolâtrie*, 173, 176. Avendaño, *Sermones*, fol. 44.

2. AAL, Idolatrías 10 (4.42), Causa contra los indios idólatras del
pueblo de San Francisco de Guantan, fols. 6, 14v.

3. Ibid., fol. 5.

4. AAL, Idolatrías 3 (6.11), Denuncia que hace Don Juan Tocas contra Hernando Hacas Cristóbal Poma Libiac, fol. 36v.

5. AAL, Idolatrías 3 (4.18), Denuncia que hace Don Juan Tocas contra Alonso Ricari, San Francisco de Cajamarquilla, 1656, fol. 7v.

6. AAL, Idolatrías 3 (6.11), Denuncia que hace Don Juan Tocas contra Hernando Hacas Cristóbal Poma Libiac, fols. 8–11.

7. AAL, Idolatrías 4 (5.6), Causa de idolatría contra los indios idólatras hechiceros del pueblo de San Francisco de Mangas, 1662, fol. 105;
AAL, Idolatrías 3 (4.19), Causa hecha a los curacas camachicos y mandones del pueblo de San Francisco de Otuco, anejo de la doctrina de
San Pedro de Hacas, 1656, fols. 11v, 24.

8. AAL, Idolatrías 2 (4.13), Causa contra Don Tomás de Acosta,
1647, fols. 3v–4, 10; AAL, Idolatrías 3 (4.19), Causa hecha a los curacas
camachicos, fols. 1–8.

9. Marzal, *La transformación*, 373.

10. AAL, Idolatrías 3 (6.11), Denuncia que hace Don Juan Tocas contra Hernando Hacas Cristóbal Poma Libiac, fols. 128–31v.

11. AAL, Idolatrías 4 (2.12), Provansa hecha a pedimiento de los indios de Hacas, Machaca, Chilcas y Cochillas, contra el licenciado
Bernardo de Noboa, 1658–60, fols. 59–66, 169–72.

12. AGI, Lima 333, Información de servicios del licenciado Bernardo
de Noboa, 24–26 November 1664.

13. AAL, Idolatrías 8 (5.17), Información y pesquisa secreta hecha
contra Bernardo de Noboa, cura vicario de San Ildefonso de la Barranca, 1668.

14. In contrast to the campaigns of 1609 to 1622, the Visitors-General were forbidden to demand from the Indians support for the costs
of the visitations. Acosta, "La extirpación," 185.

15. AAL, Idolatrías 7 (5.10), Acusación de Cristóbal Pariasca, caci-

que y governador del repartimiento de Juan de Lampián, contra Juan Sarmiento de Vivero por abusos durante su visita, 1665.

16. AAL, Idolatrías 7 (7.2), Petición hecha por el promotor fiscal que el visitador exhiba y presente ante el juzgado eclesiástico todas las causas que ha fulminado, 1666. There is evidence from another trial that complaints about the irregular financial exactions of Sarmiento had already been brought to Lima. The witness María Pomaticlla of Huarochirí had traveled in person to the capital to accuse the Visitor of charging the Indians twenty or thirty pesos for their crime of being hechiceros. If she had not brought a lawsuit, it was because of insufficient funds and because the protector general, Diego de León Pinelo, had told them that the Visitor was "a saint and would do them no harm." AAL, Idolatrías 5 (4.32), Causa de hechicería contra María Pomaticlla de Huarochirí, 1660.

17. See, for example, AAL, Idolatrías 8 (5.16), Información y pesquisa secreta hecha contra licenciado Don Diego Barreto de Aragón y Castro, visitador general de este arzobispado y cura vicario de San Bartolomé de Guacho, 1668; and the investigation against Noboa cited in note 13. Such investigations had occurred in the 1620s; see AAL, Idolatrías 1 (4.7), Información y pesquisa secreta contra los visitadores del pueblo de Santiago de la Nazca, 1623.

18. AGI, Lima 59, Letter of Archbishop Pedro de Villagómez to the king, 2 May 1663, as quoted in Marzal, *La transformación*, 222.

19. AAL, Idolatrías 2 (6.8), Autos hechos por Juan Gutiérrez de Aguilar, cura de Pira y Cajamarquilla, contra indios por idolatría, San Gerónimo de Pampas, 1646, fol. 2.

20. AAL, Idolatrías 3 (6.11), Denuncia que hace Don Juan Tocas contra Hernando Hacas Cristóbal Poma Libiac, fols. 23v–24, 52.

21. For just one example among many, see AAL, Idolatrías 3 (5.2), Causa hecha a los indios camachicos del pueblo de Santa Catalina de Pimachi, anejo de la doctrina de San Pedro de Hacas, 1656, fols. 36–37.

22. AAL, Idolatrías 3 (6.11), Denuncia que hace Don Juan Tocas contra Hernando Hacas Cristóbal Poma Libiac, fol. 21; AAL, Idolatrías 7 (2.7), Causa de idolatrías contra los indios idólatras hechiceros de Chamas y Nanis de este pueblo de San Francisco de Mangas, 1663, fols. 7v, 61–64.

23. AAL, Idolatrías 3 (4.18), Denuncia que hace Don Juan Tocas contra Alonso Ricari, fols. 5v–6.

24. See, for example, AAL, Idolatrías 7 (2.27), Causa de idolatrías contra los indios idólatras hechiceros de Chamas, fol. 38.

25. AAL, Idolatrías 3 (6.11), Denuncia que hace Don Juan Tocas contra Hernando Hacas Cristóbal Poma Libiac, fols. 9, 11, 16v, 36v, 60v.

26. Ibid., fol. 29. See also the experience of Juan Raura who was ordered to become the minister for his ayllu because his elders had died. The simple offering of sacrifices sufficed to initiate him (fol. 40v).

27. Ibid., fols. 45v–46. Curiously, the shortage of suitable candidates

for his office did not prevent him being deprived of it subsequently for maintaining sexual relations with married women. For more examples of Indians who were obliged to serve as religious specialists, see fols. 51 and 53v.

28. Bernand and Gruzinski, *De l'idolâtrie*, 190.

29. AAL, Idolatrías 3 (6.10), Causa hecha contra los camachicos de Santo Domingo de Paria, 1656, fols. 4, 6v–11v; AAL, Idolatrías 3 (4.19), Causa hecha a los curacas camachicos, fols. 24v-25; AAL, Idolatrías 3 (6.11), Denuncia que hace Don Juan Tocas contra Hernando Hacas Cristóbal Poma Libiac, fol. 12.

30. AAL, Idolatrías 3 (6.11), Denuncia que hace Don Juan Tocas contra Hernando Hacas Cristóbal Poma Libiac, fol. 22v.

31. Bernand and Gruzinski, *De l'idolâtrie*, 181.

32. AAL, Idolatrías 3 (6.10), Causa hecha contra los camachicos de Santo Domingo de Paria, fols. 6v–7; AAL, Idolatrías 3 (6.11), Denuncia que hace Don Juan Tocas contra Hernando Hacas Cristóbal Poma Libiac, fols. 14v–15, 22; AAL, Idolatrías 3 (4.19), Causa hecha a los curacas camachicos, fols. 12v-13. Hucha, the dark spot in an otherwise perfectly white llama, was (and is) the lack of something which should be there, the absence of a necessry attribute, a breach in ritual or custom. It was the predominant cause of sickness. See Urioste, "Sickness and death," 12.

33. AAL, Idolatrías 3 (6.11), Denuncia que hace Don Juan Tocas contra Hernando Hacas Cristóbal Poma Libiac, fol. 35v. See fol. 55 for another example. AAL, Idolatrías 3 (4.19), Causa hecha a los curacas camachicos, fol. 14v.

34. AAL, Idolatrías 7 (2.29), Confesión de la india María Llacsa sobre una idolatría [*sic*] llamada Tuqui Atipac "todo lo vence," San Pedro de Hacas, 1667, fols. 1–2.

35. AAL, Idolatrías 3 (6.11), Denuncia que hace Don Juan Tocas contra Hernando Hacas Cristóbal Poma Libiac, fol. 37.

36. Ibid., fols. 9v–10 (and also 33v); AAL, Idolatrías 3 (6.10), Causa hecha contra los camachicos de Santo Domingo de Paria, fols. 9v–10.

37. AAL, Idolatrías 4 (2.12), Causa de idolatrías hecha a pedimiento del fiscal eclesiástico contra los indios e indias hechiceros del pueblo de San Juan de Machaca, 1657, fol. 4v.

38. AAL, Idolatrías 3 (6.11), Denuncia que hace Don Juan Tocas contra Hernando Hacas Cristóbal Poma Libiac, fols. 9v–10, 50, 54, 66. The teachings of Alonso Ricari embodied a similar compromise by which he instructed the Indians not to go to church or to confess "any more than they were asked." AAL, Idolatrías 3 (4.19), Causa hecha a los curacas camachicos, fols. 17 and 23v; AAL, Idolatrías 3 (6.10), Causa hecha contra los camachicos de Santo Domingo de Paria, fols. 6v–7.

39. AAL, Idolatrías 3 (4.19), Causa hecha a los curacas camachicos, fol. 2v.

40. AAL, Idolatrías 4 (2.12), Causa de idolatrías . . . contra los indios . . . del pueblo de San Juan de Machaca, fols. 4v–5.

41. AAL, Idolatrías 3 (6.11), Denuncia que hace Don Juan Tocas contra Hernando Hacas Cristóbal Poma Libiac, fols. 10, 17, 22v, 25, 31, 39v, 44v, 62, 82v.

42. AAL, Idolatrías 9 (5.15), Causa de idolatría, Santiago de Maray, 1677.

43. Salomon and Urioste have stressed the dynamism of native religion when it came into contact with Christianity; as Francisco de Avila remarked, huaca cults thrived most, not in the areas where they had remained unmolested, but in the villages where Catholic priests had been most zealous. Salomon and Urioste, *Huarochirí Manuscript*, 3–4.

44. AAL, Idolatrías 9 (5.15), Causa de idolatría, Santiago de Maray, fols. 1v–3.

45. Ibid., fols. 3–4.

46. AAL, Idolatrías 5 (2.17), Declaración de Pedro Villanga, San Pedro de Pilas, 1660, fols. 1–4v.

47. AAL Idolatrías 6 (5.5), Declaración de Don Diego Pacha en razón de las idolatrías del paraje de Cañas en la doctrina de Sallan, 1662, fols. 1v–2.

48. AAL, Idolatrías 14 (3.11), Causa de idolatrías contra indios de la doctrina de San Juan de Churin, 1725, fols. 3v–4, 6v, 9. The epidemic of 1719, for example, had been very widespread and devastating.

49. See, particularly, AAL, Idolatrías 13 (3.9), Causa contra Juan de Rojas, Santiago de Carampoma, 1723, fol. 4.

50. AAL, Idolatrías 13 (3.10), Autos contra Pedro de la Cruz, alias Quiñones, y Francisco Bartolomé, por delitos de idolatría, San Agustín de Canin, 1724, fols. 3v–4v, 7–9; AAL, Idolatrías 13 (3.9), Causa contra Juan de Rojas, fol. 13; AAL, Idolatrías 14 (3.13), Causa de idolatría contra indios de la doctrina de Santiago de Andajes, 1725, fol. 5.

51. AAL, Idolatrías 13 (3.10), Autos contra Pedro de la Cruz, fols. 7v–8.

52. AAL, Idolatrías 14 (3.15), Causa contra Francisco Julcarilpo, Santiago de Carampoma, 1730, fol. 11.

53. AAL, Idolatrías 13 (3.9), Causa contra Juan de Rojas, fol. 15v.

54. Duviols discusses some of these functions in *Cultura andina*, lxxvi.

55. According to Cristóbal de Molina, these diverse functions were separated in precolonial times. Bernand and Gruzinski, *De l'idolâtrie*, 119.

56. Ibid., 189. See also MacCormack, *Religion in the Andes*, 180–81. She points out that the sheer naturalism of Spanish religious images invited Andeans to perceive them as the huacas of Christians and hence find authorization for the worship of their Andean counterparts.

Chapter Six

1. The 1690s had seen the appointment of ecclesiastical judges and even judges "specially nominated to investigate idolatrous and super-

stitious Indians and hechiceros" but no revival of the title Visitor-General of Idolatry, or the extension of the jurisdiction of the aforementioned judges outside the immediate locality of their inquiries, let alone to the entire archbishopric. See, for example, AAL, Idolatrías 12 (5.27), Cartas de Don Martín Sosa y de Don Antonio Ilario de Sosa, principal del pueblo de Vichaycocha del repartimiento de Pacaraos, 1697, fol. 7.

2. Celís was the priest of Paccho and ecclesiastical judge and vicar-general in the provinces of Checras and Cajatambo. AAL, Idolatrías 14 (3.11), Causa de idolatrías contra indios de la doctrina de San Juan de Churin, fol. 1.

3. Morcillo had already been prelate in Charcas and had occupied the position of viceroy of Peru on two occasions, in 1716 and from 1720 to 1724. See Egaña, *Historia de la Iglesia*, 2:816–17.

4. AAL, Idolatrías 13 (3.9), Causa contra Juan de Rojas, Santiago de Carampoma, 1723, fol. 1.

5. AAL, Idolatrías 14 (3.11), Causa de idolatrías contra indios de la doctrina de San Juan de Churin, fols. 1–3.

6. Ibid., fol. 21; AAL Idolatrías 14 (3.13), Causa de idolatría contra indios de la doctrina de Santiago de Andajes, 1725, fol. 18v.

7. AAL, Idolatrías 14 (3.11), Causa de idolatrías contra indios de la doctrina de San Juan de Churin, fol. 1.

8. See the edict issued in San Antonio de la Lancha; AAL, Idolatrías 14 (3.13), Causa de idolatría contra indios de la doctrina de Santiago de Andajes, fol. 2. See also the edict promulgated in the village of Santo Domingo de Nava; AAL, Idolatrías 14 (3.11), Causa de idolatrías contra indios de la doctrina de San Juan de Churin, fols. 2v–3.

9. AAL, Idolatrías 14 (3.11), Causa de idolatrías contra indios de la doctrina de San Juan de Churin, fol. 21.

10. AAL, Idolatrías 13 (3.9), Causa contra Juan de Rojas, fols. 34, 36.

11. AAL, Idolatrías 13 (3.10), Autos contra Pedro de la Cruz, alias Quiñones, y Francisco Bartolomé por delitos de idolatría, San Agustín de Canin, 1724, fols. 7–9, 21–24v, 26–29.

12. AAL, Idolatrías 13 (3.10), Autos contra Pedro de la Cruz, fols. 30–33.

13. Ibid., fols. 38–39.

14. AAL, Idolatrías 13 (3.9), Causa contra Juan de Rojas, fols. 49, 56. The sentence against Juan de Rojas has not survived, but a similar punishment must have been inflicted. We do not know the punishment inflicted on Cruz either.

15. AAL, Idolatrías 13 (3.9), Causa contra Juan de Rojas, 1723; AAL, Idolatrías 14 (3.15), Causa contra Francisco Julcarilpo, Santiago de Carampoma, 1730.

16. AAL, Idolatrías 13 (3.9), Causa contra Juan de Rojas, fols. 5–7.

17. AAL, Idolatrías 14 (3.15), Causa contra Francisco Julcarilpo, fols. 10–12, 23v–24. See Spalding, *Huarochirí*, 264–65, for an interesting analysis of Julcarilpo's case.

18. AAL, Idolatrías 14 (3.15), Causa contra Francisco Julcarilpo, fols. 2v, 43–44. For the role of Mango, see also AAL, Idolatrías 13 (3.9), Causa contra Juan de Rojas, fols. 32–33.

19. AAL, Idolatrías 14 (3.15), Causa contra Francisco Julcarilpo, fol. 50.

20. See Spalding, *Huarochirí*, 257–58, for an example of the use of this tactic by Sarmiento.

21. BN, C4284, Autos seguidos criminalmente contra unos indios del pueblo de Llucta [sic] sobre el delito de idolatría, Yura, Arequipa, 1788, fols. 1–2. Millones interpreted the actions of Mamani as characteristic of modern shamans. See Millones, "Los ganados del señor," 116. For the references to modern South American shamans, see Harner, *Hallucinogens and Shamanism*, 21, 158.

22. BN, C4284, Autos . . . contra unos indios del pueblo de Llucta, fols. 4v–5, 17. Approximately one-fourth of Jívaro men are shamans. Any adult male can become a practitioner by taking the hallucinogenic drink. See Harner, *Hallucinogens and Shamanism*, 5, 17.

23. BN, C4284, Autos . . . contra unos indios del pueblo de Llucta, fol. 4. For the 1821 case, see Millones, "Los ganados del señor," 124–36. The case is identified by Millones as "Expediente seguido contra los indígenas de Lluta y Huanca, por delito de idolatría, Arequipa, 1821." At the time of his publication, it was located in AAL, Idolatrías 5. After the reorganization of the archives, I was unable to locate and consult the case personally and hence am indebted to his analysis.

24. BN, C4284, Autos . . . contra unos indios del pueblo de Llucta, fols. 2, 15.

25. See Millones, "Los ganados del señor," 136–43.

26. Ibid., 116–17.

27. AAL, Idolatrías 14 (3.17), Causa contra Domingo Garci, San Francisco de Quiso, doctrina of San Juan de Quibi, 1741.

28. BN, C4284, Autos . . . contra unos indios del pueblo de Llucta, fols. 1–2, 13v–14. Urizar's classification of Mamani's offenses did not derive from any indigenous distinction; on the contrary, it ignored the accused's testimony that the mountain spirits had instructed him in the use of the conopas. These spirits had taught him that he would not achieve the abundant reproduction of his llamas unless he observed the ceremonies with the stone figures. It is clear that what Urizar perceived as "residual customs" were, from the native point of view, intimately connected to the "idolatry" of communication with the mountain spirits. For the native tradition, acts of communication with sacred beings were part of an inseparable whole.

29. Ibid., fols. 21v–23.

30. Ibid., fols. 21, 29–31.

31. De la Peña, *Itinerario*, 213, 217, 266–67, 276–81, 294. For the impact in Peru, see Marzal, *Historia de la antropología indigenista*, 351.

32. Kubler, "The Quechua," 400. Marzal has taken issue with Ku-

bler's argument. See Marzal, *Historia de la antropología indigenista*, 351. Elsewhere Marzal points out that it is incorrect to deduce from de la Peña's writings that he believed idolatry had completely died out. His references to *idolatrías* among the Indians make this clear. Marzal, *La transformación*, 223.

33. This reclassification may only to a certain extent be called a return to Thomist categories. De la Peña's analysis and that of the judges of 1788 differed fundamentally from the Thomist conception in their understanding of the significance of exterior idolatry. For de la Peña, the rendering of worship to creatures with exterior actions alone was not a sin of "formal idolatry" but one of "material idolatry." Such a distinction would not have been allowed by classical writers. Purely exterior idolatry, even without interior infidelity, remained idolatry nonetheless. The outward worship of idols could not be excused or tolerated merely as a survival of hollow popular custom, since outward actions could not fail to signify inward convictions. See Augustine, *City of God*, 10.19; and Aquinas, *Summa Theologiae*, 2a2ae. 92.2, 94.2, and 94.4.

34. The bishop even requested that the Inquisition should be consulted as to the most effective remedy. AGI, Quito 182, Letter of Diego Ladrón de Guevara, bishop of Cuzco, to the king, 29 April 1706, fols. 186–87.

35. For the Cajamarca trials, see Dammert Bellido, "Procesos por supersticiones," 179–200. The trials were dated 1776, 1782, and 1795. Marzal refers to several trials in the provinces of Cuzco, Trujillo, Arequipa, and Huamanga, almost all from the eighteenth century, the latest in 1786. See Marzal, *La transformación*, 218. Salomon found four trials for hechicería in the Archivo Nacional de Historia del Ecuador for the years 1704, 1705, 1730, and 1786. See Salomon, "Shamanismo y política," 489. Laviana Cuetos discovered a trial for hechicería from La Punta de Santa Elena on the Ecuadorean coast as late as 1784 to 1787. See Laviana Cuetos, "Un proceso por brujería."

Conclusion

1. Taussig, *The Devil*, 43.

2. Ibid., 170–71. See also Taussig, *Shamanism*, 143.

3. As Caro Baroja has stressed, things may be of diabolical origin and, at the same time, false. See Caro Baroja, "Witchcraft and Catholic Theology," 23.

4. Silverblatt, *Moon, Sun and Witches*, 159.

5. Ibid., 170.

6. Ibid., xxx.

7. Taussig, *The Devil*, 169.

8. Mannarelli, "Inquisición y mujeres," 142.

9. Arriaga, *La extirpación*, 206.

10. Ibid., 208.

11. Poole and Harvey, "Luna, sol y brujas," 286.

12. Silverblatt, "The Universe," 156.

13. Hernández Príncipe, "Mitología andina," 27–29, 31, 34, 36–37.

14. Silverblatt, "The Universe," 174–78. See also Silverblatt, *Moon, Sun and Witches*, 195–98.

15. Silverblatt, *Moon, Sun and Witches*, xxx. Despite the reservations expressed here, Silverblatt's work is undoubtedly extremely stimulating and thought-provoking.

16. Behar, "Sexual Witchcraft," 184.

17. Poole and Harvey, "Luna, sol y brujas," 286–87.

18. For the flight of Indian prisoners, see Duviols, *Cultura andina*, xxxvii.

19. Several victims of one of the visits of Alvaro de Lugares to the village of San Gerónimo de Omas (province of Yauyos) subsequently fell again into the net of the extirpator Sarmiento, including Inés Carpa, Pablo Ato, Juana Aycro, Pedro Villanga, Juana Conoa, María Ticllaguacho, and Juan Chapa. Chapa had already been punished twice. Both he and Ticllaguacho confessed that they had reoffended every year during the feast of Saint John and at Christmas in order that his llamas would multiply. See AAL, Idolatrías 5 (1.1), Causa de hechicería contra María Magdalena Angelina, San Francisco de Ancor, 1660, fol. 8; AAL, Idolatrías 5 (4.28), Causa de hechicería contra Pablo de Ato, San Pedro de Pilas, 1660, fol. 2; AAL, Idolatrías 5 (1.2), Acusación contra Juan Chapa por hechicería, San Pedro de Pilas, 1660, fols. 5v–9; AAL, Idolatrías 5 (4.29), Declaración de Juana Aycro, San Pedro de Pilas, 1660, fol. 1v; and AAL, Idolatrías 5 (2.17), Declaración de Pedro Villanga, San Pedro de Pilas, 1660, fols. 2, 7. The defendant María Inés had been punished twenty years before as an hechicera by the Visitor Felipe de Medina. See AAL, Idolatrías 6 (5.8), Causa de hechicería contra los indios de San Gerónimo de Sallan, 1662, fol. 6. Sebastian Quito had been brought before two previous Visitors, Francisco Gamarra and Bartolomé Jurado. See AAL, Idolatrías 6 (5.7), Causa de hechicería contra los indios de San Gerónimo de Sallan, 1662, fols. 34–38v. Cristóbal Yaguas admitted that he had already been punished as an hechicero on a previous visitation. See AAL, Idolatrías 7 (1.3), Causa contra Cristóbal Yaguas, Huamantanga, 1664, fol. 13.

20. For Hernando Ticssi Mallqui, see AAL, Idolatrías 9 (5.15), Causa de idolatría, Santiago de Maray, 1677, fol. 5v. María Llano affirmed her belief that the huacas she worshiped had the power to grant her good crops. See AAL, Idolatrías 7 (5.12), Causa de hechicería, Ihuari, 1665, fol. 14v. María Angelina, Vicente Napuri, Juan Chapa, María Ticllaguacho, and Magdalena Sachacarva had trusted with all their hearts that the mountain spirits had the power to grant their wishes. See AAL, Idolatrías 5 (1.1), Causa de hechicería contra María Magdalena Angelina, San Francisco de Ancor, 1660, fols. 2, 11; AAL, Idolatrías 5 (1.2), Acusación contra Juan Chapa por hechicería, San Pedro de Pilas, 1660,

fol. 6v; AAL, Idolatrías 5 (2.26), Causa de hechicería contra Magdalena Sacsacarva, San Bartolomé de Tupe, 1660, fol. 2.

21. The religious specialist Juan Guaman achieved public renown after punishment by Lugares on an idolatry visitation. Subsequently he became the object of accusations of maleficio. See AAL, Idolatrías 5 (4.28), Causa de hechicería contra Pablo Ato, San Pedro de Pilas, 1660, fol. 2. Cristóbal Yaguas was renowned as an hechicero because he had been imprisoned by the Visitor Pedro Quixano. He insisted that the previous accusation had fueled subsequent charges against him. Juan Francisco de Betanzos was denounced as a notorious hechicero because on a previous occasion he had appeared before the Visitor Pedro García de Verastigui. See AAL, Idolatrías 7 (1.3), Causa contra Cristóbal Yaguas, Huamantanga, 1664, fols. 1, 13.

22. For the arguments of the opponents of the Inquisition for the Indians, see Vargas Ugarte, Historia de la Iglesia, 3:319.

23. For the techniques of the Inquisition, see Bennassar, "Modelos de la mentalidad inquisitorial," 174–79.

24. Salomon has suggested that the fundamental difference between the European witch and the South American shaman was that the former was an outcast of society, whereas the latter lay at its center. By definition, European witchcraft was deviant; witches were those whose acts were abhorrent and the very negation of everything decent. Furthermore, witchcraft was attributed to the marginalized members of society: the weak, the poor, the old, the disadvantaged. By contrast, the Andean shaman was neither marginalized nor weak but powerful and influential. By definition, he or she was (and is) "the one who possesses an extraordinary amount of what is most desirable," a quality in the Andes that is often called sami or samay. The power and success that characterized shamans precluded perception of them as deviant by members of their own community. Salomon, "Shamanismo y política," 505–6.

25. If the extirpators dispensed with the juridical safeguards of the Holy Office, it was because these restrictions would have paralyzed the repression of such a ubiquitous phenomenon as Andean religious practices. Klor de Alva has stressed that the inquisitorial techniques of random investigation and selective punishment rendered the institution a poor mechanism for effectively regulating masses of unacculturated Indians. What was needed, in Peru as in Mexico, was widespread, rather than selective and exemplary, intervention. It was for this reason that the "Indian Inquisition" in Mexico was abandoned. See Klor de Alva, "Colonizing Souls," 12–15.

26. Letter of Francisco de Patiño to Archbishop Pedro de Villagómez, 14 October 1648, printed in Villagómez, Carta pastoral, 278. Taussig has stressed the supremely difficult task of supplanting pagan views of nature with Church-derived doctrines, which involved nothing less than "a revolution in the moral basis of cognition itself." If the

signs (i.e., natural phenomenon) could not be removed, then their sig-
nification had to be. "A new semiotic had to be written, as large and as
all-encompassing as the universe itself." Taussig, *The Devil*, 174–75. In
the absence of such a radical change in perception, the planting of
crosses on such indestructible numinous sites merely confirmed their
sacred status in the eyes of the Indians. See Sallnow, *Pilgrims of the
Andes*, 52.

27. It is interesting to note that one of the original meanings of the
Latin word *paganus* was "rustic." The fifth-century writer Orosius
thought that the Christian usage of this word was explained by the
fact that the countryside was still heathen after the towns had become
Christian. See Chadwick, *The Early Church*, 152. Noting this usage,
William Christian spoke of a process of "paganization" of Christianty
whereby rural pre-Christian notions of a sacred landscape reasserted
themselves over an initially cathedral-, parish-, and church-centered
religion. See Christian, *Apparitions*, 20. In the Peruvian context, Sallnow
has shown how the numinous power of ancient sacred peaks of the
Andes is manifested in the cult of advocations of Christ that lie upon
them. The cult of Señor de Qoyllur Rit'i is explicitly associated with
the great mountain peak and deity Apu Ausangate, on whose slopes
the shrine lies; the object of reverence is an unusually shaped crag
with a painting of the crucified Christ. The ritual cycle of the pilgrimage to this spot includes the ascension of the mountain by the *ukukus*,
the symbolic protectors of the pilgrims, in order to pay homage to the
apu. The sanctuary of Señor de Wank'a in the Vilcanota valley lies on
the slopes of Apu Pachatusan and also has as the focus of its devotion
a crag that bears a painting of a vision of the Christ figure. The hal-
lowing of such rocks through miraculous theophany has assimilated
unique "loci" of the Andean sacred into the Catholic cult. These
miraculous shrines remain both Christian and Andean; whereas, on
the one hand, they are Christian in their iconography, religious meaning, and clerical involvement, on the other, their location in the sacred
landscape and their incorporation into a wider cult of telluric divinities make them unambiguously Andean. The landscape was not de-
sacralized in the colonial period but, on the contrary, resacralized.
Sallnow, *Pilgrims of the Andes*, 54, 79, 235–39, 269.

28. Salomon and Urioste, *Huarochirí Manuscript*, 3–4.

29. See Harner, *Hallucinogens and Shamanism*, 25. Overt hostility toward the failures of specialists is common elsewhere. In the district of
Chinchero near Cuzco, when *pacos* fail in curing some affliction, they
may be insulted or accused of robbery, especially if they have charged
a down payment. See Esteva Fabregat, "Medicina tradicional," 46.

There are several examples among the colonial idolatry trials of curanderos accused of ill will when their healing failed. Gerónimo Pumayauri was accused of deliberate malice on the death of a patient for
whom he had prepared an herbal drink. Already a known bitter

enemy of the patient's family, he had boasted that he had been responsible for her death. See AAL, Idolatrías 12 (4.49), Causa de hechicería contra Gerónimo Pumayauri, Santa María de Jesús, 1700, fols. 1–4.

Notorious curanderos were often blamed by their enemies for the onset of apparently inexplicable illnesses. Pedro Vilcaguaman was held responsible for the ill health of two witnesses whose enmity he had incurred. Juan Ilario Chumbivilca had fallen seriously ill with no apparent explanation shortly after he had seized instruments of hechicería from the accused. Agreeing to return the confiscated items to Vilcaguaman in exchange for a cure, he became convinced that the curandero had caused his illness. Marcelo Macuychauca was sure that an inexplicable ailment that befell him was the work of Vilcaguaman, since the curandero had sworn to revenge himself after Macuychauca had denounced him before the priest.

Resentment could also be provoked by the arbitrary use of the curandero's powers. When Vilcaguaman had refused to cure his own son, his daughter-in-law, María Teresa Pumachumbi, became convinced that the curandero was the origin of the illness and, to punish him, agreed to testify against him. See AAL, Idolatrías 12 (1.13), Causa contra Pedro Vilcaguaman, Santa María de Jesús de Huarochirí, 1700, fols. 2–7, 13. The refusal of the curanderos Diego Capcha and Francisco Guaman to cure one witness had been sufficient to convince him of their responsibility for his own affliction and the death of his two sons. See AAL, Idolatrías 11 (5.25), Causa contra Diego Capcha y Francisco Guaman, Huamantanga, 1696, fol. 3.

30. Taussig, "Folk-healing," 220. Lévi-Strauss, "The Sorcerer and His Magic," and "The Effectiveness of Symbols."

31. Noting that the frequency of witchcraft increased in the Yucatán in proportion to the size of the community, Redfield argued that black magic is an expression of the insecurity of the individual in the unstable social milieu of the city. The lack of an integrated culture and the breakdown of familial and religious controls make it difficult to predict the behavior of others. Redfield, *Folk Culture of Yucatán*, 334–35.

32. Sharon, *The Wizard*, 32, 64. Referring to the Avá-Chiripá, a subgroup of the Guaraní of Paraguay, Miguel Alberto Bartolomé has also spoken of the shaman as an "intercultural agent," the "axis around which cultural identity revolves," whose "role as interpreter of religious law maintains and guarantees cultural continuity." See Bartolomé, "Shamanism among the Avá-Chiripá," 95.

33. Gruzinski, "Le filet déchiré," 524–25.

34. Bolton and Sharon, "Andean Ritual Lore," 65. The mesa of the shaman Eduardo Calderón, studied by Sharon, blends Christian and indigenous elements in one ritual complex and gives expression to "the creative synthesis between aboriginal shamanism and Christian symbology manifest in Eduardo's art." It has two principal fields, rep-

resenting good and evil, that are kept apart by a third mediating field, or neutral zone, where the opposing forces are held in balance. The left zone, symbolized by three demonic staffs, is associated with the forces of evil and negative magic. The right zone is ruled by Christ and displays images of saints, holy water, and cans of San Pedro infusion, as well as eight staffs including the swords of Saint Paul and Saint James the Elder. In the middle field are artifacts of a neutral nature—magical herbs, a mirror, and a statue of Saint Cyprian (a powerful magician who was converted to Christianity), ruler of that zone. See Sharon, "A Peruvian *Curandero's* Séance," 224 and 231. The division into fields is common among the mesas of shamans in northern coastal Peru. See Joralemon, "Altar Symbolism," 10.

35. Taussig, "Folk-healing," 221, 236.

36. Sharon, *The Wizard,* xii–xiii, 151.

37. Arriaga, *La extirpación,* 224.

38. On the exclusive demands of Taki Onqoy, see Stern, *Peru's Indian Peoples,* 58. The Andean religious tradition was one of accommodation of alien deities within the preexisting pantheon. Andean polities had already been obliged to incorporate Viracocha and Inti, for example, under Inca suzerainty. See Rowe, "Inca Culture," 272–73, 293–95.

39. For the experience of painful incongruity, see Gruzinski, "Le filet déchiré," 544.

40. Marzal, *La transformación,* 183; Millones, *Historia y poder,* 184.

41. Marzal, *La transformación,* 210–12, 274.

42. The modern anthropological literature abounds with references to the protective role of the apus or their equivalents under another name (e.g., *wamanis* or *aukis*). See, for example, Bastien, *Mountain of the Condor;* Buechler and Buechler, *Bolivian Aymara,* 90–103; Casaverde Rojas, "El mundo sobrenatural," 140–47; Condori and Gow, *Kay Pacha;* Earls, "Organization of Power in Quechua Mythology," 397–409; Mishkin, "Contemporary Quechua"; Núñez del Prado Béjar, "El mundo sobrenatural de los quechuas," 79–83.

43. Casaverde Rojas, "El mundo sobrenatural," 176.

44. Sallnow, *Pilgrims of the Andes,* 52. For the concept of "loci of sacredness," Sallnow draws heavily on the work of Christian, *Local Religion.* MacCormack has pointed out that, for the Indians, the images of the saints and the Virgin were independent living agents of supernatural power, just as the huacas had been. The holy presence immanent in the image, just as in the huaca, responded to the devotee without the intervention of any other force. The image *was* the numinous force. MacCormack, "From the Sun of the Incas," 53.

45. It is worth noting that cults of mummified ancestors were uncovered in Andagua in the *corregimiento* of Condesuyos de Arequipa as late as the middle of the eighteenth century. See Salomon, "Ancestor Cults and Resistance." The Andagua trial is also analyzed by Marzal; see Marzal, *La transformación,* 230–32. Bastien has observed

how offerings are made by the Kaatans, of the Qollahuaya region of Bolivia, to their ancestors by feeding them into the river. He interprets this as a response to the Spanish attempt to eradicate ancestor worship by burning the mummies and throwing their ashes into the rivers. Such a strategy failed because, according to the native understanding, rivers were a means of returning relics to their original time and place where they could never be destroyed. Bastien, *Mountain of the Condor,* 157–59.

46. For ceremonies in honor of Pariacaca, see Avila, *Dioses y hombres,* 121–23. For modern rites for the dead, see Bastien, *Mountain of the Condor,* 173–81; Casaverde Rojas, "El mundo sobrenatural," 199–211; Harris, "The Dead and the Devils"; Núñez del Prado Béjar, "El mundo sobrenatural de los quechuas," 108–14; and Tschopik, "Aymara of Chucuito," 213–18. Harris describes how, among the Laymi of Bolivia, certain precautions must be taken when making offerings to the dead: the corpse must be tied to prevent the escape of the ghost; coca should be chewed to prevent abduction by the ghost; pregnant women and children are excluded from the journey to the graveyard since they are particularly vulnerable to seizure by the spirit of the dead; on the way to the cemetery, the protection of the God and the saints is sought at a church or chapel; the house must be thoroughly cleansed after the departure of the corpse; and the graveyard should be avoided by all at all times but especially at night. The association between the dead and devils probably derives, first, from the insistence of Spaniards (and particularly the extirpators) that the Indian ancestors were in Hell; and, second, from Spanish superimposition of the Christian Hell on the native underworld or afterlife, referred to as Supayca guacin or Zumayhuci ("House of Supay," "House of the Dead" or "House of Shadows"), probably synonyms for Upaymarca, the eternal resting place of the dead near Lake Titicaca. See Taylor, "Supay," 47–63.

47. For example, among the Kaatans, Catholic shrines are interpreted according to the native mountain metaphor and, hence, the Catholic symbolic system has been incorporated into a preexisting native system. Bastien, *Mountain of the Condor,* 58, 63, 69, 189–97.

48. See Millones, *Historia y poder,* 179. According to Sallnow, Andean pilgrimage is an attempt to domesticate a sector of the Christian cult, to appropriate it and insert it into the sociogeographic matrix of the environment. Christian shrines are used to reconstruct space according to an image that since pre-Inca times has served as a means of modeling regional, subimperial relations. Andean patterns of self-definition in relation to others have been reasserted by means of this resacralization of the landscape. Thus Andean pilgrimage is a classic example of the means by which the native understanding of reality exploited the alien religious system so as to continue offering its own answers. Sallnow, *Pilgrims of the Andes,* 269.

GLOSSARY

Important Andean and Spanish terms that appear more than once in the text are included here. [A] denotes a word of Andean origin, [CAR] a word of Caribbean origin, [CAM] a word of Central American origin, and [S] a word of Spanish origin.

Alcalde [S]: Functionary of the Crown exercising ordinary civil jurisdiction in a territorial district, like a justice of the peace.

Alférez [S]: Steward.

Alguacil [S]: Constable; judicial official subordinate to the alcalde.

Ají [CAR]: Chili pepper (*Capsicum longum*).

Alto mesayoq [A]: Shaman who stands at the apex of the religious hierarchy and communicates with native deities and the spirits of the dead.

Amaru [A]: A destructive force, represented as a serpent, erupting from beneath the earth in an attempt to recreate balance when relations of equilibrium are not maintained in the social and natural universe.

Apu [A]: "Lord" in Quechua. As the spirit inhabiting mountain peaks, the apu is the personification of the landscape. It functions as a tutelary deity, intervening directly in the material world and requiring propitiation through regular, formal offerings. The best summary of the meaning of apu is probably Condori and Gow, *Kay Pacha*, 38–41. The concept of the apu is pre-Hispanic.

Aquelarres [S]: Collective worship of the devil by witches at mass meetings in secret places.

Audiencia [S]: Supreme judicial and administrative council.

Auto de fe [S]: Public ceremony of absolution and punishment of practitioners of native religious rites, modeled on the practice of the Inquisition.

Ayllu [A]: Kin group.

Brujo [S]: Witch.

Brujería [S]: Witchcraft.

Cabildo [S] 1. (secular): Municipal council of an Indian pueblo. 2. (ecclesiastical): Cathedral chapter.

Cacicazgo [S/CAR]: Indian chieftainship, office held by a *cacique*.

Cacique [S/CAR]: Indian headman or chieftain (synonymous with *kuraka*).

Calificador [S]: Judge of the Tribunal of the Inquisition, responsible for determining the category of an offense.

Camaquen [A]: The vital force that animated creation; see, for example, Rostworowski de Diez Canseco, *Estructuras andinas*, 10.

Capítulo [S]: Ecclesiatical lawsuit.

Carta de edicto [S]: Edict.

Cauchu [A]: "He who devours people"; native sorcerer.

Chicha [CAM]: Maize beer.

Cofradía [S]: A religious confraternity; a voluntary association of people devoted to the maintenance and veneration of a particular image and certain forms of mutual aid, founded on the contributions of members and the income of lands and livestock.

Conopa [A]: Domestic sacred entities. They take the form of small stones shaped like the animal (llama, alpaca) or crop (potatoes, maize) whose fertility is to be assured. In the Cuzco region, these personal "amulets" are known as *incaychus* and are considered to be a memento handed on from the apus. Since they are said to contain the life force of the livestock, their possession prevents the sickness of one's animals. See Sharon, *The Wizard,* 59–60; and Gow and Gow, "El alpaca."

Corregidor [S]: Chief judicial and administrative official appointed by the Crown or its local representative.

Corregimiento [S]: An administrative district governed by a corregidor.

Curandero [S]: Folk healer.

Cuy [A]: Andean guinea pig.

Doctrina [S]: A missionary indigenous parish; also catechism classes.

Doctrinero [S]: Parish priest of an Indian community.

Dogmatizadores [S]: Preachers and propagandists of native beliefs and rites.

Embaucador [S]: Impostor.

Embustero [S]: Trickster, charlatan.

Encantador [S]: Enchanter.

Fiscal [S]: 1. Judicial official of the audiencia, attorney, public prosecutor. Appointed to each diocese. 2. In Indian pueblos, a native catechist and assistant working under the supervision of the parish priest.

Hatunruna [A]: Unacculturated Andean.

Hechicería [S]: Sorcery.

Hechicero [S]: Sorcerer.

Hechizo [S]: Spell.

Huaca [A]: In pre-Columbian and colonial times, a huaca was a "sacred entity" or "object of reverence." See Garcilaso de la Vega, *Primera parte de los Comentarios reales,* 51–53. Arriaga gave an account of the different kinds of huaca in *La extirpación,* 202. Possibly the best definition of a huaca is the following by Burr C. Brundage: "A *huaca* was both a localization of power and the power itself resident in an object, mountain, grave, ancestral mummy, ceremonial city, shrine, sacred tree, cave, spring or lake of origination, river or standing stone, statue of a deity, a revered square or bit of ground where festivities were held or where a great man lived." Brundage, *Empire of the Inca,* 47. The modern Aymara Indians see almost every unusual occurrence in nature as a huaca: an animal or human born with too many or too few natural parts, the birth of twins, an egg with two yolks, children born feet-first, a very copious spring, high mountain passes, inaccessible peaks, misshapen potatoes, even large serpents. Labarre, "The Aymara Indians," 165.

Huacacamayo [A]: Minister or caretaker of deities.

Huacapvillac [A]: Interpreter of huacas' communications.

Huanca [A]: Large stone driven into the ground, commemorating a tutelary ancestor of an ayllu or group of ayllus, a primordial populator or hero of the distribution of fertile lands or of agricultural practices. It demarcated the limits of land that could be cultivated and was believed to be occupied by a soul of the legendary hero. See Duviols, *Cultura andina,* lxvi.

Idólatra [S]: Idolater.

Idolatría [S]: Idolatry.

Kuraka [A]: Indian headman or chieftain (synonymous with *cacique*).

Ladino [S]: Hispanicized Indian, particularly one who spoke Spanish.

Laicca [A]: Native religious specialist.

Layqa [A]: Native specialist in the practice of black magic.

Licenciado [S]: Licenciate, bachelor.

Machay [A]: Indigenous aboveground resting chambers, in the form of caves or niches carved out of rock, for mortal remains, mummies, and funeral offerings.

Maleficio [S]: Harmful magic.

Mallqui [A]: Mummified corpse, bones, or other remains of ancestors of ayllus.

Mallquipvillac [A]: Interpreter of *mallquis's* communications.

Mita [A]: System of forced labor whereby natives were assigned on a shift basis to work in Spanish-owned enterprises (mines, farms, textile workshops, and building projects).

Mitayo [A]: Native assigned to the mita.

Obraje [S]: Textile workshop.

Pampa mesayoq [A]: Native shaman and folk-healer.

Paqarina [A]: Mythical place of origin of each ayllu.

Procurador de los naturales [S]: Attorney for the natives. Legal representative appointed to each province to present cases on behalf of the native population.

Promotor/promotor fiscal [S]: See Fiscal 1.

Protector de los naturales [S]: see *Procurador*.

Provisor [S]: Vicar-general; an ecclesiastical judge, appointed to each diocese or archdiocese, under the jurisdiction of the bishop.

Quipu [A]: Mnemonic device, consisting of a cluster of colored and knotted threads, used for keeping statistical records in the Inca Empire and early colonial Peru.

Rapiac [A]: Native specialist who divined using human limbs.

Regidor [S]: City councillor, alderman.

Repartimiento [S]: An administrative district.

Sango [A]: Mixture of maize flour and blood used in sacrificial ritual.

Sortílego [S]: Diviner.

Sortilegio [S]: Divination.

Taki Onqoy [A]: "Dance of disease." Native religious revivalist movement that flourished in the area of Huamanga around 1565.

Taquiongos [A]: Disseminators of the message of *taki onqoy*.

Visitador General [S]: Visitor-General; inspector.

Bibliography

Manuscripts

Archivo Arzobispal de Lima (AAL)

All the following documents are to be found in the section *Procesos de hechicerías e idolatrías* (AAL, *Idolatrías*). The numbers in parentheses indicate the reference numbers in use at the time I consulted the documents in 1990 (the first number corresponds to the *legajo* or bundle, and the second number to the *expediente* or case). The documents have since been reorganized. For a comprehensive index of the current classifications see Laura Gutiérrez Arbulú, *Indice de la sección hechicerías e idolatrías del Archivo Arzobispal de Lima*, in Ramos and Urbano, *Catolicismo*, 105–36.

AAL, Idolatrías 1 (2.6), Información secreta contra los visitadores de la idolatría hecha en la villa de Carrión de Velasco (province of Chancay), 1622.

AAL, Idolatrías 1 (4.5), Causa contra Juan Caxaatoc, San Miguel de Ullucmayo, 1617.

AAL, Idolatrías 1 (4.7), Información y pesquisa secreta contra los visitadores del pueblo de Santiago de la Nazca, 1623.

AAL, Idolatrías 1 (4.10), Causa contra indios sobre idolatría, Santo Tomás de Auquimarca (province of Checras), 1644.

AAL, Idolatrías 1 (6.5), Autos hechos en virtud de comisión de Andres García de Zurita contra los visitadores eclesiásticos de la idolatría, Cajatambo (province of Cajatambo), 1623.

AAL, Idolatrías 2 (2.10), Causa de hechicería contra Inés Carva, Pomacocha (province of Canta), 1650.

AAL, Idolatrías 2 (4.13), Causa de idolatría contra Don Tomás de Acosta, cacique de segunda persona de este repartimiento de Checras, Santiago de Maray (province of Chancay), 1647.

AAL, Idolatrías 2 (4.14), Causa contra Juana Icha de hechizos y pactos expresos con un demonio Apu Parato, Pomacocha (province of Canta), 1650.

AAL, Idolatrías 2 (6.8), Autos hechos por Juan Gutiérrez de Aguilar, cura de Pira y Cajamarquilla contra indios por idolatría, San Gerónimo de Pampas (province of Huaylas), 1646.

AAL, Idolatrías 3 (2.11), Causa de hechicería contra Rodrigo de Guzmán Rupachagua, Huamantanga (province of Canta), 1656.

AAL, Idolatrías 3 (4.18), Denuncia que hace Don Juan Tocas contra Alonso Ricari, San Francisco de Cajamarquilla (province of Cajatambo), 1656. Printed in Duviols, *Cultura andina*, 5–39.

AAL, Idolatrías 3 (4.19), Causa hecha a los curacas camachicos y mandones del pueblo de San Francisco de Otuco, anejo de la doctrina de San Pedro de Hacas (province of Cajatambo), 1656, fols. 11v and 24. Printed in Duviols, *Cultura andina*, 43–81.

AAL, Idolatrías 3 (5.2), Causa hecha a los indios camachicos del pueblo de Santa Catalina de Pimachi, anejo de la doctrina de San Pedro de Hacas (province of Cajatambo), 1656. Printed in Duviols, *Cultura andina*, 109–33.

AAL, Idolatrías 3 (6.10), Causa hecha contra los camachicos de Santo Domingo de Paria (province of Cajatambo), 1656. Printed in Duviols, *Cultura andina*, 85–108.

AAL, Idolatrías 3 (6.11), Denuncia que hace Don Juan Tocas contra Hernando Hacas Cristóbal Poma Libiac, 1656. Printed in Duviols, *Cultura andina*, 137–261.

AAL, Idolatrías 4 (2.12), Causa de idolatrías hecha a pedimiento del fiscal eclesiástico contra los indios e indias hechiceros del pueblo de San Juan de Machaca (province of Cajatambo), 1657. Printed in Duviols, *Cultura andina*, 265–90.

AAL, Idolatrías 4 (2.12), Provansa hecha a pedimiento de los indios de Hacas, Machaca, Chilcas y Cochillas (province of Cajatambo), contra el licenciado Bernardo de Noboa, 1658–60. Extracts printed in Duviols, *Cultura andina*, 305–21.

AAL, Idolatrías 4 (4.23), Causa contra Francisco Malqui, San Pedro de Caras, 1659.

AAL, Idolatrías 4 (5.6), Causa de idolatría contra los indios idólatras hechiceros del pueblo de San Francisco de Mangas (province of Cajatambo), 1662. Extracts printed in Duviols, *Cultura andina*, 325–91.

AAL, Idolatrías 4 (6.14), Causa de hechicero contra Diego Caxa Guaman, San José de Chorrillo, province of Huarochirí, 1659.

AAL, Idolatrías 5 (1.1), Causa de hechicería contra María Magdalena Angelina, San Francisco de Ancor (province of Yauyos), 1660.

AAL, Idolatrías 5 (1.2), Acusación contra Juan Chapa por hechicería, San Pedro de Pilas (province of Yauyos), 1660.

AAL, Idolatrías 5 (2.17), Declaración de Pedro Villanga, San Pedro de Pilas (province of Yauyos), 1660.

AAL, Idolatrías 5 (2.18), Causa de hechicería contra Francisca Mayguay, San Pedro de Pilas (province Of Yauyos), 1660.

AAL, Idolatrías 5 (2.26), Causa de hechicería contra Magdalena Sacsacarva, San Bartolomé de Tupe (province of Yauyos), 1660.

AAL, Idolatrías 5 (3.1), Causa de hechicería contra Isabel Choqui, San Lorenzo de Quinti (province of Huarochirí), 1660.

AAL, Idolatrías 5 (4.24) Causa de hechicería contra Isabel Concepción, San Lorenzo de Quinti (province of Huarochirí), 1660.

AAL, Idolatrías 5 (4.28), Causa de hechicería contra Pablo de Ato, San Pedro de Pilas (province of Yauyos), 1660.

AAL, Idolatrías 5 (4.29), Declaración de Juana Aycro, San Pedro de Pilas (province of Yauyos), 1660.

AAL, Idolatrías 5 (4.32), Causa de hechicería contra María Pomaticlla, San Lorenzo de Huarochirí (province of Huarochirí), 1660.

AAL, Idolatrías 6 (3.3), Causa contra Agustín Carbajal, León de Huánuco, 1662.

AAL, Idolatrías 6 (5.5), Declaración de Don Diego Pacha en razón de las idolatrías del paraje de Cañas, San Gerónimo de Sallan (province of Yauyos), 1662.

AAL, Idolatrías 6 (5.7), Causa de hechicería contra los indios de San Gerónimo de Sallan (province of Chancay), 1662.

AAL, Idolatrías 6 (5.8), Causa de hechicería contra los indios de San Gerónimo de Sallan (province of Chancay), 1662 (same title as above).

AAL, Idolatrías 6 (6.18), Causa contra Juana de los Reyes, Asunción de Ambar (province of Cajatambo), 1662.

AAL, Idolatrías 6 (7.1), Causa de idolatría en Santiago de Lunahuana (corregimiento de Cañete), 1661.

AAL, Idolatrías 6 (7.3), Causa contra Don Leandro Pomachagua, governador de cinco repartimientos, por hechicerías (province of Huamalíes), 1666.

AAL, Idolatrías 7 (1.3), Causa contra Cristóbal Yaguas, Huamantanga (province of Canta), 1664.

AAL, Idolatrías 7 (2.27), Causa de idolatrías contra los indios idólatras hechiceros de Chamas y Nanis de este pueblo de San Francisco de Mangas (province of Cajatambo), 1663. Printed in Duviols, *Cultura andina,* 395–419.

AAL, Idolatrías 7 (2.29), Confesión de la india María Llacsa sobre una idolatría [*sic*] llamada Tuqui Atipac *todo lo vence,* San Pedro de Hacas (province of Cajatambo), 1667.

AAL, Idolatrías 7 (3.4), Pleitos y causas de hechicerías que sigue Don Luis de Villavicencio, cura de la provincia de Pachas, contra Don Leandro Pomachagua, governador del repartimiento de la doctrina, acusado de favorecer a los indios hechiceros (province of Huamalíes), 1667.

AAL, Idolatrías 7 (4.35), Causa contra Leandro Pomachagua, governador del pueblo de Pachas, acusado de permitir idolatrías a Luis Guánuco (province of Huamalíes), 1667.

AAL, Idolatrías 7 (4.36), Causa contra María Sania, Santo Domingo de Cochalaraos (province of Yauyos), 1667.

AAL, Idolatrías 7 (5.10), Acusación de Cristóbal Pariasca, cacique y governador del repartimiento de Juan de Lampián (province de Canta), contra Juan Sarmiento de Vivero por abusos durante su visita, 1665.

AAL, Idolatrías 7 (5.12), Causa de hechicería, Ihuari (province of Chancay), 1665.

AAL, Idolatrías 7 (7.2), Petición hecha por el promotor fiscal que el visitador exhiba y presente ante el juzgado eclesiástico todas las causas que ha fulminado, 1666.

AAL, Idolatrías 8 (5.16), Información y pesquisa secreta hecha contra licenciado Don Diego Barreto de Aragón y Castro, visitador general de este arzobispado y cura vicario de San Bartolomé de Guacho (province of Chancay), 1668.

AAL, Idolatrías 8 (5.17), Información y pesquisa secreta hecha contra Bernardo de Noboa, cura vicario de San Ildefonso de la Barranca (province of Chancay), 1668.

AAL, Idolatrías 8 (6.24), El fiscal contra Don Francisco de Vergara, cacique del repartimiento de Santo Domingo de Ocros (province of Cajatambo), 1665.

AAL, Idolatrías 8 (7.6), Causa contra Juana de Mayo, Lima, 1668.

AAL, Idolatrías 9 (2.31), Pleito contra Don Francisco de Vergara, governador del pueblo de Santo Domingo de Ocros (province of Cajatambo), 1669.

AAL, Idolatrías 9 (4.38), Causa contra Pasquala de Salsedo, Lima, 1669.

AAL, Idolatrías 9 (4.40), Causa contra Francisca Tomasa, Lima, 1670.

AAL, Idolatrías 9 (4.41), Auto y pleito contra Don Lorenzo Guaraca, cacique del pueblo de Mangas (province of Cajatambo), 1671.

AAL, Idolatrías 9 (5.14), Auto contra Don Juan Soclac y Doña María Chumpi (province of Chancay), 1676.

AAL, Idolatrías 9 (5.15), Causa de idolatría, Santiago de Maray (province of Chancay), 1677.

AAL, Idolatrías 10 (1.8), Causa contra María de la Cruz, Hananhuanca (province of Jauja), 1691.

AAL, Idolatrías 10 (1.9), Proceso contra Pedro Guaman, Diego Yacan y Juliana, indios (province of Jauja), 1690.

AAL, Idolatrías 10 (4.42), Causa contra los indios idólatras del pueblo de San Francisco de Guantan (province of Yauyos), 1680.

AAL, Idolatrías 11 (2.32), Causa contra Francisca Huaylas y María de la Cruz, Lima, 1691.

AAL, Idolatrías 11 (5.25), Causa contra Domingo Capcha y Francisco Guaman, Huamantanga (province of Canta), 1696.

AAL, Idolatrías 11 (7.19), Causa contra Juan Picho, cacique principal y governador del repartimiento de Hurinhuanca en el valle de Jauja (province of Jauja), 1691.

AAL, Idolatrías 12 (1.13), Causa contra Pedro Vilcaguaman, Santa María de Jesús de Huarochirí (province of Huarochirí), 1700.

AAL, Idolatrías 12 (2.33), Causa contra Don Miguel Menacho y Don Juan de Guzmán, caciques principales del repartimiento de Huamantanga (province of Canta), 1696.

AAL, Idolatrías 12 (4.47), Causa de hechicería contra Juana Augustina, San Luis de Huari, 1697.

AAL, Idolatrías 12 (4.49), Causa de hechicería contra Gerónimo Pumayauri, Santa María de Jesús de Huarochirí (province of Huarochirí), 1700.

AAL, Idolatrías 12 (5.27), Cartas de Don Martín Sosa y de Don Antonio Ilario de Sosa, principal del pueblo de Vichaycocha del repartimiento de Pacaraos (province of Canta), 1697.

AAL, Idolatrías 13 (3.6), Causa contra Juan Vásques, Lima, 1710.

AAL, Idolatrías 13 (3.9), Causa contra Juan de Rojas, Santiago de Carampoma (province of Huarochirí), 1723.

AAL, Idolatrías 13 (3.10), Autos contra Pedro de la Cruz, alias Quiñones, y Francisco Bartolomé, por delitos de idolatría, San Agustín de Canin (province of Checras), 1724.

AAL, Idolatrías 14 (3.11), Causa de idolatrías contra indios de la doctrina de San Juan de Churin (province of Cajatambo), 1725.

AAL, Idolatrías 14 (3.13), Causa de idolatría contra indios de la doctrina de Santiago de Andajes (province of Cajatambo), 1725.

AAL, Idolatrías 14 (3.15) Causa contra Francisco Julcarilpo, Santiago de Carampoma (province of Huarochirí), 1730.

AAL, Idolatrías 14 (3.17), Causa contra Domingo Garci, San Francisco de Quiso, doctrina of San Juan de Quibi, (province of Canta), 1741.

Archivo General de Indias (Sevilla) (AGI)

AGI, Lima 38, Letter of Francisco de Cabrera, bishop of Trujillo, to the congress of the Company of Jesus, 9 July 1618.

AGI, Lima 38, Letter of Viceroy Esquilache to the king, 23 March 1619.

AGI, Lima 59, Letter of Archbishop Pedro de Villagómez to the king, 10 July 1658.

AGI, Lima 59, Letter of Archbishop Pedro de Villagómez to the king, 2 May 1663.

AGI, Lima 98, Letter of the audiencia of Lima to the king, 30 October 1626.

AGI, Lima 301, Letter of Archbishop Bartolomé Lobo Guerrero to the king, 20 April 1611.

AGI, Lima 301, Manifestación que hicieron todos los indios de un pueblo en razón de ser idólatras ante el visitador de la idolatría, Concepción de Chupas, 1614.

AGI, Lima 302, Letter of Archbishop Gonzalo de Campo to the king, 8 October 1626.

AGI, Lima 302, Letter of Fray Gaspar de la Torre, provincial of the Mercedarians, to the king, 30 October 1626.

AGI, Lima 302, Two letters of Archbishop Hernando Arias de Ugarte to the king, 27 May 1632 and 13 May 1633.

AGI, Lima 303, Relación que hizo Felipe de Medina de las idolatrías descubiertas en Huacho, 25 March 1650.

AGI, Lima 303, Letter of Archbishop Pedro de Villagómez to the king, 28 August 1654.

AGI, Lima 305, Letter of Lorenzo Perez de Grado, bishop of Cuzco, to the king, 18 March 1623.

AGI, Lima 306, Relación de la visita que hizo Manuel de Mollinedo, obispo de Cuzco, 20 November 1674.

AGI, Lima 307, Constituciones synodales del obispado de Trujillo del Perú, 1623.

AGI, Lima 308, Two letters of Francisco de Verdugo, bishop of Huamanga, to the king, 20 April 1621 and 2 February 1626.

AGI, Lima 308, Constituciones synodales del obispado de Huamanga, 5 August 1629.

AGI, Lima 308, *Carta de edicto* issued by Francisco de Godoy, bishop of Huamanga, 15 June 1652.

AGI, Lima 308, Letters of Francisco de Godoy, bishop of Huamanga, to the king, 15 July 1652, 10 July 1656, and 18 June 1657.

AGI, Lima 309, Letter of Pedro de Perea, bishop of Arequipa, to the king, March 1620.

AGI, Lima 310, Letter of the cabildo eclesiástico of Lima to the king, 8 May 1623.

AGI, Lima 311, Letter of the cabildo eclesiástico of Lima to the king, 25 March 1650.

AGI, Lima 325, Letter of Francisco de la Serna, provincial of the Augustinians, to the king, 9 May 1622.

AGI, Lima 332, Letter of Hernando de Avendaño to the king, 5 August 1653.

AGI, Lima 333, Información de servicios del licenciado Bernardo de Noboa, 24–26 November 1664. Printed in Duviols, *Cultura andina*, 421–35.

AGI, Quito 182, Letter of Diego Ladrón de Guevara, bishop of Cuzco, to the king, 29 April 1706.

Archivo Histórico Nacional (Madrid) (AHN)

AHN, Inquisición Lima, Libs. 1031 and 1032.

Archivum Romanum Societatis Iesu (Roma) (ARSI)

ARSI, Nuevo Reino de Granada y Quito 14, Descripción del Nuevo Reino de Granada de las indias occidentales . . . y de la misión que desde la Nueva España hicieron a él los Padres Alvaro de Medrano y Francisco de Figueroa, sacerdotes de la misma compañía de Jesús. (1598?)

ARSI, Peruana Litterae Annuae V 1651–74, Annual Letter for 1660–61; Annual Letter for 1664–66.

Biblioteca Nacional (Lima) (BN)

BN, B612, Testimonio del expediente sobre la denuncia de incesto, idolatría y otros excesos cometidos por el cacique de Santiago de Aija, Diego Yaruparia, Santiago de Aija (province of Huaylas), 1672.

BN, B1400, Por las preguntas siguientes se examinan los testigos que fueron presentados por parte de Don Juan de Campos Vilcatapayo, principal del pueblo de San Pedro de Quipan del repartimiento de Huamantanga (province of Canta), en los autos que sigue con Don Juan de Guzmán y Don Miguel Menacho sobre el cacicazgo y gobierno de dicho repartimiento, Lima, 1695.

BN, B1701, Declaraciones sobre la práctica de la hechicería e idolatría por los indios del pueblo de Chichas (province of Condesuyos de Arequipa), 1671.

BN, C4284, Autos seguidos criminalmente contra unos indios del pueblo de Llucta [sic] sobre el delito de idolatría, Yura, Arequipa, 1788.

Real Academia de la Historia (Madrid) (RAH)

RAH, Jesuitas, Letras anuas, Perú, 1618.

Primary Printed Sources

Acosta, José de. *De procuranda Indorum salute:* Corpus hispanorum de pace. 2 vols. Madrid: CSIC, 1984–87.

―――. *Historia natural y moral de las Indias.* 2d rev. ed. Ed. Edmundo O'Gorman. Mexico: Fondo de Cultura Económica, 1962.

Albornoz, Cristóbal de. *Las informaciones de Cristóbal de Albornoz (1569–84).* In Millones, *El retorno.*

―――. *Instrucción para descubrir todas las huacas del Perú y sus camayos y haciendas (1583, 1584).* In Urbano and Duviols, *Fábulas y mitos,* 161–98.

Aquinas, Saint Thomas. *Summa theologiae.* Ed. Thomas Gilby O.P. 50 vols. London: Eyre and Spottiswoode, 1964–81.

Arriaga, Pablo José de. *La extirpación de la idolatría del Perú.* In *Crónicas peruanas de interés indígena,* ed. Francisco Esteve Barba. Biblioteca de Autores Españoles, vol. 209. Madrid: Atlas, 1968.

Augustine, Saint. *City of God.* Trans. Henry Bettenson. Harmondsworth: Penguin, 1986.

―――. *On Christian Doctrine.* Trans. Durant W. Robertson Jr. New York: Liberal Arts Press, 1958.

Augustinians. *Relación de la religión y ritos del Perú hecha por los primeros religiosos Agustinos.* Colección de documentos inéditos relativos al descubrimiento, conquista y colonización de las posesiones españolas en América y Oceania, 3:5–58. Madrid: Manuel B. de Quirós, 1865.

Avendaño, Hernando de. *Sermones de los Misterios de Nuestra Santa Fe Católica en lengua Castellana y General del Inca.* Lima: Jorge López de Herrera, 1649.

Avila, Francisco de. *Dioses y hombres de Huarochirí: Narración quechua recogida por Francisco de Avila.* Trans. José María Arguedas. 2d ed. Lima: Museo Nacional de Historia/Instituto de Estudios Peruanos, 1975.

Calancha, Antonio de la. *Corónica moralizada del Orden de San Agustín en el Perú.* 5 vols. Lima: Ignacio Prado Pastor, 1974–81.

Castañega, Martín de. *Tratado de las supersticiones y hechicerías.* Madrid: Sociedad de Bibliófilos Españoles, 1946.

Ciruelo, Pedro. *Reprobación de las supersticiones y hechicerías.* Madrid: Joyas Bibliográficas, 1952.

Cobo, Bernabé. *Historia del nuevo mundo.* Biblioteca de Autores Españoles, vols. 91–92. Madrid: Atlas, 1956.

del Río, Martín. *Disquisitionum magicarum libri sex.* Venice, 1616.

Durán, Diego. *The Book of the Gods and the Ancient Calendar.* Civilization of the American Indian Series 102. Trans. Doris Heyden and Fernando Horcasitas. Norman: University of Oklahoma Press, 1971.

———. *Historia de las Indias de Nueva España e Islas de la Tierra Firme.* Ed. Angel M. Garibay. 2 vols. Mexico: Porrúa, 1967.

Eymerich, Nicolás. *Directorium inquisitorum.* Montpellier: F. Aviñón, 1821.

Garcilaso de la Vega, El Inca. *Primera parte de los Comentarios reales de los Incas.* Biblioteca Clásicos del Perú. Ed. César Pacheco Vélez. Lima: Banco de Crédito del Perú, 1985.

Guaman Poma de Ayala, Felipe. *El primer nueva corónica y buen gobierno.* Ed. John V. Murra, Rolena Adorno, and Jorge Urioste. 3 vols. Mexico: Siglo Veintiuno, 1980.

Hernández Príncipe, Rodrigo. "Mitología andina," *Inca* 1.1. Lima: Museo de Arqueología, Universidad Nacional Mayor de San Marcos, 1923.

———. "Relación de la visita del pueblo de Santa María Magdalena de Marca [Province of Huaylas], 1621." In Hernández Príncipe, "Mitología andina," 65–68. Reprinted in Duviols, *Cultura andina,* 479–82.

las Casas, Bartolomé de. *Apologética historia sumaria.* Ed. Edmundo O'Gorman. 3d ed. 2 vols. Mexico: UNAM, 1967.

————. *Del único modo de atraer a todos los pueblos a la verdadera religión.* Ed. Agustín Millares Carlo and Lewis Hanke. Mexico: FCE, 1975.

Molina, Cristóbal de. *Relación de las fábulas y ritos de los Incas.* In Urbano and Duviols, *Fábulas y mitos,* 47–134.

Peña Montenegro, Alonso de la. *Itinerario para párrochos de indios.* Madrid: Joseph Fernández de Buendía, 1678.

Ramos Gavilán, Alonso. *Historia del celebre santuario de Nuestra Señora de Copacabana.* Lima: Geronymo de Contreras, 1621.

Solórzano Pereira, Juan de. *Política indiana.* Biblioteca de Autores Españoles, vols. 252–256. Madrid: Atlas, 1972.

Villagómez, Pedro de. *Carta pastoral de exhortación e instrucción contra las idolatrías de los indios del arzobispado de Lima.* Colección de libros y documentos referentes a la historia del Perú, vol. 12. Ed. Carlos. A. Romero and Horacio H. Urteaga. Lima: Sanmartí, 1919.

Vitoria, Francisco de. *De la magia.* In *Obras: Relecciones teológicas.* Biblioteca de Autores Cristianos, vol. 198. Ed. T. Urdanoz. Madrid: Editorial Católica, 1960.

Secondary Works

Acosta, Antonio. "Los clérigos doctrineros y la economía colonial (Lima 1600–1630)." *Allpanchis* 19 (1982): 118–41.

————. "Los doctrineros y la extirpación de la religión en el arzobispado de Lima, 1600–1620." *Jahrbuch für Geschichte von Staat, Wirtschaft und Gesellschaft Lateinamerikas* 19 (1982): 69–109.

————. "La extirpación de las idolatrías en el Perú. Origen y desarrollo de las campañas. A propósito de *Cultura andina y represión* de Pierre Duviols." *Revista andina* (July 1987): 171–95.

Aguirre Beltrán, Gonzalo. *Medicina y magia: El proceso de aculturación en la estructura colonial.* Mexico: Instituto Nacional Indigenista, 1973.

Alcalá, Angel, ed. *La Inquisición española y mentalidad inquisitorial.* Barcelona: Ariel, 1984.

Armas Medina, Fernando de. *Cristianización del Perú (1532–1600).* Seville: Escuela de Estudios Hispano-Americanos, 1953.

Barnett, Homer G. *Innovation: The Basis of Cultural Change.* New York: McGraw-Hill, 1953.

Bartolomé, Miguel Alberto. "Shamanism among the Avá-Chi-ripá." In Browman and Schwarz, *Spirits, Shamans and Stars,* 95–148.

Bastien, Joseph W. *Mountain of the Condor: Metaphor and Ritual in an Andean Ayllu.* American Ethnological Society Monographs 64. St. Paul, Minn.: West Publishing Company, 1978.

Behar, Ruth. "Sex and Sin, Witchcraft and the Devil in Late-Colonial Mexico." *American Ethnologist* 14, no. 1 (February 1987): 34–54.

————. "Sexual Witchcraft, Colonialism and Women's Powers: Views from the Mexican Inquisition." In *Sexuality and Marriage in Colonial Latin America,* ed. Asunción Lavrin, 178–206. Lincoln: University of Nebraska Press, 1989.

Bennassar, Bartolomé. "Modelos de la mentalidad inquisitorial: Métodos de su 'pedagogia del miedo.'" In Alcalá, *La Inquisición española,* 174–79.

Bernand, Carmen, and Serge Gruzinski. *De l'idolâtrie: Une archéologie des sciences réligieuses.* Paris: Seuil, 1988.

Blázquez Miguel, Juan. *Hechicería y superstición en Castilla la Mancha.* Toledo: Servicio de Publicaciones de la Junta de Comunidades de Castilla-la Mancha, 1986.

————. *Inquisición y brujería en la Yecla del siglo XVIII.* Yecla: Ayuntamiento patr. Cultura, 1984.

Bolton, Ralph, and Douglas Sharon. "Andean Ritual Lore: An Introduction." *Journal of Latin American Lore* 2, no. 1 (1976): 63–69.

Brading, David. *The First America: The Spanish Monarchy, Creole Patriots and the Liberal State 1492–1867.* Cambridge: Cambridge University Press, 1991.

Browman, David L., and Ronald A. Schwarz, eds. *Spirits, Shamans and Stars: Perspectives from South America.* The Hague: Mouton, 1979.

Brundage, Burr C. *Empire of the Inca.* Norman: University of Oklahoma Press, 1963.

Buechler, Hans C., and Judith M. Buechler. *The Bolivian Aymara.* New York: Holt, Rinehart and Winston, 1978.

Caro Baroja, Julio. *Brujería vasca.* 3d ed. San Sebastián: Txertoa, 1985.

————. *Las brujas y su mundo.* 9th ed. Madrid: Alianza, 1990.

————. *El Señor Inquisidor y otras vidas por oficio.* 3d ed. Madrid: Alianza, 1988.

————. *Vidas mágicas e Inquisición.* Madrid: Taurus, 1967.

————. "Witchcraft and Catholic Theology." In *Early Modern European Witchcraft: Centres and Peripheries,* ed. Bengt Ankarloo and Gustav Henningsen, 19–43. Oxford: Clarendon Press, 1990.

Casaverde Rojas, Juvenal. "El mundo sobrenatural en una comunidad." *Allpanchis* 2 (1970): 125–236.

Castañeda Delgado, Paulino. "Bartolomé Lobo Guerrero, tercer arzobispo de Lima." *Anuario de estudios americanos* 33 (1976): 60–83.

Castañeda Delgado, Paulino, and Pilar Hernández Aparicio. *La Inquisición de Lima (1570–1635).* Madrid: Deimos, 1989.

Chadwick, Henry. *The Early Church.* Penguin History of the Church 1. Harmondsworth: Penguin, 1990.

Christian, William A., Jr. *Apparitions in Late Medieval and Renaissance Spain.* Princeton: Princeton University Press, 1981.

————. *Local Religion in Sixteenth-Century Spain.* Princeton: Princeton University Press, 1981.

Condori, Bernabé, and Rosalind Gow. *Kay Pacha: Tradición oral andina.* Cuzco: Centro de Estudios Rurales Andinos "Bartolomé de Las Casas," 1976.

Contreras, Jaime. *El Santo Oficio de la Inquisición en Galicia 1560–1700: Poder, sociedad y cultura.* Madrid: Akal, 1982.

Cook, Noble David. "Migration in Colonial Peru: An Overview." In Robinson, *Migration in Colonial Spanish America,* 41–61.

Dammert Bellido, J. "Procesos por supersticiones en la provincia de Cajamarca en la segunda mitad del siglo dieciocho." *Allpanchis* 6 (1974): 179–200.

Doore, Gary. "The Ancient Wisdom in Shamanic Cultures: An Interview with Michael Harner Conducted by Gary Doore." In Nicholson, *Shamanism,* 3–16.

Durkheim, Emile. *Elementary Forms of the Religious Life.* Trans. J. W. Swain. London: Allen and Unwin, 1915.

Duviols, Pierre. *Cultura andina y represión: Procesos y visitas de idolatrías y hechicerías, Cajatambo, siglo XVII.* Cuzco: Centro de Estudios Rurales Andinos "Bartolomé de Las Casas," 1986.

———. *La lutte contre les religions autochtones dans le Pérou colonial: L'extirpation de l'idolâtrie entre 1532 et 1660*. Lima: Institut Français d'Etudes Andines, 1971.

———. "La visite des idolâtries de Concepción de Chupas (Pérou, 1614)." *Journal de la Société des Américanistes* 55 (1966): 497–510.

Earls, John. "The Organization of Power in Quechua Mythology." In *Ideología mesiánica del mundo andino*, ed. Juan M. Ossio, 397–409. Lima: Ignacio Prado Pastor, 1973.

Earls, John, and Irene Silverblatt. "La realidad física y social en la cosmología andina." *Proceedings of the 42d International Congress of Americanists* 4 (1976): 299–325.

Egaña, Antonio de. *Historia de la Iglesia en la América española desde el descubrimiento hasta comienzos del siglo XIX*. Biblioteca de Autores Cristianos. 2 vols. Madrid: Editorial Católica, 1966.

Eliade, Mircea. *Shamanism: Archaic Techniques of Ecstasy*. Trans. Willard R. Trask. London: Routledge and Kegan Paul, 1964.

Elkin, Adolphus P. *Aboriginal Men of High Degree*. The John Murtagh Macrossan Memorial Lectures for 1944. Sydney: Australasian Publishing Co., 1945.

Esteva Fabregat, Claudio. "Medicina tradicional, curanderismo y brujería en Chinchero (Perú)." *Anuario de Estudios Americanos* 27 (1970): 19–60.

Evans, Brian. "Migration Processes in Upper Peru in the Seventeenth Century." In Robinson, *Migration in Colonial Spanish America*, 62–85.

Farriss, Nancy M. *Maya Society under Colonial Rule: The Collective Enterprise of Survival*. Princeton: Princeton University Press, 1984.

Furst, Peter T., ed. *Flesh of the Gods: The Ritual Use of Hallucinogens*. London: Allen and Unwin, 1972.

García, Juan Carlos. "Apuntes para una biografía del bachiller Rodrigo Hernández Príncipe, extirpador de idolatrías." In Ramos and Urbano, *Catolicismo*, 241–61.

García Cárcel, Ricardo. *Herejía y sociedad en el siglo XVI: La Inquisición en Valencia 1530–1609*. Barcelona: Ediciones Peninsula, 1980.

Ginzburg, Carlo. *The Night Battles: Witchcraft and Agrarian Cults in the Sixteenth and Seventeenth Centuries.* Trans. John and Anne Tedeschi. Baltimore: Johns Hopkins University Press, 1983.

Glenn, Paul J. *A Tour of the Summa.* St. Louis: B. Herder, 1960.

Goñi Gaztambide, José. "El tratado *De superstitionibus* de Martín de Andosilla." *Cuadernos de etnología y etnografía de Navarra 9* (1971).

Gow, David, and Rosalind Gow. "El alpaca en el mito y el ritual." *Allpanchis 7* (1975).

Greenleaf, Richard E. "Historiography of the Mexican Inquisition: Evolution of Interpretations and Methodologies." In Perry and Cruz, *Cultural Encounters*, 248–76.

Gruzinski, Serge. *La colonisation de l'imaginaire: Sociétés indigénes et occidentalisation dans le Mexique espagnol XVI–XVIII siécle.* Paris: Gallimard, 1988. Published in English as *The Conquest of Mexico: the Incorporation of Indian Societies into the Western World, Sixteenth to Eighteenth Centuries.* Trans. Eileen Corrigan. Cambridge: Polity, 1993.

———. "Le filet déchiré: Sociétés indigénes, occidentalisation et domination coloniale dans le Mexique central." 4 vols. Ph.D. dissertation, University of Paris I, 1985.

———. *Man-Gods in the Mexican Highlands: Indian Power and Colonial Society 1520–1800.* Trans. Eileen Corrigan. Stanford: Stanford University Press, 1989.

Guibovich Pérez, Pedro. "La carrera de un visitador de idolatrías en el siglo XVII: Fernando de Avendaño (1580?–1655)." In Ramos and Urbano, *Catolicismo*, 169–240.

Guilhem, Claire. "La Inquisición y la devaluación del verbo femenino." In *La Inquisición española: Poder político y control social*, ed. Bartolomé Bennassar, 171–207. Barcelona: Crítica, 1981.

Harner, Michael J., ed. *Hallucinogens and Shamanism.* New York: Oxford University Press, 1973.

———. *The Way of the Shaman: A Guide to Power and Healing.* San Francisco: Bantam Books, 1980.

Harris, Olivia. "The Dead and the Devils among the Bolivian Laymi." In *Death and the Regeneration of Life*, ed. Maurice Bloch and Jonathan Parry. Cambridge: Cambridge University Press, 1982.

Henningsen, Gustav. *The Witches' Advocate: Basque Witchcraft and the Spanish Inquisition (1609–1614)*. Reno: University of Nevada Press, 1980.

Herskovits, Melville J. *Man and His Works: The Science of Cultural Anthropology*. New York: A. A. Knopf, 1948.

Huertas Vallejos, Lorenzo. *La religión en una sociedad rural andina (siglo XVII)*. Ayacucho: Universidad Nacional de San Cristóbal de Huamanga, 1981.

Hultkrantz, Ake. "Ecological and Phenomenological Aspects of Shamanism." In *Shamanism in Siberia*, ed. Vilmos Dioszegi and Mihali Hoppal, 27–58. Budapest: Akademiai Kiado, 1978.

Joralemon, D. "Altar Symbolism in Peruvian Ritual Healing." *Journal of Latin American Lore* 11, no. 1 (1985): 3–29.

Kamen, Henry. "Notas sobre brujería y sexualidad y la Inquisición." In Alcalá, *La Inquisición española*, 226–36.

Klor de Alva, J. Jorge. "Colonizing Souls: The Failure of the Indian Inquisition and the Rise of Penitential Discipline." In Perry and Cruz, *Cultural Encounters*, 3–22.

———. "Spiritual Conflict and Accommodation in New Spain: Toward a Typology of Aztec Responses to Christianity." In *The Inca and Aztec States, 1400–1800: Anthropology and History*, ed. George A. Collier, Renato I. Rosaldo and John D. Wirth, 345–66. New York: Academic Press, 1982.

Kubler, George. "The Quechua in the Colonial World." In Steward, *Handbook of South American Indians*, 331–410.

Labarre, Weston. "The Aymara Indians of the Lake Titicaca Plateau, Bolivia." *American Anthropologist* 50 (1948).

Laviana Cuetos, Maria Luisa. "Un proceso por brujería en la costa ecuatoriana a fines del siglo XVIII: La punta de Santa Elena, 1784–1787." *Anuario de estudios americanos* 46 (1989): 93–129.

Lévi-Strauss, Claude. "The Sorcerer and His Magic." In *Structural Anthropology* 1, 167–85. 2 vols. Trans. Claire Jacobson and Brooke G. Schoepf. London: Allen Lane, Penguin, 1968–77.

———. "The Effectiveness of Symbols." In *Structural Anthropology* 1, 186–205. 2 vols. Trans. Claire Jacobson and Brooke G. Schoepf. London: Allen Lane, Penguin, 1968–77.

Lewis, Ioan M. *Ecstatic Religion: An Anthropological Study of*

Spirit Possession and Shamanism. Harmondsworth: Penguin, 1971.

Lisón Tolosana, Carmelo. *Brujería, estructura social y simbolismo en Galicia*. Madrid: Akal, 1987.

Lockhart, James. *Spanish Peru, 1532–1560: A Colonial Society*. Madison: University of Wisconsin Press, 1968.

————. *The Nahuas after the Conquest: A Social and Cultural History of the Indians of Central Mexico, Sixteenth through Eighteenth Centuries*. Stanford: Stanford University Press, 1992.

Luna, Luis Eduardo. *Vegetalismo: Shamanism among the Mestizo Population of the Peruvian Amazon*. Stockholm Studies in Comparative Religion 27. Stockholm: Almqvist and Wiksell International, 1986.

MacCormack, Sabine. "From the Sun of the Incas to the Virgin of Copacabana." *Representations* 8 (1984): 30–60.

————. "'The Heart Has Its Reasons': Predicaments of Missionary Christianity in Early Colonial Peru." *Hispanic American Historical Review* 65 (1985): 443–466.

————. *Religion in the Andes: Vision and Imagination in Early Colonial Peru*. Princeton: Princeton University Press, 1991.

Madsen, William. "Religious Syncretism." In *Handbook of Middle American Indians*. Vol. 6, *Social Anthropology*, ed. Robert Wauchope, 369–91. Austin: University of Texas Press, 1967.

Mannarelli, María Emma. "Inquisición y mujeres: Las hechiceras en el Perú durante el siglo XVII." *Revista andina* (July 1985): 141–55.

Marzal, Manuel. *Historia de la antropología indigenista: México y Perú*. 3d ed. Lima: Pontificia Universidad Católica del Perú, 1989.

————. *La transformación religiosa peruana*. Lima: Pontificia Universidad Católica del Perú, 1983.

Mauss, Marcel. *A General Theory of Magic*. Trans. Robert Brain. London: Routledge and Kegan Paul, 1972.

Medina, José T. *Historia del Tribunal de la Inquisición de Lima: 1569–1820*. 2d ed. 2 vols. Santiago de Chile: Fondo Histórico y Bibliográfico J. T. Medina, 1956.

————. *La imprenta en Lima: 1584–1824*. 4 vols. Amsterdam: N. Israel, 1965.

Millones, Luis. "Los ganados del señor: Mecanismos de poder

en las comunidades andinas en los siglos XVIII y XIX."
América indígena 39 (1979): 107–43.

———. *Historia y poder en los Andes centrales (desde los orígenes al siglo XVII)*. Madrid: Alianza, 1987.

———. "Religion and Power in the Andes: Idolatrous Curacas of the Central Sierra." *Ethnohistory* 26 (1979): 243–63.

Millones, Luis, ed. *El retorno de las huacas: Estudios y documentos sobre el Taki Onqoy, siglo XVI*. Lima: Instituto de Estudios Peruanos/Sociedad Peruana de Psicoanálisis, 1990.

Mills, Kenneth. *An Evil Lost to View? An Investigation of Post-Evangelisation Andean Religion in Mid-Colonial Peru*. Liverpool: Institute of Latin American Studies, 1994.

———. "The Limits of Religious Coercion in Mid-Colonial Peru." *Past and Present* 145 (November 1994): 84–121.

Mishkin, Bernard. "The Contemporary Quechua." In Steward, *Handbook of South American Indians*, 411–70.

Monahan, William B. *The Moral Theology of St. Thomas Aquinas*. 3 vols. Worcester and London: Trinity Press, 1942.

Monter, E. William. *Frontiers of Heresy: The Spanish Inquisition from the Basque Lands to Sicily*. Cambridge: Cambridge University Press, 1990.

———. *Ritual, Myth and Magic in Early Modern Europe*. Athens: Ohio University Press, 1983.

Nicholson, Shirley, ed. *Shamanism: An Expanded View of Reality*. London: Theosophical Publishing House, 1987.

Noll, Richard. "The Presence of Spirits in Magic and Madness." In Nicholson, *Shamanism*, 47–61.

Nutini, Hugo G. *Todos Santos in Rural Tlaxcala: A Syncretic, Expressive and Symbolic Analysis of the Cult of the Dead*. Princeton: Princeton University Press, 1988.

Núñez del Prado Béjar, Juan Victor. "El mundo sobrenatural de los quechuas del sur del Perú, a través de la comunidad de Qotobamba." *Allpanchis* 2 (1970): 79–114.

Perry, Mary E., and Anne J. Cruz, eds. *Cultural Encounters: The Impact of the Inquisition in Spain and the New World*. Berkeley and Los Angeles: University of California Press, 1991.

Poole, Deborah A., and Penelope Harvey. "Luna, sol y brujas: Estudios andinos e historiografía de resistencia." *Revista andina* (July 1988): 277–98.

Ramos, Gabriela. "Política eclesiástica y extirpación de idolatrías: Discursos y silencios en torno al Taqui Onqoy." In Ramos and Urbano, *Catolicismo*, 137–68.

Ramos, Gabriela, and Henrique Urbano, eds. *Catolicismo y Extirpación de Idolatrías, siglos XVI-XVIII: Charcas, Chile, México, Perú*. Cuzco: Centro de Estudios Regionales Andinos "Bartolomé de las Casas," 1993.

Redfield, Robert. *The Folk Culture of Yucatán*. Chicago: University of Chicago Press, 1942.

Reguera, Iñaki. *La Inquisición española en el País Vasco*. San Sebastian: Txertoa, 1984.

Robinson, David J. "Indian Migration in Eighteenth-Century Yucatán: The Open Nature of the Closed Corporate Community." In Robinson, *Studies in Spanish American Population History*, 149–73.

Robinson, David J., ed. *Migration in Colonial Spanish America*. Cambridge: Cambridge University Press, 1990.

———. *Studies in Spanish American Population History*. Dellplain Latin American Studies 8. Boulder, Colo.: Westview Press, 1981.

Rostworowski de Diez Canseco, María. *Estructuras andinas del poder: Ideología religiosa y política*. Lima: Instituto de Estudios Peruanos, 1983.

Rowe, John H. "Inca Culture at the Time of the Spanish Conquest." In Steward, *Handbook of South American Indians*, 183–330.

Sallnow, Michael J. *Pilgrims of the Andes: Regional Cults in Cuzco*. Washington, D.C.: Smithsonian Institution Press, 1987.

Salomon, Frank. "Ancestor Cults and Resistance to the State in Arequipa, ca. 1748–1754." In *Resistance, Rebellion and Consciousness in the Andean Peasant World, Eighteenth to Twentieth Centuries*, ed. Steve J. Stern, 148–65. Madison: University of Wisconsin Press, 1987.

———. "Shamanismo y política en la última época colonial del Ecuador." *Revista cultural del Banco Central del Ecuador* 21b (1985): 487–509; also published in English in *American Ethnologist* 10 (1983): 413–28.

Salomon, Frank, and George L. Urioste, eds. *The Huarochirí Manuscript: A Testament of Ancient and Colonial Andean Religion*. Austin: University of Texas Press, 1991.

Sánchez, Ana. *Amancebados, hechiceros y rebeldes (Chancay, siglo XVII)*. Cusco: Centro de Estudios Regionales Andinos "Bartolomé de las Casas." 1991.

Sharon, Douglas. "A Peruvian *Curandero's* Séance: Power and Balance." In Browman and Schwarz, *Spirits, Shamans and Stars*, 223–32.

——. *The Wizard of the Four Winds: A Shaman's Story*. New York: Free Press, 1978.

Silverblatt, Irene M. *Moon, Sun and Witches: Gender, Ideologies and Class in Inca and Colonial Peru*. Princeton: Princeton University Press, 1987.

——. "Peru: The Colonial Andes." In *Witchcraft and Sorcery of the American Native Peoples*, ed. Deward E. Walker, Jr., 311–22. Idaho: University of Idaho Press, 1989.

——. "'The Universe has turned inside out. . . . There is no justice for us here': Andean Women under Spanish Rule." In *Women and Colonization: Anthropological Perspectives*, ed. Mona Etienne and Eleanor Leacock, 149–85. New York: Praeger, 1980.

Spalding, Karen. *Huarochirí: An Andean Society under Inca and Spanish Rule*. Stanford: Stanford University Press, 1984.

——. "Social Climbers: Changing Patterns of Mobility among the Indians of Colonial Peru." *Hispanic American Historical Review* 50 (1970): 645–64.

Stern, Steve J. *Peru's Indian Peoples and the Challenge of Spanish Conquest: Huamanga to 1640*. Madison: University of Wisconsin Press, 1982.

Steward, Julien H., ed. *Handbook of South American Indians*. Vol. 2, *The Andean Civilizations*. Washington D.C.: Smithsonian Institution, Bureau of American Ethnology, 1946.

Taussig, Michael T. *The Devil and Commodity Fetishism in South America*. Chapel Hill: University of North Carolina Press, 1980.

——. "Folk-healing and the Structure of Conquest in South-West Colombia." *Journal of Latin American Lore* 6 (1980): 217–78.

——. *Shamanism, Colonialism and the Wild Man: A Study in Terror and Healing*. Chicago: University of Chicago Press, 1987.

Taylor, Gerald. "Supay." *Amerindia* 5 (1980): 47–63.

Tschopik, Harold. "The Aymara of Chucuito, Peru: 1. Magic." *Anthropological Papers, American Museum of Natural History* 44: 137–308. New York: American Museum of Natural History, 1951.

Turner, Victor. *The Forest of Symbols: Aspects of Ndembu Ritual.* Ithaca: Cornell University Press, 1967.

Urbano, Henrique, and Pierre Duviols, eds. *Fábulas y mitos de los Incas.* Crónicas de América 48. Madrid: Historia 16, 1989

Urioste, George L. "Sickness and Death in Preconquest Andean Cosmology: The Huarochirí Oral Tradition." In *Health in the Andes,* ed. Joseph W. Bastien and John M. Donahue, 9–18. Washington D.C., 1981.

Urton, Gary. *At the Crossroads of the Earth and the Sky: An Andean Cosmology.* Austin: University of Texas Press, 1981.

Vargas Ugarte, Ruben. *Los Concilios Limenses, 1551–1772.* 3 vols. Lima: Instituto de Investigaciones Históricas, 1951–54.

———. *Historia de la Iglesia en el Perú.* 5 vols. Burgos: Aldecoa, 1953–62.

Varón, Rafael. "El Taki Onqoy: Las raíces andinas de un fenómeno colonial." In Millones, *El retorno,* 331–405.

Wachtel, Nathan. *The Vision of the Vanquished: The Spanish Conquest of Peru through Indian Eyes, 1530–1570.* Trans. Ben and Sian Reynolds. Hassocks: Harvester Press, 1977.

Walsh, Roger N. *The Spirit of Shamanism.* London: Mandala, 1990.

Wightman, Ann M. "'. . . residente en esa ciudad . . .': Urban Migrants in Colonial Cuzco." In Robinson, *Migration in Colonial Spanish America,* 86–111.

———. *Indigenous Migration and Social Change: The Forasteros of Cuzco, 1570–1720.* Durham: Duke University Press, 1990.

Wolf, Eric. "Types of Latin American Peasantry." *American Anthropologist* 57 (1955): 452–71.

Zemon Davis, Natalie. *Society and Culture in Early Modern France.* Stanford: Stanford University Press, 1975.

INDEX